IL DOTTORE

IL DOTTORE

The Double Life of a Mafia Doctor

RON FELBER

BARRICADE
BOOKS

Fort Lee • New Jersey

DISCLAIMER:

The account that follows is entirely true. Some of the names have been changed to protect privacy.

The doctor himself has returned to the East Coast and is one of the top cardiac surgeons in the country, working at a major hospital. The decision not to use his real name was made because to do so would suggest that he was cashing in on his notorious past.

All the facts about him as described in the pages that follow are accurate.

—Lyle Stuart
June 2004

Published by Barricade Books Inc.
185 Bridge Plaza North
Suite 308-A
Fort Lee, NJ 07024

www.barricadebooks.com

Library of Congress Cataloging-in-Publication Data
Felber, Ron.
    Il dottore : the double life of a Mafia doctor / Ron Felber.
      p. cm.
    Includes bibliographical references and index.
    ISBN 1-56980-278-5
      1. Litner, Elliot. 2. Cardiologists--New York, N.Y.--Biography.
      3. Mafia--New York, N.Y.--Biography. I.Title.
RC666.72.L554F5 2004
364.1'092--dc22
    [B]   2004053629
First Printing
Manufactured in the United States of America

CONTENTS

CONTENTS

FOREWORD

The idea for writing *Il Dottore* was given to me by Bill Bonanno, author of *Bound by Honor, A Mafioso's Story*. The son of godfather and Commission founder, Joseph Bonanno, in addition to writing, he was involved in film and having read a manuscript of mine titled *The Privacy War* became interested in the possibility of a movie. We were meeting at Anthony's, a restaurant in Tucson, Arizona, to discuss the project when, in the course of conversation, he mentioned an acquaintance who'd led an intriguing life and now was willing to have a book written about it.

At first, I was cool toward the notion of writing yet another "Mafia book." Certainly anything that needed to be said on the subject had been committed to paper by more capable authors than myself ranging from Gay Talese, *Honor Thy Father*; to Mario Puzo, *The Godfather*; and Joseph Bonanno, *A Man of Honor*. Nevertheless, since I was living in New Jersey, as was Dr. Elliot Litner, I agreed to meet with him to see what kind of chemistry developed.

To my delight, I found Elliot to be brilliant, likable, and

remarkably "human." Contrary to what one might assume about the stereotype for a man raised on the periphery of organized crime and who had by choice opted to lead a double life, I became enamored with the notion of it. A "double" life. What did it mean? Were there people in this world for whom one life was simply not enough? People whose hunger for living allowed them, perhaps even compelled them, to be two different men? If that was the case, what was the penalty for living *too* much? Once ethical considerations vanished from one's radar screen and the borders of individuality were wiped clean, what was it like to be two people, one living the life of a high-society Manhattan physician with wife and children, the other living the life of a sex addict and inveterate gambler working secretly for the Mafia?

The introduction that Bill Bonanno offered, I understood after meeting Elliot, was an opportunity to explore a world that few will ever live or even know about. It was an invitation to see the world of La Cosa Nostra through the eyes of an outsider, a self-confessed "nerd" who hailed from the Bronx in New York and through a series of choices and coincidences evolved into an "everyman" historian capable of walking one through a Mafia house of mirrors as unfamiliar and frightening to him as it would be to any potential reader.

From that point on, Elliot Litner and I worked together on this project. He drove me to his old haunts on Jerome Avenue in the Bronx and even to the "backies" where as a young boy, his brother, Steve, their pals, Jewish and Italian, and he would ride cardboard boxes down the garbage heaps, their version of Swiss Alps. As important, I spent hours taping the events that made up his life, past and current, putting those accounts today—with the benefit of hindsight—into their historical context, while getting to know him as a person and his family going back to their emigration from Russia immediately following the Revolution.

Beyond that, during my two years of research, I had the good fortune to get to know Bill and meet his father, Joseph, shortly before he died. Having taken my nephews along on the trip, we found ourselves at Joseph Bonanno's home where the feisty godfather, then in his mid-nineties, told anecdotes about Al Capone, the Kennedys, and a priceless gem about having once bribed President Calvin Coolidge. Prior to that, I had, of course, instructed my nephews, Matt, fifteen, and Colin, ten, to be "polite" and on their "best behavior." Once we'd finished talking and were about to leave, I was careful to point out that I wanted them to "shake hands" and say "thank you" for the hospitality.

As it turned out, the conversation was enthralling, and at its conclusion, Colin and Matt lined up dutifully in front of me to bid farewell to the retired godfather. As Bill, and his nephew, Frank, looked on, Colin stepped forward expecting to shake hands when to his shock and amazement, the old man turned his right cheek to him. Colin was mortified, not having a clue about what he should do, but wanting to remain ever polite, simply stood there in silence. It was then that his older brother nudged him. *"He wants you to kiss him, stupid,"* he exhorted. At which time, Colin looked into the eyes of the grizzled Joseph Bonanno, whose cheek was still showing, then turning to me in total desperation, asked, *"Where?"*

Our good-byes were suitably arranged in the moments that followed, and we all had a good-natured laugh about the comedies of everyday life. Still, sensing at that moment the possibilities for historical intimacy that Elliot's story offered, I vowed then to write something more than just another Mafia book. I wanted to capture not just his life, but the Cosa Nostra way of life from his unique perspective, interweaving the exploits of Rudolph Giuliani, for example, known to him through his career as a well-respected Manhattan surgeon, with those of John Gotti, known to him through his alternate life as Il Dottore, the Mafia doctor.

In the final analysis, then, I was determined to discover who this man was. How could he be so driven by the need to heal and achieve social acceptability in his visible life, yet demonstrate such destructive tendencies, steeped up to his eyeballs in what, at best, could be described as moral ambiguity in his invisible one? Was there a price to pay for living *too* much? The answer would come for Elliot Litner in the unlikely specter of heart patient Ralph Scopo, union official and capo for the Columbo crime family, whom he would be coerced both to murder and to save on the operating table of New York City's Mount Sinai Hospital in December 1986.

What was the price for cutting a Faustian deal with New York high society and the godfathers of La Cosa Nostra? This was the mystery I set out to solve in the biography of a physician forced to probe for "truth" amid the inner workings of the Mafia, the hidden agendas of American hypocrisy, and the darkest recesses of his own spirituality.

R. F.

Mendham, New Jersey

August 2004

1

THE COMMISSION

"Giuliani had achieved a national visibility he'd craved his entire life."

—Foley Square, February 27, 1985, 10:35 A.M.

A buzz of speculation swirled around U.S. Attorney Rudolph Giuliani as he stood on the Federal Courthouse steps in Manhattan. Flanked by FBI Director William Webster, the news conference had a carnival air about it as television and newspaper reporters roiled around New York's top federal lawman calling out questions, popping camera flashbulbs, and shooting videotape as he tried to wave them down.

"The New York City Bar Association called you 'overzealous' and said your use of RICO has led to abuses. What do you say about that?" asked David Margolick then of the *New York Times*.

"I'd say they're provincial and should stop acting like a trade organization," Rudy shot back, casting a quick grin in Webster's direction.

"What about John Gotti?" called out *NBC*'s Gabe Pressman. "There're reports that with Castellano out of the picture, he's the new boss of bosses."

"No comment."

"You wanna be mayor? That's the word down at City Hall," shouted *Newsday*'s Lenny Levitt.

"I've been U.S. attorney less than a year, Lenny. Why don't you give me a break?" Rudy answered, then directing himself to the crowd and Webster, who stood by his side bemused, "Come on, guys!" he exhorted. "Let's get a little organized here!"

The night before, on February 26, 1985, fifty major mob leaders were busted and hauled before a swarm of cameras in Foley Square. Today, Giuliani was about to rock the world of organized crime again by announcing grand jury indictments against the bosses of New York's five ruling Mafia families.

"This is a great day for law enforcement," Giuliani proudly declared, "but a bad day, probably the worst ever, for the Mafia because we have not only attacked the 'heart,' but the 'brain' of La Cosa Nostra."

Based on taped evidence, he asserted, the U.S. Attorney's Office would prove that the heads of five Mafia families essentially ran the construction industry in New York, collecting two percent of the price of every significant contract in the state.

Giuliani then presented the indictment charging the bosses with running a RICO enterprise known, since its formation in 1931, as the Commission. Indicted were Paul "Big Paul" Castellano (Gambino Family); Anthony "Fat Tony" Salerno (Genovese Family); Gennaro "Gerry Lang" Langella (Columbo Family); Anthony "Tony Ducks" Corallo (Lucchese Family); Philip "Rusty" Rustelli (Bonanno Family). In other words, every ruling godfather in the state.

On that day and the next, Giuliani appeared on ABC's "Evening News," "Nightline," "Good Morning America," and CBS's "Morning News" boasting about his prosecutorial triumph. In those forty-eight hours, he achieved a national visibility he'd craved and worked for his entire life.

Then it happened. An event that would forever link Elliot Litner's fate with the destinies of two of this generation's most extraordinary men: future New York City Mayor Rudolph Giuliani and John Gotti, *Time* magazine's "Teflon Don" and heir apparent to the throne of the nation's most powerful Mafia crime family.

On November 13, 1986, in the midst of the Commission trial, Ralph Scopo, president of the Concrete Workers' District Council, complained of nausea and numbness in his right arm. Then, while listening to prosecution tapes of himself secretly recorded by the FBI, he stood and clutched his chest, seized by a knifelike thrust of excruciating pain. He turned to his left toward Asst. U.S. Attorney Michael Chertoff as if to say something, then to his right, robotic, as he tried to move out from behind the defense desk. Finally, reaching for the oak rail behind him, he fell forward, then collapsed to the courtroom floor, suffering a heart attack.

Coronary patient Ralph Scopo lay motionless on the operating table at Mount Sinai Hospital, chest bare, electrodes attached to the back of his shoulders, intravenous needles inserted into his right arm and left wrist. Fifty-six years old, grossly overweight, and a three pack-a-day smoker, Giuliani's pride and joy had collapsed four weeks earlier, headlines in the morning papers screaming SCOPO HEART ATTACK DISRUPTS RACKETEERING TRIAL. But there was much more to it than racketeering. This case was an attempt by the FBI and New York City's Organized Crime Task Force to bring down the Commission, the "bosses" of the five La Cosa Nostra families that governed organized crime in New York and possibly the nation.

In the background played "The Wanderer," a 1961 hit by Dion in place of Verdi or Puccini, Elliot's usual fare. The anesthesiologist jerked Scopo's head back so the blunt blade of the L-shaped laryngoscope could be put in his throat and a one-half-inch endotracheal tube inserted past his vocal chords. A balloon on the tube's lower end inflated, creating an airtight seal as Clark Hinterlieter, the resident surgeon, inserted a Foley catheter through Scopo's penis into his bladder, then nodded to Dr. Elliot Litner, the chief operating surgeon.

Litner glanced to his right where outside Operating Room #2 the Giuliani team of three federal investigators led by Special Agent Peter Hogan awaited the operation's outcome like vultures. Then, to his left where John Gotti's right hand, Sammy "the Bull" Gravano, and two of his underlings loomed nearby the patient's waiting room pacing the floor with equal intensity. The Brooks Brothers Ivy Leaguers versus the polyester suit gumbas, Litner mused sardonically, the voice in his head sounding like a cross between Woody Allen and a manic Jerry Lewis. *"How the hell did a nerdy, Jewish kid from the Bronx get caught up in a mess like this?"* he anguished. The feds want Scopo alive to prosecute and "twist" into a government witness against New York's five families. The goodfellas don't want him leaving this operating room alive. Either way, it's understood, Litner was a dead man.

Dion warbled in the background about Flo on the left, Mary on the right, and Janie being the girl he'll be with tonight. When Janie asks who he loves the best, Dion tears open his shirt to show Rosie on his chest.

> *'Cause I'm the wanderer,*
> *Yeah the wanderer,*
> *I go around, around, around . . .*

The chest was open; the heart-lung machine ready to go. It was impossible to stall any longer. It was time for Elliot Litner, a man who could have been the poster boy for moral ambiguity, to choose between life or death: loyalty to La Cosa Nostra or devotion to his Hippocratic oath.

"Fifty cc's going in to test the line," the technician announced.

"On bypass," Litner commanded, "start cooling."

Almost immediately, Scopo's heart slowed.

Judy Harrow, his surgical nurse, held the shiny stainless-steel needle up in the air. She depressed the syringe plunger, and a stream of clear liquid potassium spurted from it.

She handed it to Litner.

This was it. The moment of truth, for if ever there was a time to see to it that Scopo never awakened from his drug-induced sleep to testify, this was that time.

Litner took the syringe into his right hand, clamped the aorta, then injected the icy fluid directly into the vessels below the blockages in Scopo's lower aorta.

Ralph Scopo's heart had stopped beating!

2

BRONX BOY
DISCOVERS BODY

"These gangsters are going to kill my little Ellie."

Harley Hotel
Cleveland, Ohio
March 8, 1987

T he tiny hotel room was overrun with the waste generated by a man who'd given up living, and it showed as he stood naked before the full-length mirror that covered the pine wardrobe before him. Elliot Litner had become part of the environment since he'd gone into hiding, as much a part of the decadent décor as the used styrofoam McDonald's hamburger shells, crushed Big Mac wrappers, and half-empty beer cans that adorned the place: a human wreck, both physically and psychologically.

For nearly three decades, he'd maintained secret relationships with America's most notorious criminals, smuggling precious gems from Brazil, disposing of sensitive medical records, and acting as a courier transporting counterfeit stocks, bonds, and who knew what else from Switzerland and other parts of Europe. He'd been a personal physician to

Carlo Gambino, worked with *capo di tutti capi* Paul Castellano, and tended to business for garment district boss Al Rosengarten, as well as Mafia up-and-comer John "Johnny Boy" Gotti.

More, he'd reaped the rewards of those efforts, shooting craps gratis at the Sands in Las Vegas and Resorts in Atlantic City, $1,000 a throw; partying at Studio 54 with Cybill Shepherd, Richard Gere, and Roy Cohn; engaging in three-somes, and even foursomes, at Plato's Retreat with the most beautiful women in the world. *Christ almighty, it was like being a fuckin' rock star.*

But suddenly it came to a screeching halt. The Mafia empire tumbled down around him like a house of cards. And for him, it had all come down to the life of a single potential government witness who Gotti, himself, had ordered to be hit. A man named Ralph Scopo.

Elliot's eyes scanned the human wreck he'd become, eyes ringed and lifeless from lack of sleep and paranoia, face unshaven, pot belly swollen, and even his penis, once the pride and joy of his life, hanging ludicrously shriveled. He sat down naked and alone on the Spartan wooden chair set before a desk as stripped and bare as his ravaged brain these days and nights to begin writing the notes that would become the basis of *Il Dottore: The Double Life of a Mafia Doctor.*

When did Elliot Litner's involvement with the Mafia, or La Cosa Nostra as it's sometimes called, first begin? Very early. In 1953, to be exact, at the age of five, when he was play-ing Cowboys and Indians with his older brother, Steven, in a deserted lot near their tenement apartment on Anthony Avenue in the Bronx, New York.

It was there that he witnessed a gun deal gone bad, lead-ing to the murder of one man by two others. *Bam! Bam!! Bam!!!* He heard the sound of the final bullets shot into the back of the man's head. Then, maybe to make identification more difficult or as a last gesture of contempt, a rock the size of a watermelon dropped onto his skull, crushing it in a pool of blood, bone, and brain tissue.

That's when they noticed Elliot, a skinny, little Jewish kid, Roy Rogers's six-shooter in hand, standing petrified with fear, not ten feet from them. Both men were huge—broad shouldered, dressed in dark overcoats and hats.

"You didn't see nothin', did you, kid?" the man with the pistol asked.

Elliot shook his head "no," shaking, literally, in his shoes.

"Good," the man said shoving a $10 bill in the boy's shirt pocket. "You remember that. You didn't see nothin'."

Then they drove off in a black Cadillac leaving him wondering if anything had happened at all, but knowing that it must have. "Where else would a dead body come from?" he asked himself. Moments later, his brother returned complaining loudly about his lack of enthusiasm for Cowboys and Indians when he noticed Elliot's stunned expression.

"Hey," he said. "You peed in your pants!"

Once he could bring himself to speak, Elliot showed his brother the body.

"Jesus," Steven muttered. "It really is a dead body—and you saw who did it, Elliot."

"No. No, I didn't," he stammered remembering his pledge. "I didn't see nothin'. I didn't see no one."

From there, Steve, who immediately saw star status in the murder, took credit for finding the body since his little brother was too frightened to care and offered no objection. Together they made a beeline for their Uncle Lou's luncheonette on Webster Avenue.

"I found a dead body! I found a dead body!" Steve proclaimed.

9

"Shut up," his Uncle Lou shouted back. "You're going to make people lose their appetites!"

Undeterred, Steve left for their Uncle Saul's laundry, just down the block on 174th Street, with Elliot in tow.

"I found a dead man. He was shot. I found him. Now we've got to call the police!"

Saul, who owned the laundry where their father worked as a driver, couldn't fathom what they were trying to tell him.

"Marty," he said turning to their eighteen-year-old cousin, "go back to the lot with them, and see what they're talking about."

The three went to the deserted lot, filled with garbage and debris, and Marty couldn't believe his eyes.

"My God, Steve," he managed to utter, "you really did find a dead body! You're like," he thought for a minute, "like a *movie star!*"

They were not movie stars, and in truth, though the term "nerd" had yet to be coined, if you were to look up nerd in the dictionary, a photo of him, Elliot Litner, scrawny and bookish, with thick, black-rimmed glasses, would undoubtedly be staring back at you. Still, finding a dead body and witnessing a murder in those days was front-page news, and though the police, who later arrived, came to learn the truth of what happened, Elliot kept his vow of silence even after intense questioning. It was this stance that earned him notoriety and an odd kind of respect in the neighborhood as a kid who could be trusted and wouldn't "rat."

The next morning, headlines in papers ranging from the *New York Mirror* to the *Daily News* carried the headline Bronx Boy Discovers Body. Then below, Gangland Victim Murdered in Gun Deal Gone Bad. But if notoriety would get him free penny candies at Moe Greenberg's corner candy store, it was obviously something his mother, Etta, could do without.

"Abe, I tell you these gangsters are going to come and kill my lil' Ellie," she wailed to his father. "I know it, I know it as sure as God is in 'eaven!"

The gangsters didn't come. They didn't have to. They were already there. This was the Bronx, stomping grounds for such notorious mob figures as Dutch Schultz and Abner "Longy" Zwillman; chosen location for the coronation of *capo di tutti capi* Salvatore Maranzano as "boss of bosses" attended by Charlie "Lucky" Luciano, Tom Gagliano, Joseph Profaci, Vincent Mangano, and Joseph Bonanno—in other words, anyone that was anyone in the Italian underworld. The mob's infiltration of New York had started long before that.

The Sicilian Mafiosi, symbolized by the "Black Hand," had been well-known in the boroughs of Brooklyn and the Bronx since the turn of the century extorting immigrant shopkeepers, hijacking goods, and kidnapping wealthy businessmen for ransom. Even the great Italian tenor, Enrico Caruso, became a victim when during an engagement at the Metropolitan Opera, shortly before World War I, he received a Black Hand letter demanding $2,000. He paid without resistance. Then a second demand, this time for $15,000 arrived, compelling him to meet with the police, who captured two prominent Italian businessmen as they attempted to retrieve the money from beneath the steps of a deserted factory. It was one of the few successes by law enforcement against the early New York Mafia, but Caruso, despite his fame, required police and private protection for years to come.

Still, while Elliot was doing his best to survive in the Bronx, working with his brother at Uncle Saul's laundry and reading biographies about Pasteur, Curie, and Einstein, there were two other kids whose lives would later become entwined with his living just a few miles away. One was John Gotti born, like him, in a rented tenement apartment in the

Bronx. The other was Rudy Giuliani, living in a modest two-family brick house in East Flatbush, Brooklyn. Interestingly, even then, both were admiring historical icons placed at poles exactly opposite one another. Gotti's hero was Chicago crime lord, Al Capone, and Giuliani's, the ambitious and cunning New York prosecutor-turned-governor, Thomas E. Dewey.

In days to come, of necessity, Elliot would become an expert on Rudolph Giuliani. Born in New York, the son of Harold and Helen, Giuliani's family had by the early 1950s relocated to a two-bedroom Cape Cod house in Garden City, Long Island. Rudy was enrolled at St. Anne's, a Catholic school run by the Sacred Heart of Mary nuns, where students were required to wear uniforms consisting of navy blue pants, a white shirt, and blue tie. There he learned the value of discipline above most everything else. Along with teaching discipline during the Cold War era, the sisters' secondary agenda was imbuing the ability to isolate an enemy, Communism in this case, and despise it to the core.

In those early days, and through his adolescent years at Bishop Loughlin Memorial High School where he was taught by Christian Brothers, Rudy, much as his hero Thomas Dewey, developed a love of opera even while his father pushed him toward more "manly" endeavors such as boxing and baseball. Encouragement to compete was hardly needed, however, as the academic requirements at Bishop Loughlin were rigorous and unforgiving. The walls of the classrooms bore just two symbols, a crucifix and an American flag.

John Gotti's childhood was ultimately "different," but intrinsically the "same," as if a chemical formulation of identical constituents had been mixed at dissimilar proportions creating an alternate version of the same amalgam.

Described at the zenith of his career as "Al Capone in an $1,800 suit," John "Johnny Boy" Gotti was anything but dapper while growing up in the Bronx with twelve brothers and sisters. His father was a low-earning man of Neapolitan origin, barely able to provide for the thirteen children he'd fathered in less than sixteen years. "The guy never worked a fuckin' day in his life. He was a rolling stone. He never provided for the family," Gotti once complained in an FBI-taped conversation with underboss Sammy Gravano. "He never did nothin'. He never earned nothin'. And he never had nothin'!"

When he was ten, the Gotti family moved, not to Long Island like Giuliani's, but to a rented Brooklyn house in East New York where La Cosa Nostra was as intertwined with its citizens as the Catholic Church. Gotti's parents cared little about his education, and by the time he was fourteen, he was committing petty crimes and sporting a tattoo of a serpent on his right shoulder. At sixteen, he quit Franklin Lane High School to run full-time with a gang called the Fulton-Rockaway Boys. They stole cars, dealt in stolen merchandise, ripped off stores, and rolled drunks stepping out of gambling parlors.

Other members included guys who would become life-long criminal associates like Angelo Ruggiero, known as "Quack-Quack" because he couldn't keep his mouth shut, and Wilfred "Willie Boy" Johnson, a sometimes professional boxer, who would loom large in the life of both John Gotti and Elliot Litner as Il Dottore, the Mafia doctor.

3

INITIATION

"You're a guy who can be trusted, and that makes you one of us."

As a young boy, Elliot lived an extremely sheltered life, and if there was a line drawn that sequestered him, his aunts, uncles, and parents from the rest of society, it was the parameters of the Bronx itself. Rarely did his father or mother, both Jews who had emigrated from the Kiev province of Russia, venture outside the borough. Why should they? His dad worked eighty hours a week at Uncle Saul's laundry. His mother, a genius when it came to cooking, spent her time filling their tiny kitchen with the intoxicating aromas of her specialties: *noodle kugel*, a pudding of noodles and eggs; *matzobrei*, matzo fried with eggs into a pancake; and *rosca*, Elliot's favorite, big round sweet rolls with sesame seeds.

His world, and that of his brother, Steven, five years older than he, was also self-contained: P.S. 28, two blocks from the six-story apartment house where they lived on Anthony Avenue; Saul's laundry; Uncle Lou's luncheonette; 174th Street where they played stickball; and the "backies," their word for the mountainous garbage dumps they sledded down on cardboard boxes for fun after school. That was the extent of their universe, all separated by Tremont Avenue, the main thoroughfare before the coming of the Cross Bronx Expressway, where, if they valued life and limb, all forms of motion stopped. It was verboten. They were forbidden from crossing such a dangerously trafficked street.

The neighborhood itself was made up predominantly of Jewish merchants. There were very few blue-collar types among the Jews. For those services, there was the next largest population, the Italians, who just as the Irish became cops, seemed to prefer employment as masons, carpenters, bricklayers, and on occasion, *something else.*

Exactly what "something else" meant didn't occur to Elliot until much later, but among the Italian kids and their families, there was one occupation that seemed ineffable.

"My dad works at the laundry. Where does your dad work?"

Silence. Shuffling of feet. "He don't really work nowhere. He does a little of this and a little of that."

"Oh," Elliot would say, as if some secret understanding had passed between them, thinking that maybe he was *what?* A Catholic priest?

That was the way it was in many respects between Italians and Jews in the Bronx at that time. No question, there were differences in culture and religion, but there were also many values they shared. Their parents, for one, had brought with them the European experience along with the monumental decision to move to America. And while they were Americanized, they had both acquired century-old habits from the Old Country that bonded Jews and Italians into a respect for family values that they felt all around them on a daily basis.

No better example of the symbiosis that existed between them was the fact that for the Orthodox Jews, during the High

Holy Days and bar mitzvahs, Italians would often act as Shabbes goys who turned the lights on and off on the Sabbath for those whose orthodoxy forbade it.

But the cooperation didn't end there—at least not for Elliot. While he was a totally subpar athlete and about as tough as tofu when it came to fighting, he was always an extraordinary student and would get 100 percent and A+ for nearly every subject, except gym, on his report card. Phrases like quid pro quo meant nothing to him then, but the basic arrangement went something like this. At their next-door neighbor, Mr. Micelli's request, Elliot would tutor his son, Nicky, and others to help get them through exams. In turn, they'd protect him from neighborhood tough guys who viewed him as an easy mark for lunch and spending money.

It was at about that time that Elliot discovered the opposite sex, and for a fourteen-year-old, it was quite a discovery. Her name was Helga Schmidt, and if a name like *Helga* stirs visions of a large, redhead with horned helmet and loud singing voice, this was not a Helga of the Teutonic-Amazon variety. Far from it, for she was, to him, like a goddess. Her hair was long and golden, her face radiant, and when she smiled, paradise opened up to him.

As important, Helga was what adults at the time called "mature." This meant that she had breasts, *two of them*, that swelled from her chest like the choicest fruit on the vine. Simply outstanding. And, one day, Elliot actually touched one, or at least, brushed up against it during a study hall when she reached across a tabletop to get a mathematics book. Elliot looked at her. She looked at him. And, miraculously, Helga smiled. It was a sweet, vaguely coquettish glance that immediately evaporated when everyone at the table who'd seen their encounter laughed and teased until she rushed away, embarrassed.

Unfortunately, Helga's brother, Max, who was captain of the football team and a bully in the Goebbels tradition, was not so amused. After school that day, he waited for Elliot, along with four or five members of the team, mostly Irish. The football players circled Elliot in the schoolyard while Max, who was with him in the center, began shoving.

"You Jew purr-vert! You like to touch the tits of the girls, huh?"

Shove—no response.

"So, you tink you can get a feee-l from my little sistah, Jew boy, is that it?"

Shove—no response.

Well, not only did Max talk like Arnold Schwarzenegger, he was built like him and seeing that his friends were getting restless, finally rolled up his huge fist and hit Elliot hard in the stomach. That, of course, doubled him up. Then, Max clasped his two hands together in the shape of one gigantic fist and slammed it down onto the back of Elliot's head. At that point, totally nauseous and gasping for air, Elliot was down, but not so incapacitated that he couldn't see Nick Micelli, Joey Ficshetti, Sal DiGregorio, and Little Eddy Sabella charging up the concrete hill where P.S. 28 stood to descend upon the varsity bullies.

One by one, the German and Irish guys were handled or fled as Nicky, who was shorter than Max, but broader and strong as a bull, broke through, throwing Max to the ground like a rag doll.

Slowly Elliot got to his feet, horrified by Nicky's ferocity as he beat Max's face with his rock-hard fists, then got up and kicked him, joined by the others once Max's fair-weather friends had been vanquished.

Rolled into a ball, Max was surrounded as they wailed into his body, taking full-scale kicks into his arms, back, and ribs once they were exposed.

"Hey! Nicky!!" Elliot screamed. "Enough! This guy's balls are coming out of his eye sockets for Jesus's sake! Stop it! Stop it already!"

And they did, but not before Nicky grabbed Max by the front of his shirt and lifted him so that Max's face was no more than two inches from his. "Listen, you Nazi bastard," he seethed. "If you or any of your fucking friends ever lay a hand on Elliot Litner again, you're dead, understand? This kid is 'protected.' He's one of us, *capisci?*"

Max nodded, licking blood away from the side of his mouth as Nicky shook him. *"Capisci?"* he demanded.

"Yah. Yah, *capisci,*" Max finally uttered.

Then Nicky lowered him down to the ground, and once he collected himself, Max left to the shoves, smacks, and jeers of the others who had now formed a circle around him.

"Elliot," Nicky said, then turning to him with the care and sincerity of a *zayde*, blood brother, "are you all right? Did they hurt you?"

"No, no, Nicky," he said, so shy that he was embarrassed to even look up at him.

"Nothing like this will ever happen to you again, Elliot. You have my word on that. You're a good kid—*solid.* You help us, and you never tell anyone, even when they ask. You're a guy who can be trusted, and that makes you one of us."

Elliot nodded, then looked into Nicky's eyes understanding that he genuinely meant it. For whatever reason, Nicky had feelings for him. And, in an odd way, he was proud not only of the friendship, but that given Nicky and the group's prominence in the school, he didn't have to be afraid anymore. Not of Max. Or one dozen Max's. For Elliot, this was a kind of epiphany.

4

BIRTH OF THE
AMERICAN MAFIA

*"It was only later that Elliot learned Officer Kahler was a 'bag' man,
and Salvatore Micelli a caporégime."*

O f course, as Elliot would come to understand much later,
the "special" relationship Jews and Italians shared wasn't
restricted to the Bronx, or New York for that matter.
Historically, the symbiosis built around power and money
between the two ethnic groups went back at least to the hey-
day of Chicago underworld boss Johnny Torrio and a hood-
lum genius named Arnold Rothstein.

Torrio, who was nicknamed "the Fox," was born in New
York's Lower East Side in 1882, but gravitated to Chicago
where he went to work for Chicago crime boss "Big Jim"
Colosimo running gambling operations, brothels, and narcotic distribution. Street smart and ruthless when he had to
be, Torrio climbed his way through the ranks of Big Jim's
operations preaching an approach considerably different
from his boss and most others working in the business of
crime at the time.

Torrio believed that "violence leads only to more violence," though it was he who arranged Colosimo's assassination by a young hood named Frankie Yale so he could take

over his operation. Afterward, seeing, as many did, that Prohibition was a bonanza for crime lords like himself, he formed distribution alliances in Chicago, Detroit, and Canada, counterfeiting legal U.S. government alcohol certificates, buying distilleries in England and Scotland to control supply, and carving up the city of Chicago into inviolable territories to lessen mob tensions and maintain a "permanent" peace.

The old joke goes "Jesus saves, but Moses invests," and maybe there's some truth to it because while Johnny Torrio saw a future for the Mafiosi in multinational corporations, it was Arnold Rothstein, a Jew, who articulated a vision of what organized crime could someday become.

Rothstein was nicknamed "the Brain" because it was he who brought La Cosa Nostra to entirely new levels. Active, as were Al Capone and Torrio, in bootlegging, Rothstein expanded the world of crime into Wall Street, counterfeiting stock certificates, selling worthless bonds, making millions per year on the sale of stolen Liberty Bonds issued by the federal government during World War I. Not content with indirect control of most bootlegging operations in New York, stolen and counterfeit Liberty Bonds began showing up in Cuba, England, Nassau, France, and the Near East to purchase liquor and narcotics worldwide.

A great believer in cooperation over violence, Rothstein saw crime as a corporation exercising limited use of force and called for the creation among his gangland counterparts of a multiethnic, multinational federation. Truly the world of Arnold Rothstein was a limitless one uninhibited by morals or prejudice, leaving no stone unturned, no business opportunity unexploited.

Significantly, the views of Rothstein and Torrio would influence, and be shared by, New York's Sicilian born Mafioso Salvatore Maranzano. In 1931, as *capo di tutti capi*, Maranzano created five Mafia "families," not "gangs" or "mobs" in New

York. A scholarly man who spoke six languages including Greek and Latin, Maranzano structured the American Mafia after Julius Caesar's military legions calling it Cosa Nostra, "our thing." Under the fathers of each family, there would be an underboss and under him, would be several lieutenants, called *caporégime*, in charge of an estimated 3,500 soldiers at the time.

Later, after years of a bloody conflict known as the Castellamarese War and Maranzano's assassination arranged by Charles "Lucky" Luciano, Joseph Bonanno put forward a system to prevent further bloodshed through negotiation of internal disputes. "I suggested it be called the *Commizione del Pace*, Sicilian for Commission of Peace," Bonanno confided to Elliot during a conversation at his home in Tucson, "to which Luciano, a shrewd, but illiterate street thug from Manhattan's Lower East Side, responded, 'I don't even know how to pronounce it. Just call it the fucking Commission.'"

Little did any of them realize that it was this body, made up of the fathers of New York City's five families, that years later would provide federal investigators the landscape and target for the American Mafia's unraveling, along with their own.

So, even before Bugsy Siegel, who invented Las Vegas, or Meyer Lansky, who took mob influence in real estate and gambling to its pinnacle, there was Arnold Rothstein, as good a crook as any Italian, who like him, was maybe not so tough as he was liberal in his own personal approach about what was "right" and what was "wrong."

Like Arnold, too, it was Elliot's brains that got him more and more entrenched with the Mafia, but there was one major difference. In Rothstein's case, he was the brains behind all that was going on around him. Like a kid playing his favorite video game—always in control. For Elliot, the relationships he maintained with the sons of "made" men like Nick Micelli weren't because he controlled them, but because he enjoyed them.

In some ways back then, he was not unlike Jerry Lewis as *The Nutty Professor*. While his grades were As and his SAT scores approached 1,600, he couldn't get pretty girls or gamble or gain the respect (and fear) of his peers, but they could. And when he hung out with them, though he never drank, he, too, would be "cool." That's when he *did* go to the local nightclubs and *did* get the girls and was viewed with respect and, yes, even fear. *What a rush!* And all he had to do was write a few term papers or tutor Joey or Eddy or Sal so they could pass their math exam in high school or whatever community college they might wind up attending.

Not a bad accommodation, and there seemed little wrong with it, Elliot reasoned back then. No one got hurt, after all, and for him, it was like drinking the Nutty Professor's potion. Miraculously, he was no longer skinny Elliot Litner, Abe and Etta's son, *schlepping* his way through the Bronx, but Buddy Love, cruisin' in a Thunderbird convertible, swingin' with the best lookin' chicks, and having the time of his life.

If Elliot's primary school was the classroom, his other school was "the Corner." This was where, hanging out with Nicky, Joey Ficshetti, Sal, and Little Eddy, he learned what was really going on in the world beyond his uncle's laundry. There they would meet to discuss anything from baseball, Yankee slugger Mickey Mantle was their hero; to girls, always a topic of interest; and music, largely dominated by Elvis, and their favorite Italo-American recording group, the Four Seasons.

The debate surrounding baseball might have the guys comparing Mantle to Willie Mays, of the long-departed San Francisco Giants, or Whitey Ford to Sandy Koufax, of the long-departed and now-despised Los Angeles Dodgers. But one debate that never lasted long compared the East Coast's Frankie Valli and the Seasons to the West Coast's Brian Wilson and the Beach Boys.

"Ya know," Stanley Finelli, lead singer for their own street-corner doo-wop group, would begin, "I truly believe the Beach Boys are faggots. Ev-ah see the clothes they wear?" He shook his head just thinking about it.

To which Joey Ficshetti would add, "Did ya see 'em on Ed Sullivan? I swear to Christ, there's a twinkle in Brian Wilson's eye. No straight guy could ev-ah look like that!"

Then, if he was allowed by his parents to "hang out," which was almost never, Elliot might put an intellectual spin on the subject with something like, "Yeah, I agree with both of you. In fact," he would say, eyes narrowing for effect, "I read somewhere, *National Geographic* I think, that there are more homosexuals on the beaches of California than any-place in the world except, of course, for Greenwich Village."

Nodding, convinced, Joey would put a cap on it. "Exactly. That's the reason there ain't no fuckin' way that any-fuckin'-body would ev-ah compare the music of a cock nibbler like Brian Wilson to a bona-fide paisan like Frankie Valli, am I right or wrong?"

After graduation from high school, Elliot attended Syracuse University on a full scholarship, but before he left the Bronx and Long Island behind, Nicky's dad, Salvatore Micelli, asked him to stop by to see him. Nicky was there, of course, with his mom, never known as anything but Mrs. Micelli, and so was Officer Kahler, the local cop, who'd watched him grow up in the neighborhood. Unbelievably, he sat at the Micellis' kitchen table counting money—cash—and stacking it into piles.

"Elliot, Elliot," greeted Mr. Micelli. "We're so proud of you goin' off to a good school upstate like Syracuse college."

"And on full scholarship," Mrs. Micelli added, rushing over to hug him.

Nicky looked on, genuinely happy for him and not dis-pleased himself at the opportunity, now that school was over, to do a little of *dis* and *dat* with his father.

"Hi, Elliot," Officer Kahler called out from the kitchen, continuing his counting.

Elliot waved.

"So, anyway," Mr. Micelli sighed, "I just wanted to tell you, personal, how we appreciate the help you gave little Nicky gettin' him through some tough spots and coverin' for him that time those *scherzi* down there at the high school accused youse of cheatin'."

"Yeah, Elliot, you remember?" Nicky fondly recalled. "You said we had the same ans-sas because we spent the week studyin' together! That was a good one, Elliot. A gem of an ans-sa!"

"So, anyway," Mr. Micelli repeated, like he always did at the start of a new sentence, "Mrs. Micelli and me know, well, we know your dad don't have a lot, so we decided to give you a little somethin' so you can buy books or warm clothes for when you go upstate in the cold."

With that, he reached into his pocket, pulled out a roll of $20 bills and handed it to Elliot. Then, wrapping his two big hands around Elliot's little one, he looked directly into his eyes, nodding his approval like the proudest of fathers.

"But, but, Mr. Micelli," Elliot protested in the high-pitched, nasal voice he happened to have been born with, "that's all the money you have in your pocket."

To which Mr. Micelli replied, very matter of factly, "Yeah, but I got two pockets!"

They all laughed. Nicky, Mr. and Mrs. Micelli, Elliot and even Officer Kahler, sitting at the Micellis' kitchen table still counting cash and stacking it into neat piles.

Later Elliot learned that Officer Kahler was what was called a "bagman," collecting "pad" from Mafia *caporégime*, like Salvatore Micelli, and spreading it among his fellow patrolmen.

5

INTO THE MIRROR

"He shook hands with Aniello 'Neil' Dellacroce on what would be his first step into La Cosa Nostra."

A ttending Syracuse University in the fall of 1964 on full scholarship was a source of pride for Elliot as he looked back on all that had gone wrong in his life. He'd achieved straight As through high school and 800s on both the verbal and mathematics testing for the SATs. Unlike many students at that time, Elliot was never the type to be distracted by the politics of the day—civil rights, Vietnam, women's liberation, and student protests. He was detached from it, uninterested, and that for him, was kind of a blessing since it was learning that came naturally and the acquisition of knowledge that brought him joy.

So far as campus life, he didn't need or desire anything else, except maybe women, but there would be plenty of time for that later. History, literature, and foreign language studies were all important, but his true passion was science. The logic of math, the mysteries of chemistry and biology were, to him, like a portal into a brash new world, different from anything to which he was accustomed.

From a scientific standpoint, it was exciting. But there was another reason, one that wasn't, maybe, so noble. He understood that the sciences led to medical school, medical school to a medical degree, and a medical degree to the kind of money and status no one in his family had ever seen or lived to enjoy either in the Bronx or Vinograd, Russia, from where the Litner family had emigrated.

Close as his family was growing up, it was not uncommon for his father or Uncle Saul, the colorful owner of the laundry that supported them, to tell stories of life in Russia, both tragic and somehow funny at the same time. In some ways, Elliot believed it might have been this crazy and often futile history that influenced many of the choices, both good and bad, made during his university days and afterward.

One story he remembered had to do with Saul and his grandfather, who was in the egg business. During the winter months, his grandfather used to buy all the eggs he could from the Russian peasants and store them away so they wouldn't spoil. During the spring and summer when the roads were clear of snow, he would go to Kiev, the capital of Ukraine, hire a horse and wagon, load it with eggs, and take them to the open market where they were sold to the public like on a street in New York. On one particular afternoon after all the eggs were sold, his grandfather reached into his pocket to count the money, but there was nothing there. Somehow, he realized, that while he was busy with customers, putting money in his pocket from the sale, there were two pickpockets right behind him—and as soon as he put the money in his pocket, they took it out, just as fast!

The next time his grandfather opened for business, he spotted the two crooks, who he called *ganuvim*, bums. Every time he made a sale this time, he put the money in his pocket, but kept his hand in there so they couldn't get to the money. He kept on working with one hand like that all day.

After a while, the crooks, tired of waiting for him to take his hand off the money, decided to take a different approach.

One of the them came to the front where his grandfather stood and was ready to rough him up, but the old man stared at him and said in Russian, "*Bilshe ne produrish,*" which meant "you're not going to fool me anymore." So the crook took his grandfather's hat, put two handfuls of eggs in it, then put it back on his head breaking all of them, thinking that when those eggs started dripping over his face, grandfather would take his hand out of his pocket, and the robber would get to the money. But the old man was determined and remained on the spot, his hand firmly in the pocket with the money, a dozen yolks dripping down his face until his day's work was over and he could take his profits home.

Of course, there were other stories, not so amusing about Saul and Elliot's father battling their way through Russia to Romania, along with thousands of other Jews, being shot at and beaten by soldiers on their escape to America. No doubt, those tales stay with a man. They toughen him up to the realities of life and sharpen his survival instincts so that when he sees a way out, an opportunity, he doesn't just seize it, he holds on to it for dear life. In a way, it was like that for Elliot at Syracuse where he graduated cum laude and went on to Downstate Medical School in Brooklyn, where, at twenty-one-years old, he became the youngest student ever to graduate.

Through his undergraduate years, Elliot kept in touch with his friends in the old neighborhood despite the fact that his parents had by then, like so many other first-generation immigrants, moved to the rapidly expanding suburbs of Long Island. While they were, along with Uncle Saul, now in Hempstead, Elliot was back to his old stomping grounds, serious as ever, attending Downstate, but living it up when Nicky, Sal, and the other guys came by to party or just cruise in

Brooklyn, Queens, or Lower Manhattan in Nicky's brand-new Chevy Camaro.

Gone were the days of Elvis, the Beatles, and rock 'n' roll. This was a new period entirely—the age of disco, with clubs opening almost as fast as somebody could come up with a name: Ondine's, Shepherd's, Cheetah, the Scene, and a place called the Loft, run by pioneer disco entrepreneur, David Mancuso, in Manhattan's Lower East Side. Though only a prelude to the opening of Studio 54 by Steve Rubell and Ian Schrager, for Elliot it was like Alice stepping through the looking glass, a time that marked the beginning of what some would call his double life—the hopelessly serious medical student "nerd," Elliot Litner, and the young, hip Mafioso wannabe, Il Dottore.

At the time, it never occurred to him to ask why. Why did they have him around? To be sure, they'd grown up together, but aside from being the scrawny Jewish kid, dressed in black pants, white shirt, and brown penny loafers, who seemed more like a mascot for the group than a member, was there something beyond that? More, why did it never occur to him that they, all of them, were treated "special" when they entered these clubs? Maybe Elliot was naive and maybe he just didn't want to know, but the fact, as he would later discern, was that most of these clubs were owned directly or indirectly by the Gambino Family, the largest and most powerful in the nation.

Just how Carlo Gambino had come to accumulate his fortune seemed to Elliot, at least at that time, unbridled capitalism in its purest form. There were several ways: The first had to do with Don Carlo's business genius in the Arnold Rothstein sense. Business was business, money was money, so when he surmised that New York's homosexual population was without bars to socialize, he financed and opened dozens of gay clubs where they could drink, listen to music, dance, and make love if they chose. Understanding the other side of the coin, Gambino also had no compunctions about blackmailing the more prominent among them, one being longtime FBI Director J. Edgar Hoover.

A second method of making big bucks was family loansharking operations where sums of money, small and large, would be lent at interest rates of 200 percent or more to financially strapped club owners. If they couldn't pay, the collateral would be appropriated, usually the establishment itself. Finally, there was the Hotel and Restaurant Employee International, a union the family controlled since the 1940s. This enabled the Gambinos to shake down restaurants, topless bars, nightclubs, and hotels in return for granting union peace.

All in all, most of the Bronx, nearly all of Brooklyn, and many of the major industries in Manhattan ranging from construction to garbage collection and the garment industry were mobbed up. No wonder they were treated so well.

It was in June 1971 that Elliot began interning as a general surgical resident in the Department of Surgery at Jewish Hospital and Medical Center in Brooklyn. The work was exhausting, but each day he learned something new. Whether it was a routine tonsillectomy or something as dangerous as a debridement and excision for a bullet wound carried out during life-threatening surgery, he realized that he loved not only the satisfaction of a well-executed procedure, but the excitement of a life-and-death situation, particularly when the stakes were high and the surgery he was performing became a true gamble.

One procedure, illegal prior to the Supreme Court's *Roe v. Wade* decision, was abortion. It was to discuss this subject that Sal DiGregorio, at the behest of Nicky's dad, Sal, invited Elliot to dinner at a restaurant called Tommaso's in the Bay Ridge section of Brooklyn to meet with a man referred to only as "Neil." It wasn't a tough sell. "Are you kidding?" Elliot asked. "I make $100 a month as an intern at this slave hospital. Tommaso's is a class place. Where else am I going to get a meal like that for free?"

When he got to Tommaso's, a smallish, gray-pallored man with icy blue eyes sat at a table alone. The place was buzzing with conversation and the clanking of silverware, pots, and pans from the nearby kitchen. The maître d' was waiting and brought him to the booth.

The man, probably in his late fifties, and dressed in a non-descript gray suit, half-rose, then extended his hand. "My name is Neil. Sal Micelli, you know him?"

Elliot nodded, a little self-conscious. "Yes, Mr. Micelli, sure."

"Well, he told me you're a bright young kid, just outta medical school, who could probably use a little extra cash."

He looked into Elliot's eyes, and again Elliot was struck by the starkness of his stare. Neil was a tough cookie, there was no question about that, but despite his language, which was laced almost every other word with a "fuck" or a "goddamn," he had his own brand of charm, his own kind of sincerity.

From there, while he ate a plate of pasta and Elliot wolfed down a seafood dish called cioppino, Neil proceeded to talk about a type of arrangement that would be a "win-win" for everybody. Young girls were getting pregnant, many out of wedlock, some married, who for whatever reason—emotional, financial—didn't want to carry the fetus to term. Forget that the law for the moment prohibited abortion, this was a matter of convention, a way of thinking that changed with the times. What about the girl? Neil asked. Because of these conventions, young girls were performing abortions on themselves or going to quacks and untrained practitioners who were oftentimes little more than butchers.

What if, Neil proposed, he and his business partners were to find sterile, hospital-grade conditions where young women could quietly have their problem taken care of without putting their lives in jeopardy? What if Elliot helped to recruit young underpaid surgeons like himself to perform this service and got a fee for every doctor he recruited and on each of the procedures they performed? Wouldn't that be a win-win? Wouldn't he be helping these distraught young women, maybe saving their lives, while helping to fund the careers of young resident physicians at the same time?

Elliot thought about what he said and then considered the two lives he'd already begun living. On the one hand, he was working his fingers to the bone while barely sustaining himself. On the other, he was driving in red Corvettes, partying in the best discos with the prettiest women, and living like a movie star. The choice, for him, was not difficult. He decided that between surviving like the Nutty Professor and living it up like Buddy Love, he would choose: both. Why, after all, should he have to lead just one life or the other? Why should he stand like his grandfather with egg dripping down his face holding his money with one hand and his dick with the other making *bubkis* while others thrived? If not him, somebody would do it.

So Elliot agreed and shook hands that night with Aniello "Neil" Dellacroce, future underboss to Paul Castellano and mentor to John Gotti, on what would be his first step out of normal everyday society and his first step into the world of La Cosa Nostra.

6

BOSS OF BOSSES

"We like Elliot Litner."

It was Adam Smith who first theorized that "supply plus demand equals good business." And that was the way it was for the Gambino abortion enterprise. Women, most of them wealthy, must have been getting knocked up all over the place because the network of clinics the Gambino Family set up spread like wildfire throughout the Bronx, Brooklyn, Queens, and Manhattan. They were getting $3,000 to $4,000 per procedure, and no matter how many clinics were opened, the demand seemed to exceed supply to the point where Elliot ran out of candidates to perform the operations.

From Jewish Hospital to Mount Sinai in New York and even Jersey hospitals like the General Hospital Center at Passaic, he couldn't recruit fast enough. Aside from the pent-up demand for sanitary locations, confidential transactions, and professionally able practitioners, the Gambinos had it all figured out, converting the backrooms of the storefront locations already established for numbers and gambling operations into outpatient surgical centers. They had the geographies covered and, as today's marketing gurus recommend, had strategically focused "points of distribution" aligned for their services. For each of the procedures performed by physicians Elliot recruited, 5 percent of their earnings went to him. Now, it wasn't like he was about to send Deloitté and Touche in for a full accounting of income, but from $100 a month, his income grew to $5,000 a month in a matter of six months. Not bad for a poor kid from the Bronx!

While Elliot was making money hand over fist, the two men who were destined to change his life, Rudolph Giuliani and John Gotti, were also developing as young men into what they were earmarked to become in the future.

During the early 1960s, Rudy Giuliani idolized Jack Kennedy and skipped classes along with fellow classmates to shake hands with the president, who was speaking at a garment district rally. While there is no way of knowing how much Rudy knew about his father's past, knowledge of Harold Giuliani's mob associations may have influenced him even then because after JFK's assassination, Rudy became obsessed with Attorney General Robert Kennedy while attending Manhattan College. The reason, he confided to girlfriend Kathy Livermore, was the "moral conviction" RFK showed in prosecuting the mob-infested Teamsters Union.

As a student at New York University law school, while most classmates were being mesmerized by the music of Bob Dylan and the Rolling Stones, Rudy Giuliani was infatuated by idols of another kind: the careers of former federal prosecutor and New York governor, Thomas Dewey, and Robert Kennedy. In both cases, it would take something less than a penetrating study to pull either man from their pedestals, at least in terms of their careers as district attorney and attorney general. Both men, burning to the core with political ambition, had achieved their greatest prosecutorial victories undermining the very systems they were sworn to uphold.

To those who understood the inner workings of the conviction then-District Attorney Thomas Dewey gained over mobster Charles "Lucky" Luciano, the headlines had a hollow ring. Charged with sixty-two counts of compulsory prostitution entailing a network of some 200 brothels that employed 1,000 prostitutes and grossed more than $12 million annually, by the time Luciano's appeal was denied, even some prosecutors came to believe he was framed.

One witness, a career criminal named Joe Bendix, claimed he'd personally been offered a job by Lucky with the ring and had heard him boast how he controlled it. More damaging was the testimony of Cokey "Flo" Brown, a prostitute, who declared that she'd been sleeping with Luciano at his Waldorf-Astoria suite and heard him bragging that he had "organized cathouses around the city to operate more efficiently than A & P." Upon cross-examination, it was discovered that Bendix had never met Luciano and that Cokey "Flo" Brown didn't know where the Waldorf was located.

Nevertheless, using his own fiery brand of self-righteous rhetoric that asked jurors to convict Lucky not of "vice," but of "racketeering" for which he was never charged, Lucky Luciano was convicted and sentenced to thirty to fifty years in state prison, the longest sentence ever handed down for prostitution.

In the case of RFK, the prosecution of mob-connected Teamster Union leader Jimmy Hoffa seemed more a personal vendetta than a triumph of justice where illegal wiretaps, witness tampering, and bribes were used to gain a conviction. This was not the first time the Kennedys had transgressed against the fathers, nor would it be the last.

As early as 1959, Joseph Kennedy made contact with Joseph Bonanno, then chairman of the Commission, through intermediate Lawrence O'Brien. JFK was going on a fundraising tour looking to bolster his campaign for the Democratic nomination for president, O'Brien told Bonanno, and he wanted the Commission's backing in order to gain labor union support. "There'll be resistance," Bonanno said. "Bobby has already proven his political ambition as a prosecutor during the McClellan hearings and embarrassed many of our friends." Still, Bonanno, understanding that Joseph Kennedy, himself a former bootlegger with ties to Frank Costello, could be an important resource if his son was elected, promised to see what he could do.

The result was the Commission's financial and political backing at critical moments in JFK's campaign: a win in the all-important West Virginia primary and in Illinois during the general election where 80 percent of Illinois' largest county, Cook, went for Kennedy in a state won by just 8,000 votes. Almost immediately after the election, once he was named attorney general, Bobby declared an all-out war against "organized crime" beginning a relentless prosecution of Hoffa, Chicago's Sam Giancana, and New Orleans' boss Carlos Marcello in what was viewed as a calculated strategy to ride the Mafia hobbyhorse to headlines and higher office. The double-cross would not be forgotten.

Soon afterward, while Rudy Giuliani was clerking for U.S. District Judge Lloyd F. McMahon and Elliot's career was burgeoning having been named "Outstanding Surgical Resident" at the Jewish Hospital and Medical Center, the third cog in destiny's wheel, John Gotti, was also making a name for himself.

By the early 1960s, Gotti, his brother, Gene, and Ruggiero were seen as up-and-comers by the Fatico brothers, Carmine and Daniel, operating out of a Brooklyn storefront called the Club. Active in hijacking, loansharking, and murder for hire, the Faticos were interested in Gotti's fearlessness and put it to the test as he, Gene, and Ruggiero became full-time hijackers stealing virtually anything that moved from Long Island's Kennedy Airport. A string of arrests followed for petty crimes like unlawful entry, possession of bookmaking records, and petit larceny. In 1967, with Albert Anastasia having been assassinated in a "whack job" choreographed by Vito Genovese and Carlo Gambino, Gotti became a family associate working for Carmine Fatico and the man he reported to as *caporégime*, Aniello "Neil" Dellacroce.

Gotti became enamored of Dellacroce, a "man's man," who was Carlo Gambino's second in command. Dellacroce was a tough customer even by Mafia standards. He spoke in expletives and threats that few doubted he would carry out. A cold-blooded murderer who'd once posed as a Catholic priest to gain entrance into the room of the man he would assassinate, Dellacroce and Gotti took an immediate liking to one another akin to father and son.

If it was a sense of style that Gotti gleaned from Dellacroce, it was Al Capone, also from Naples, whom he idolized and was probably closest to in bearing. While stories of Capone's generosity are not uncommon, tales of his ferocity are more easy to come by because, unlike his mentor, Johnny Torrio, he believed in excessive force to gain his ends. A man of gargantuan appetites for food, liquor, gambling, and women, Capone was exactly the loud, brash, and stereotypical Neapolitan that Sicilian traditionalists like Maranzano and Bonanno sought to keep out of powerful positions within La Cosa Nostra. Capone's bets on horses, dice, roulette, and other games of chance were rarely less than $1,000 each and often as much as $100,000. He drove around Chicago in a bulletproof, armor-plated car custom made for him by General Motors. He tipped newsboys $10, hatcheck girls $20, and waiters $100 from a huge roll of bills he carried in his pocket.

Displays of his fury, both private and public, were of such magnitude that they became instantaneous headlines and the stuff of folklore. In May 1928, Capone held a banquet at the Hawthorne Inn in Cicero, Illinois, inviting a group of suspected conspirators. Once they'd eaten and drunk to satiation, his aides suddenly surrounded his guests and tied them to their chairs. Then, Capone picked up a baseball bat and with slow and cool deliberation, beat each one of them to death. Even men like Bugs Moran seemed shocked when on Valentine's Day, nine months later, four men dressed in police uniforms, lined six of Moran's soldiers and an innocent bystander against the wall of the S-M-C Cartage Company warehouse, riddled them with machine-gun bullets, then fired a shotgun at close range into the faces of those who were still moving. "There's only one man who kills like that," Bugs Moran later told police. "'The Beast,' Al Capone."

Stories not unlike these would circulate among Elliot's associates about John Gotti as he worked his way up the Mafia ladder, earning his "bones" through murders equally brutal. But that would be later. The problem Johnny Boy faced in the fall of 1969 was a thirty-month stay in Lewisburg Penitentiary for December 1967 and February 1968 hijacking convictions, followed by an interstate theft and kidnapping conviction just two months later. Soon after his release from prison in 1972, however, the irrepressible Teflon Don would strategize a way into the heart of Don Carlo Gambino and position himself for all the fame his hero, Capone, had achieved while living up to the worst fears of all the godfathers before him.

By 1972, as Gotti and Giuliani were making names for themselves at opposite poles of American society, Elliot saw his reputation among Manhattan's medical elite growing exponentially with honors like the Medical Center of Brooklyn's Research Committee Award and the Boehinger-

Ingelhein Scholar Award given by the American College of Chest Physicians. Though meetings with goodfellas from the old neighborhood became infrequent, his childhood reputation of being a man who could be trusted was enhanced by his successful dealings with Dellacroce so that he was now considered a full-fledged "associate" of the Gambino Family.

During that early period of his double life, Elliot's involvement with the mob remained limited to three key areas: one, treating Gambino Family members because they knew he was a top-flight physician; two, recruiting young interns for their thriving illegal abortion trade; three, disposing of evidence and sensitive medical records. Evidence could be a spent bullet recovered from a gunshot victim, which might prove embarrassing if reported to the police. Sensitive information could be a drug overdose, the physical presence of illegal drugs on a patient's person, or the very fact that a particular man, someone fleeing the police, for example, had ever come into the emergency room for treatment.

As they say, there was no "heavy lifting" until a hot summer night in June when a knock sounded at the door of Elliot's two-bedroom apartment sometime around midnight. Even with money coming in from other interests, he spent twelve to fifteen hours a day at the hospital, so he'd already fallen into a sound sleep.

Groggy, Elliot looked through the peephole in his apartment door and was startled to see three intimidating men. The biggest, pounding with his closed fist, was in his midforties, square faced and broad of frame. He wore a dark suit and looked like a bodybuilder. The other two were younger, maybe in their late twenties, with long slicked-back black hair, black slacks with shirts opened down to the fifth button, gold crucifixes dangling.

"Dr. Litner? Dr. Litner!"

"Yes . . ."

"Neil said you would help us. We need you to see someone. It's important."

Reluctantly, Elliot opened the door, "Jesus, it must be midnight . . ."

"We know that," the large man answered stepping in through the door as the others who didn't seem to understand much of what was being said stood in the hallway, "but we need to go now. Like I said, we're friends of Neil, Sal, too. There's a sick man who needs to see you."

"Can't your friend go to the hospital?"

The large man just stared. "Uh-uh," he finally answered.

Elliot nodded, electing against his better judgment, to go, but understanding at the same time that deep inside him there was a tiny flame that ratcheted up a notch. Who could they be talking about? What could have happened to cause them to wake him in the middle of the night and start throwing the names around that they had? Whatever it was had to be something important, and as he threw on a pair of Levis, a pullover shirt, and Adidas, he couldn't help but feel a rush of exhilaration. "Where was the phone booth?" he wondered because just then he was beginning to feel a lot like Clark Kent changing into Superman or at least someone far different from skinny, brainy Elliot Litner, and in the end, if only secretly, he knew that was just fine with him.

Elliot left his apartment. Parked directly in front of the building was a black Lincoln Town Car, engine running, waiting for him.

"I'll sit in the front," the large man muttered. "You get in the back with them."

Elliot didn't ask his name or anyone else's. That was part of the game, but the man who'd done the talking volunteered his was Lou "Cos" Coscarelli. Silently Elliot walked to the back of the car as one of the two greasers opened the door and the other got in from the street side sandwiching him between them.

The car doors had barely slammed shut when the guy to his right took something that looked like a black scarf out of his pocket and turned to him.

"Hey! Wha-wha-what is this about?" Elliot asked, looking and sounding a lot more like Woody Allen than either Clark Kent or the man of steel.

"It's a hood you got to wear," Lou explained half turning to him. "You got to have that on for your own protection."

"You're joking?"

"No, I ain't joking. But don't worry, Doc. We like you, or we wouldn't be here. *Now put on the hood!*"

He nodded to the greaser who handed the black hood to Elliot so he could put it on himself.

The ride was quiet, though occasionally Lou would speak Sicilian to the two men in the back who sat in stoic silence. It was then that Elliot realized they spoke no English at all and had probably been taken right off the boat.

Finally the Lincoln pulled into what seemed to be a driveway. "Okay, we're here," Lou confirmed, and with car doors opening and slamming shut, Elliot was led up a short walkway. "You keep that on, Doc," Lou said, referring to the hood, "until I say you can take it off, got it?"

Elliot nodded, inhaling the salty early-morning mist of what could only be Sheepshead Bay. They were on Ocean Avenue in one of those row houses that lined the street directly opposite the Bay, he was thinking. The front door was opened by an elderly Italian woman, then closed behind them, the sound of her concerned voice speaking whispered Sicilian filling his ears.

"You can take that off now," said Lou, helping him

remove the hood, and though Elliot thought most any light now would be blinding, it surprised him that his eyes barely had to adjust so dimly lit was this home.

"Follow me, please," the woman, who looked both kind and maternal, said in a soft voice, leading the entourage into a small, cluttered living room.

The walls were covered with paintings done in dark oils. The room itself was crammed with heavy, antiquated furniture. A brick fireplace was lined with photographs on the mantel of the same man at various stages of his life and career: a family portrait with his wife, the woman who'd accompanied them, two sons, a daughter, and him, a thin, sly-looking man with a large hawk nose and keen, crafty brown eyes. Others pictured him in the company of what seemed to be powerful men dressed in old-fashioned, double-breasted suits with wide lapels, some wearing hats with black bands tilted forward, and camel-hair topcoats, probably taken in the late 1930s or early 1940s.

Elliot's eyes fell upon the man pictured in these photos, now in his seventies, lying on a couch holding his abdomen in obvious misery. His wife stood over him shaking her head with worry. As Elliot approached, he waved her off, and she left the room entirely. This was Carlo Gambino, *capo di tutti capi*, the boss of Mafia bosses and most powerful criminal in America.

If Elliot was stunned for the moment, his healing instincts took over almost immediately. "It's your abdomen, isn't it? Your stomach?"

The old man nodded.

"Let me see," he said moving Gambino's hand aside and loosening his pajama bottoms.

The moment he touched the Mafia boss, Elliot could feel the air in the room electrify as a flood of urgent-sounding

Sicilian cascaded back and forth between those in the room who were watching.

"Hey!" he said turning. "I've got to examine him, don't I?"

"All right, all right," Lou mitigated, "do what you need to, but let me know along the way, *capesci?*"

Elliot didn't answer, but instead explored the old man's abdominal region. His stomach was swollen. His aorta was pulsating, and there was tenderness in the mid to lower abdomen. He could feel his bladder. All in all, Elliot realized this man was in serious trouble, and maybe so was he. He reached into his medical bag and pulled out a pair of latex gloves. "I've got to do a rectal," he told the men behind him.

Lou looked at him suspiciously. "What are you talkin' about, a rectal?"

Elliot gestured with his index finger moving it into his closed palm. "I have to ... feel inside his rectum."

Lou's eyes bulged. He turned to his cohorts, spoke in staccato Sicilian, and that's when the floodgates opened, as each man reacted, one making an angry move toward Elliot, restrained by Lou, his English-speaking interpreter.

"Now let me get this straight, Doc. You want to stick your finger up the boss' ass, is that it? 'Cause if that's it, there ain't no fucking way I'm gonna let you do that!"

"Look, Lou, I think your boss has what's called an abdominal aortic aneurysm that may burst. If he does, he's got to go to the hospital right now. I've got to catheterize him to take the urine out to relieve his pain and discomfort. If I don't do those things very soon, he will die."

"*No, Doc, no!*" the bodyguard moaned.

Lou turned away, pulling a cigarette from his shirt pocket. But before he could light it, Carlo Gambino's frail, clawlike hand tugged at his arm. The old man simply nodded as it seemed he always did rather than speak, either in Sicilian or

English. It was then that it dawned on Elliot. The reason Don Carlo never spoke, but had others address him by physical signals, Sicilian, or coded phrases, was his fear of FBI surveillance: bugs, wiretaps, parabolic microphones. None of them did any good if you never spoke, using other forms of communication instead.

Elliot rolled the old man over, pulled down his loosened pajama bottoms, and then did the unthinkable. He put his finger up Carlo Gambino's rectum while a room full of his bodyguards and protectors watched. The old man let out a low moan, then cursed in Sicilian as Elliot felt the bulging arterial walls confirming what he feared. There was a real possibility that Gambino's aorta would rupture before he could do anything.

"I can help, but we have to get him to the medical center fast. If I call ahead, we can have everything waiting. They'll take him to an emergency operating room where I can catheterize him and relieve his pain. Then he'll go to the operating room to have his aneurysm repaired. He'll be in the hospital for a while."

Lou shook his huge head from side to side with absolute resolve. "He can't stay."

"What?"

"Nobody can know he's sick, Doc. He already had problems with his heart last year. Before that, too. He can't be sick again, see what I'm saying? It would not be a good thing for us. Or for you."

"For me? Wha-what are you? Are you threatening me?"

"No, Doc. We're trusting you. If he does stay, there can't be no paper on it, *capesci?*"

"Okay. There won't be. No record of admittance. No medical record. For tonight and until he leaves the hospital, your boss will be like the Invisible Man."

"Thank you, Doc," said Lou clasping Elliot's hand with a

sincerity that seemed to pour from his heart. "The things they say about you, they're all true."

It was then that Don Carlo whispered a phrase to his aide just loud enough for Elliot to hear. *"We like Elliot Litner,"* the old man uttered to the others as he was being helped up off the sofa before leaving the house for the waiting Lincoln.

Those words were, to Elliot and in the world of La Cosa Nostra, the highest compliment you could pay anyone. To say, "I" like you, means that you are liked by an individual. To say, "We" like you, is to say that the family respects you, that you are one of them.

It was a gesture Elliot remembered truly appreciating as he followed through on his solemn promise. The boss of bosses was admitted to Brooklyn Jewish Hospital under an alias that night. All records pertaining to his treatment and surgical procedures were destroyed as soon as they were written.

7

SURGEON 1

"It was like being a fucking rock star!"

Carlo Gambino died about eighteen months after Elliot's first encounter with him, not from the aortic aneurysm, but from a heart attack on October 15, 1975, at his summer home in Massapequa, Long Island. During that time, Elliot would tend to his routine medical problems as best he could while a team of heart specialists from Columbia Presbyterian Hospital in Manhattan attempted to sustain the Mafia boss' deteriorating heart. Nevertheless, that night was the beginning of Elliot's initiation into the Gambino Family. *"We like Elliot Litner."* The words stuck in his mind and gave him a kind of comfort, like he truly belonged to something secretive and unique.

Obviously, being Jewish, he could never be a made man, but that didn't matter to Elliot. It was odd, but somehow, for some reason kept secret even from him, Elliot really loved these guys. He loved the excitement and the daring associated with standing outside of society, breaking all the rules, prospering, partying, doing whatever sex or drugs or anything that a man felt like. It was called living "the life." Yet even though Carlo

Gambino was one of its superstars, men like him, Maranzano, Bonanno, Vito Genovese, and others of the Sicilian tradition, kept to themselves, never showing off their wealth, rarely displaying their power, living humbly outside the parameters of the federal government, its laws and restrictions, quietly ruling their world, the secret society called the Mafia.

As time went on, Elliot got to know more about the old man to whose medical needs he tended. A man of incredible entrepreneurial energy, even the greasers that accompanied him to his home in Sheepshead Bay that first time were some of the dozens Gambino kept around as near-slaves, called "Zips," all part of a multimillion-dollar illegal immigration network he had conceived and operated since the mid-1930s. In retrospect, nothing should have surprised Elliot.

Carlo had grown up in an area of Palermo so dominated by the "Men of Honor" that it was considered off limits to police and military. Since boyhood, he had heard of the exploits of Sicilian crime bosses in America, their rapid rise and fabulous wealth. Then, in November 1921, after already having been initiated into the Mafia, Gambino was smuggled aboard the S.S. *Vincenzo Florio* bound for New York to join his mother's Castellano relatives. Almost immediately, Carlo, living near the Brooklyn Navy Yard where Luciano and Capone got their start, was introduced to Tommy "Three Fingers" Lucchese and the world of basement stills, protection rackets, speakeasies, and a path to power.

By the mid-1920s, Gambino's business acumen had ingratiated him to Joe Masseria, a major player in New York's burgeoning illegal liquor trade. Joe the Boss, a gruff man noted for his poor hygiene and sloppy appearance, was the exact opposite of archrival Salvatore Maranzano. It was no secret they despised one another, and soon a turf war over liquor jurisdictions was elevated to the bloodiest of battles.

SURGEON 1

The Castellamarese War, so named because of the coastal town of Sicily where they were born, was fast becoming a stalemate, until Maranzano, hearing of Gambino's superior abilities, cut a secret deal: Join forces with the Maranzano side and from the inside, arrange Masseria's assassination. Gambino agreed, offering to twist Luciano and Genovese, supporters of Masseria at that time, but only if Maranzano would give them protection and "respect" in return for their treachery. Maranzano agreed, and in April 1931, Masseria was lured by Luciano to the Nuova Villa Tammaro restaurant in Coney Island where the ambush was planned. Sedated with massive quantities of food and wine, the gluttonous Masseria was still eating when Luciano excused himself for the men's room and four assailants burst inside, guns blazing, killing Joe the Boss in front of dozens of stunned customers. Minutes later, Luciano returned to the table feigning shock at what had happened.

Gambino's chief quality may have been his cleverness or *fuberia*, supreme craftiness in Sicilian, a characteristic he claimed to have gleaned from his reading of Machiavelli's *The Prince*. "You have to be like a lion and a fox," Elliot once heard him advise a group of young Mafiosi. "The lion scares away the wolves. The fox recognizes traps. If you are a lion and a fox, nothing will stop you." Few things did, and the engineering of Albert Anastasia's assassination, which gained him a place on the Commission, was vintage Gambino, allowing Vito Genovese's ambition to elevate him much as Luciano had done twenty-five years earlier.

Carlo pondered Genovese's resolve to overtake the "Mad Hatter" as Anastasia had been dubbed for his escapades with Murder, Inc., a virtual killing machine at the time. Gambino recognized that Anastasia, while shrewd, was pathologically violent and not long on strategy as Genovese was. Soon, he devised an assassination plan that would insulate him and Genovese from the murder. He approached the godfather of another family, Joe Profaci, who detested Anastasia, and through him recruited three of his most brutal killers, the Gallo brothers: Crazy Joe, Louie, and Kid Blast.

On October 25, 1957, while Anastasia was being shaved at the Central Hotel (now the Park Sheraton) barbershop with a hot towel over his face, two of the Gallo brothers entered, blowing Anastasia out of his chair with five shots to his head and back. Miraculously still alive, Anastasia got up and lunged at his killers' reflection in the mirror, then collapsed in a pool of blood, taking a final coup de grâce from Crazy Joe Gallo to the back of his head. Once again, Carlo Gambino was nowhere to be seen, his fingerprints nowhere to be uncovered, though it was he who pulled the strings.

Gambino's empire was built block by block from that time, not only within the families, but in the awesome financial network he created afterward. One of Carlo's spectacular coups involved a ration stamp racket during World War II. He dispatched a team of safecrackers to the Office of Price Administration. They stole millions of dollars worth of stamps necessary for consumers to purchase gasoline, meat, even tires for cars. Once OPA administrators learned that the mob was an eager buyer of stolen stamps, contacts were cultivated for a steady supply sold ultimately on the black market. With the huge profits he made selling bootlegged liquor and ration stamps, Carlo then invested in meat markets, restaurants, nightclubs, trucking companies, and construction firms. It was Gambino Family activities in that same New York City construction arena that one day would put Elliot's career and those of Rudolph Giuliani and John Gotti on a collision course.

Back then, however, those problems were beyond the ken

of the frantic, and pleasurable, pace that Elliot was keeping. With the *Roe v. Wade* Supreme Court decision, the need for illegal abortion clinics ended, but that and even the death of Carlo Gambino had a negligible effect on the young doctor's lifestyle.

The family's faith in Elliot had widened to include a large circle of "under the table" patients while the new godfather, Paul Castellano, seemed no less fond of his talents than Don Carlo. Beyond that, Elliot's legitimate medical career was no less exciting. His articles on cutting-edge innovations in cardiac surgery appearing in *Contemporary Surgeon* and *Clinical Perspectives*. On the basis of that work and the reputation he'd made for himself at Jewish Hospital, Elliot was named a thoracic surgical resident at Mount Sinai Hospital in Manhattan.

Life was good. Though he was still putting in his twelve to fifteen hours in surgery, at night, with the disco scene in full bloom and the opening of Studio 54, Elliot was living the wanton lifestyle of a young Mafioso prince. Nothing was out of bounds. There were no restrictions. Cruising in his own 1976 red Corvette with a vanity plate that read SURGEON 1, the midseventies were one giant party, continuous and uninterrupted, to him. He still saw some of his *gumbas* from his Bronx-Brooklyn connection. But once in Manhattan, he began traveling in different circles.

One of the men who took an immediate liking to him at Mount Sinai was Dr. Francis Silvio, a member of the team of thoracic surgeons working at the hospital. Frank had emigrated from Palermo, Italy, and looked like a man who should be named Silvio, with a combed-back mane of white hair, a short, compact build, and a Martin Scorsese face. Beyond that, Frank Silvio was a madman. He had a home in Westchester County where his wife, Dorothy, and two daughters, Theresa and Marie, lived, as well as a Park Avenue apartment. He spent much of his time performing nonstop cardiac surgeries and an equal amount partying.

The other, a more staid relationship, almost like father and son, was with Al Rosengarten, who was a garment district mogul and Mount Sinai board member. From the first moment Elliot was introduced to him by Dr. Simon Dak, director of cardiology, Mr. Rosengarten seemed to take a personal interest in his progress within the hospital. It was a relationship that would eventually help elevate Elliot to the post of associate director of the department, a position that would have him socializing with Manhattan's crème de la crème at American Heart Foundation and New York Surgical Society fundraisers held at New York's most prestigious hotels including the Plaza, Waldorf-Astoria, and Sherry-Netherland.

Still, it didn't take long to realize that his friendship and "underworld" life with Frank Silvio was one hell of a lot more exciting than boring banquet speeches from the likes of then up-and-coming New York prosecutor Rudy Giuliani and certainly more fun. Silvio and he were like Batman and Robin back then, inseparable and clearly the dynamic duo when it came to uninhibited sex, drugs, and gambling at places like the Sands in Las Vegas and Resorts in Atlantic City where Frank, who was also connected, and he would play craps at $1,000 a throw, hopping from casino to casino, dropping as much as $20,000 in a single night. But, really, who cared? They were on a fast track with no end in sight, already making upward of $500,000 annually with Silvio in his midfifties and Elliot having just turned thirty! More, Elliot truly loved gambling, the thrill of it, and to both of them, he supposed, who gambled with human life in surgeries six, maybe eight times a day, what was so important about money?

The only thing Elliot loved more than gambling was sex— and there was plenty of that, too, because it was at around that time that a new sex club opened called Plato's Retreat. The club's main room comprised a huge oblong of cojoined mattresses, a Jacuzzi, and a pool where a guy could have whole groups of women attack, then throw him in the middle of a swarming multipartner sexual encounter. "Group Grope," they called it, and if a man was a little patient, everyone had their turn being licked, sucked, and fucked by absolute strangers, many of them among Manhattan's hippest, most beautiful people with the music of Donna Summer blaring, strobe lights flashing, and lines of cocaine served on mirrored trays with straws as if they were shot glasses full of Jose Cuervo.

Of course, Elliot realized even then, that many would say, "Hey, what's this guy about anyway? Has he no morals whatsoever?" To which, he would have answered, "No, I don't!" He had no "morals" in the conventional sense. He was amoral. Unlike Silvio, who used methamphetamines the way most people used sugar, Elliot didn't take drugs. He worked his ass off inside and outside the hospital after spending his youth playing with his brother and friends in a garbage dump. He passionately strived to teach and learn everything he could about his chosen profession while spending two-thirds of each working day performing surgeries, knowing that any misjudgment on his part was potentially life threatening. Now that was stress.

Yes, Elliot liked sex, hot and uninhibited. Yes, he loved gambling whether it was cards, craps, roulette, or two cockroaches racing across a tabletop. It gave him a thrill to risk this easy-come, easy-go commodity called money on something yet to be determined, something he couldn't control, and yes, which if he did with reckless abandon would probably destroy him. But that was exactly what he loved about it. It was the jeopardy that it put him in, and he wondered at times if the reason he so relished that high had something to do with an atavistic feeling because of what his family had endured during their struggle for survival in Russia.

He could write about the postrevolution horrors they experienced once Lenin and Trotsky had defeated the tsar, who also was not so fond of Jews; of the promises of a "chicken in every pot"; or the rampant anti-Semitism that followed with the slogan "Kill the Jews and Save Russia" plastered on posters that lined storefronts. He could also write about how his father as a young boy was beaten to a bloody pulp in Vinograd and driven by Cossack soldiers on horses into the town's synagogue which was set afire with hundreds of Jews still inside and how he miraculously escaped. But he'd prefer to put down on paper an anecdote that was told many times more often because it illustrates how these incredibly resilient people survived, constantly finding the humor in impossible situations.

It seemed, according to Saul anyway, that with the revolution over and the tsar gone, the Russian instigators told the peasants to take everything they wanted from the rich. There was nobody to stop them, so it was almost impossible to estimate the robbing and killing that went on. They stole anything that wasn't nailed down, and whatever they didn't take, they destroyed. Generally, Russian peasants lived in very small houses, so tiny that it was necessary to bend over to get inside.

During that period of anarchy, a not-so-bright Russian peasant that Saul knew brought home a very large mirror that he'd robbed from a rich home. He couldn't bring it into his small house. The only thing he could do was to store the mirror in his barn where he kept his cows and, of course, a bull. When the bull came into the barn and looked into the mirror, he was shocked to see competition for the cows that he didn't relish. The bull charged and went flying through the peasant's new mirror—and this was the end of Saul's story about a mirror full of bull!

Okay, Elliot realized, this was not "Saturday Night Live" material, but to their humble family in the Bronx, it was hilarious, and the lesson was learned that fortune, family, and even life were fleeting. It could end at any time, often for no discernible reason, so why take it so seriously? Do your best, work hard, and help people if you can, but for God's sake, have a little fun. And though circumstances and maybe life itself had changed Elliot's perspective since his days in the Bronx, it was fun he and Silvio were after, and there was no crazier place to find it than Studio 54.

8

STUDIO 54

"What a world! What a society! How could anyone take it seriously?"

I t was Silvio who introduced Elliot to Steve Rubell about six
months after the club opened, and it was already the place to
be. Almost from the beginning, there were long lines at the
entrance. Elliot remembered someone saying that even real
celebrities like Burt Reynolds were having trouble getting in
that night. But Frank knew a guy named Dominick Montiglio,
a Gambino enforcer until he went into the witness protection
program, and when he appeared with them, all obstacles parted like the Red Sea. They were inside Studio 54 with no trouble getting past the cadre of bouncers and wannabes ever
again.

These were the golden days for Rubell, disco, and
arguably New York's night scene, unless you were willing to
go back to the 1920s. On a given night, you could find Mick
Jagger, Andy Warhol, Diana Ross, Liz Smith, you name the
celebrity, some of them so out of it, or caught up in the fer-
vor of pulsating music and strobe-light-madness, that they
acted as if they were anonymous. Suddenly, they felt free to
make out or have sex with strangers in the grungy VIP base-

ment or on the balconies that hovered over the dance floor where tubes studded with crackling light bulbs were rising and descending, and just above that, a giant spoon made its rhythmic journey up into the insatiable nose of the Man-In-The-Moon stage prop towering in the background.

It was an incredible place where anything could happen and often did. It was, at least to Elliot's knowledge, the first broadly accepted club where being openly gay not only wasn't frowned upon, but was encouraged. Studio employees, waiters, and busboys bounced around bare chested in sneakers and gym shorts. A Jewish couple was made up to be Nazi vampires, she sporting a swastika on her panties. A man danced beside her in a Spider Man outfit with HERPES VIRUS inscribed on his chest as singer-actress Cher, wearing a see-through wedding dress, slow-danced with a sumptuous blonde, a single breast exposed. No wonder known gay men like Truman Capote, Rudolf Nureyev, Andy Warhol, Elton John, and not the least among them, Mafia attorney Roy Cohn, although publicly gay, felt so at home.

It was there that Elliot first met Cohn, sitting on one of the contiguous couches that snaked through the VIP Room, wearing his trademark leopard-spotted bow tie, a sequined blazer, and jeans, nuzzling with Steve Rubell, as he expostulated on the fate of the then-unknown hijacker-murderer, John Gotti. Elliot was with Frank Silvio, who the notorious attorney seemed to know quite well, and also, by happenstance, Dominick Montiglio. Cohn, who'd cut his teeth on alleged American Communists as chief counsel to Joseph McCarthy during the senator's infamous hearings, was a gun for hire and by the lights of many, a truly evil man. He'd earned his archconservative bona fides during those Senate hearing witch hunts, but cemented them with deep friendships, and some say love affairs, with FBI Director J. Edgar

Hoover and New York's Cardinal Francis Spellman. During those days, however, Cohn was earning his daily bread defending prominent mob figures including Genovese boss "Fat Tony" Salerno, Bonanno boss Carmine "Nino" Galante, and Gambino Family members Carmine Fatico, Aniello Dellacroce, and more recently, Gotti.

It was that night, through Cohn, that Elliot first heard about John Gotti. More, he came to understand Gotti's cunning in parlaying his modest credentials as "acting captain" of Fatico's crew working out of the Bergin Hunt and Fish Club in Ozone Park, Queens, to a genuine player held in high regard by the big boss Carlo Gambino, still alive at the time.

"In May 1972 while Gotti was still in Lewisburg on a hijacking charge, Carlo's twenty-nine-year-old nephew, Emmanuel, was grabbed off a Manhattan street and kidnapped," Cohn, confided to a covey of them in hushed tones. "The kidnappers contacted Emanuel's wife demanding $350,000 ransom of which she delivered $100,000, only to find his body excavated from the grounds of a New Jersey dump eight months later. The guy responsible, the Gambinos believed, was Jimmy McBratney, a member of the Westies, an Irish street gang, who'd kidnapped one of their Staten Island loan sharks a month before. So, reacting to the affront to his family's honor, the old man puts out a goddamned contract on McBratney that Gotti, now released from Lewisburg, jumps all over along with his two buddies, Angelo Ruggiero and Ralph Galione."

Cohn went on to say that Gotti's plan was to kidnap McBratney, then take him to a Brooklyn Navy Yard warehouse that would serve as both a torture and execution chamber because to him an insult to Gambino's power of that magnitude deserved more than just dying.

"I mean," Cohn said, "John wanted to get medieval on

him, but instead what happened was that family members spotted McBratney at a Staten Island bar and tipped off Gotti. John and his two accomplices then entered the bar in plain sight of something like a dozen customers and pretending to be plainclothes detectives, tell McBratney he's under arrest. When they try to handcuff him, all hell breaks loose until Gotti and Ruggiero pin him against a wall while Galione fires three shots into McBratney's head, killing him instantly in plain sight of the barmaid and a roomful of others.

"From there, Gotti went 'into the wind,' until June 1974 when he was arrested by FBI agents who turned him over to the NYPD. Out of gratitude, Carlo Gambino, himself, demanded that family capos chip in to retain me," Cohn bragged, "because they knew I had friends in high places including state judges and higher-ups at the FBI through my deep friendship with Mr. Hoover. Leaning heavy on every goddamned one of those, I had Johnny plea bargain what could have been seen by some as an open-and-shut organized crime hit down to attempted manslaughter."

"True," Cohn concluded, "John was sentenced to four years, but that really meant only two years with good behavior served at Green Haven Correctional Facility, practically his backyard. A good move, all of this, on Gotti's part. I tell you, this guy's got a future." Cohn understood what Gotti clearly knew, that the family was now indebted to him, and his standing within La Cosa Nostra had been cemented with the boss of bosses.

Beyond the scuttlebutt about Gotti, another interesting thing happened later that night. A bleach blonde, who looked to be in her late forties, approached Rubell and chastised him for being in the arms of Cohn. "Do you know what he is?" she loudly upbraided. "He's a killer! He killed Abe Feller and Stan Kaplan, him and those Nazi bastards on the McCarthy committee!" Studio 54 was not famous for violence, but there was no shortage of security. A bodyguard quickly whisked her away, still screaming, "He's a killer, that bastard! A killer!" Then, Rubell turned to Cohn, kissed him on the mouth, and said to the group, "Yes, but he's *my* killer."

That was the kind of hypocrisy that had already made Elliot realize what bullshit society really was. Here was the elite of the fashion world, America's most prestigious attorneys, lawmakers, models, stockbrokers, entrepreneurs, Mafia chieftains, and at the end of it, they were all complicit, part and parcel of the same hypocrisy. Hoover and Cohn were thick as thieves, Cohn and Rubell were lovers, along with New York's powerful Catholic Cardinal Spellman. Carlo Gambino pays big bucks to Cohn who after touting the American dream and prosecuting innocent men before the Senate as Communists, cajoles, bribes, or threatens who knows whom so that John Gotti gets away with murder, all of which makes two Manhattan heart surgeons look on in dumb amazement. What a world! What a society! How could anyone take any of it seriously?

9

BABANIA

"It's true what they say about you, Dottore. Inside, you are one of us."

Despite the craziness that kept Frank Silvio and Elliot occupied, often until the early hours of the morning, they remained conscientious about their work. How did they stay alert and on top of their game physically—they were surgeons—and mentally? Silvio had his methamphetamines. Elliot had his basic metabolism and diet cola, which for him was at least as effective. In those days, it would not be uncommon for them to take a limo to Atlantic City after ten at night, only to return the next morning at six, shower, brush teeth, and be prepping for surgery by eight. That was simply the way they lived. Silvio and Elliot understood that and everything else about each other, though they rarely discussed Mafia family connections. Sometimes, Elliot would work emergency. Other times, if Elliot had prescheduled procedures, he'd be called on by Frank to handle situations that were other than standard.

One situation happened early along in his residency at Mount Sinai when he was called to emergency over the hospital PA system. When he got there, the room was in chaos with two nurses and an intern struggling with a hysterical teenager with long black hair who looked to be seventeen or eighteen. The kid was bleeding badly from the right shoulder, and the stress he was putting on the arm was doing him no good at all.

"Let me go!" he was screaming. "Let me the fuck outta here!"

Understanding the situation, Elliot grabbed the boy's arm, trying to calm him, while applying pressure with his fingers against the wound. "Get me Demerol," he shouted to the nurse. "Stat!"

"I gotta get outta here," the kid kept insisting. "You don't understand? I gotta get out now!"

"You'll get out all right, in a hearse, unless you let us treat that arm."

But before the boy could respond, a second kid was wheeled into the room on a gurney, groggy and muttering incoherently from what appeared to be a head injury.

The gurney was wheeled next to Elliot as he continued working on the first boy, when the eyes of the two teenagers met, then locked in lethal recognition.

"You fucking cocksucker!" the second boy screamed at the patient they were working on. Then he sat up on the gurney and pulled a gun from out of the crotch of his jeans.

Pandemonium broke out. Nurses screamed. One orderly who'd been called to help dove to the floor while everyone else backed away toward the door. Except Elliot. He was still holding the wounded boy's bicep, trying to stop the jets of blood pulsing from out of his slashed artery.

"Put the gun down!" Elliot demanded in a voice that he'd never heard come from out of his mouth before.

"Fuck you!" the young hood screamed back at him. "I'm going to kill you, Tommy, you motherfucker!"

Then, as he took aim, Elliot let go of his patient's arm. Immediately, by luck, the blood that had been suppressed for the past several minutes shot like a crimson geyser into the gunman's face, flustering him for the split second. By reflex, Elliot swung his right hand with all of the force he could muster at the gun, knocking it from the kid's hand.

The .38 revolver skidded across the linoleum and was retrieved by an intern as an armed security guard grabbed the would-be killer in a bear hug, finally restraining him.

In a matter of seconds, the assailant was removed and placed in a secured room with guards and a physician while Elliot returned to the problem at hand, the sliced artery in his patient's right arm.

"Let's sew this kid up," he said tearing loose what remained of the teenager's shirt and applying a surgical clamp to the wound.

As the nurse turned to prepare a local anesthetic and sutures, he felt the boy slip an envelope into the oversized side pocket of his lab coat.

"Please take this, Doc," the kid whispered. "It can't be found on me, Dottore! I'm trusting you."

Elliot didn't say a word as he applied the anesthetic and sutures in what for him was a routine procedure. The boy, Tommy Ruggiero, would be all right. He would regain the use of his arm, perhaps with some physical therapy, but nothing worse than that.

Elliot left the emergency room and found Silvio talking with two men, one of whom he recognized as John Gotti's pal, Angelo Ruggiero, a heavyset man out of the blue-collar crew under Neil Dellacroce.

They looked up, then Frank came to him. "Hey, this situation with the kid. Everyone would rather if it never happened."

"Never happened? Christ, Frank, half of the 103rd Precinct is here right now."

"I understand, and we've already arranged for both to leave without a lot of commotion. If you could see to it that the medical chart disappears, I know that Angelo, the boy's uncle, would be extremely grateful."

Elliot looked at his new friend and nodded. "Consider it done."

Later, when the police came to take their report, Elliot told them nothing. "Two boys had come in with minor injuries sustained perhaps in a fistfight, then disappeared in all of the excitement."

"Where to?"

"I couldn't imagine, busy as emergency had been at the time."

They seemed satisfied.

That night Elliot took the medical charts and put them in the top drawer of his desk, not giving a second thought to the envelope in the pocket of his lab coat until the next morning when Tommy's uncle appeared standing in the doorway to his office. He closed the door behind him.

"Mr. Ruggiero . . ."

He nodded.

Without a word, Elliot placed the envelope and medical charts on his desktop.

"Did you look inside the envelope?" Ruggiero asked.

He shook his head.

"Open it."

Elliot did. It contained a stack of cash and a large plastic baggy filled with several ounces of fine white powder.

"*Babania*," Ruggiero said, using the slang for heroin. "You understand, Dottore? For me, this could have been trouble. My nephew was involved in a drug deal went bad." Ruggiero took the heroin from the desktop and left the money. "But believe me, he'll be punished, but he won't go to jail, and he will not cause me embarrassment. For that, I thank you, Dottore. It's true what they say about you. Inside you are one of us."

"Quack-Quack" Ruggiero shook Elliot's hand, turned, and left the office, leaving him sitting there behind his desk staring at more than $5,000 in crisp, new $100 bills. Unfortunately for Angelo, this was not his first nor would it be his last involvement with *babania* and distribution of hard-core drugs outside the family.

10

GIULIANI AT THE
WALDORF

*"True, some of his pals respected no law outside the underworld. Men
like Rudy, they just couldn't be trusted."*

Maybe we're all molded by our backgrounds and early life
experiences, or maybe each of us is just a little crazy,
Elliot speculated, recalling how he and his first wife,
Hanna, had met. His family didn't put much stock in appear-
ances and society standing. It was what you were inside that
counted. So the prospect of rubbing elbows with Manhattan's
elite never interested him nearly so much as continuing to
innovate in his chosen field of thoracic surgery. In a broad
field that concentrates on heart, lung, and circulatory system
disorders, there was a lot of room to innovate. In fact, it was
his work in the area of cardioplegia, a procedure that slows
the heart by decreasing the blood's temperature during aortocoronary bypass surgery, and intraoperative echocardiography, a way of using ultrasound to study the heart, that
inspired Dr. Dak to name him associate director of cardiac
surgery.

Of course, along with the promotion came social respon-
sibilities on behalf of the hospital that had him attending
award dinners and fundraisers for dozens of professional soci-

eties, which is why he was at one such function held by the American Medical Association at the Waldorf-Astoria. And that's where he met Hanna Shapiro, daughter of Manhattan obstetrician-to-socialites Mort Shapiro. It was also the first time Elliot laid eyes on a young up-and-coming prosecutor named Rudy Giuliani.

From Elliot's side, the evening was unsurprisingly banal: hors d'oeuvres and martinis laced with self-aggrandizing speeches by medical professionals convinced the world couldn't survive a day without them, followed by a filet mignon dinner and yet more diatribes set to the backdrop of overly eager career climbers hobnobbing their way up New York's precarious social ladder. The clear standout among them, Elliot remembered calculating even then, was thirty-four-year-old Rudolph Giuliani, fresh back from a two-year stint at the Justice Department in Washington, now officially "white-shoed" as a partner in the Manhattan law firm of Patterson, Belknap, Webb and Tyler.

Elliot had heard about Giuliani's exploits in the early 1970s "flipping" corrupt cops for the Knapp Commission from Nicky Micelli and others, and understood him to be an easy guy to either love or hate upon first impression. That night they barely shook hands after being introduced by Dr. Dak. Of what interest could a socially backward, adolescent-looking Jewish physician like him be to an up-and-coming wannabe like Rudy? Still, Elliot, seated near the speakers' podium, couldn't help observing him as he smoked a cigar and sipped Scotch, waxing eloquent about his crime-fighting days to a cult mockingly called the Rudettes by his fellow law partners, five young women who worked dawn to dark for him often spilling over to late night for steaks at the "21" Club, then partying into the wee hours at many of the same discos Silvio and Elliot frequented.

Giuliani had worked with detective Carl Bogan, whose career inspired the "Kojak" TV series, around the time of the French Connection case in which 300 pounds of heroin, procured with Gambino Family money, had been stolen from the police property room. That fiasco, coupled with the Knapp Commission report, cast a citywide pall of distrust over the NYPD, and Rudy knew how to make the most of it.

Bogan taught Giuliani how to flip witnesses, turning them from defendants to undercover agents. The technique, pioneered by Elliot's Studio 54 crony Roy Cohn during the McCarthy hearings, involved putting a suspect under oath, then bombarding him with questions, many related to an alleged crime, but others of a personal nature, the more embarrassing the better. To hide a cheating wife's indiscretion or protect a loved one from unnecessary implication, the investigator's job was to manipulate a cop into perjuring himself. The strategy was simple: If you can't get him for corruption, get him for perjury, a crime that carried a five-year prison term, a daunting prospect for cops. They usually agreed to become undercover informers in exchange for immunity.

It was mastery of this kind of intimidation that shaped Giuliani's reputation as Southern District U.S. attorney when Bob Leuci, another cop caught in the Knapp Commission web, became an undercover informer wearing a wire for the NYPD's Special Investigating Unit (SIU). Working as a good cop-bad cop team, Rudy and Thomas Puccio, U.S. attorney for the Eastern District, plied Leuci for dirt on his fellow cops, eventually bringing him to the brink of suicide, as he attempted to survive the Kafkaesque world of trust for betrayal.

Leuci's story would be told in Robert Daley's 1978 bestseller-movie, *Prince of the City*, casting Rudy as a moral crusader bringing scores of corrupt New York City cops to justice. In reality, Giuliani never prosecuted a single cop case involving Leuci because most had already been tried before he took his position or were handled by the special state prosecutor. Nevertheless, Rudy boasted that he'd convicted forty-three cops. In truth, the total number of cops convicted during the period he ran the corruption unit was only ten. But numbers like that held little sway with the media, so Giuliani invented more impressive ones then cloaked them in a self-formulated mythology used like a shield to protect himself from the truth about his family's own Mafia ties.

While Elliot gazed at the prosecutor that night at the Waldorf, he wondered if Giuliani was elaborating on childhood stories told to him by Adelina, his grandmother, about an insidious "monster" called the Mafia and the time his great-grandfather Vincenzo Stanchi received a note from the Black Hand signed with the ominous coal-smeared handprint demanding money for protection. Or another, involving her late husband, Luigi, a baker, who after being extorted, could pay no more and committed suicide. "Given five years and the right resources, a prosecutor like me could bring the Mafia to its knees!" Elliot would later hear Giuliani brag on national television.

No, Elliot didn't like Rudy Giuliani, he decided then. True, some of his own pals were rough around the edges and of a kind that respected no law outside the underworld, but at least they weren't hypocrites. They had a code, and for the most part, they lived by it. Men like Rudy, they just couldn't be trusted.

Elliot's eyes probed the ballroom at the Waldorf, filled with music and dancing, until they fixed on a more compelling sight, the table where Dr. Dak; Mount Sinai board member and garment district mogul, Al Rosengarten; and high-society obstetrician, Mort Shapiro, were sitting. But it wasn't the three men that caught his attention, it was the young woman sitting beside Dr. Shapiro.

Elliot knew that Mort's wife had died from cancer two years earlier. So who was this raven-haired beauty with skin as white as alabaster and eyes coal black and piercing as lasers? A girlfriend? She looked to be in her early twenties, he guessed, and that wasn't like Mort, a straight shooter still getting over his wife's passing. No, this had to be a daughter, Elliot reasoned, slowly rising from his chair and gliding across the room as if on a cloud.

"Dr. Litner!" the short, plump Dr. Dak resonated in his deep-voiced, Romanian accent. "I wondered if you'd come by to say hello!"

Elliot nodded in rote as Al Rosengarten, the most "mobbed up" of anyone he knew outside the Gambino Family's inner circle, shook his hand heartily, followed by Dr. Shapiro, and finally the girl, his daughter, Hanna.

"It's nice to meet you," he heard himself utter.

She looked at him warily, not a shy girl, then extended her hand confident, self-assured, and exactly unlike him.

Who knows? Maybe it was his shyness or self-deprecating humor that Hanna found attractive. Maybe it was his mind, clear and focused, at least when it came to medicine. But one way or the other, they chatted under the watchful gaze of the three men, danced just once, then left the crowded ballroom for a stroll in the cool night air around Park Avenue. Miraculously, Hanna seemed to enjoy being with him! They talked about his work as a surgeon at Mount Sinai, but she seemed most interested, and amused, by Elliot's stories about Uncle Saul and his laundry business, and Lou with his luncheonette, Steven and he bluffing their way into Yankee Stadium to see the 1961 World Series, their escapades out behind their apartment building in the backies, and almost anything that had to do with growing up dirt poor in the Bronx. It was a background that being raised as the daughter of a prominent physician in a Prospect Park brownstone, alongside the likes of former New York Gov. Hugh Carey, actress Margaux Hemingway, and Russian concert pianist Vladimir Horowitz, absolutely and forever precluded.

From Elliot's side, he was all too delighted just to have a girlfriend that somebody hadn't paid to be with him. But Hanna wasn't just a girl. She was a stunner! Tall and slim, with fine features, and a magnificent figure accentuated by clothes fashioned by New York's finest designers. Hanna was not only beautiful, but well educated with an undergraduate degree from Vassar and an N.Y.U. master's degree in education. More, she was captivating. Enthusiastic about skiing and horses, it was clear she was her father's daughter, sharing with Elliot her own family exploits, so unlike his, canoeing Hudson Bay in Canada, journeying up the Amazon with her dad to locations no white child had ever seen.

To him, she was intriguing! Intoxicating! And soon he found himself visiting Hanna and her dad at that Prospect Park brownstone on weekends and as often during the week that his hectic schedule allowed. Together, they attended plays at Lincoln Center where Mort had a box. The same for concerts at Carnegie Hall, after which they'd pass the night talking for hours about art, literature, and their deepest feelings and dreams for the future.

One topic that Elliot never broached with Hanna, however, was his "other" life: the friends and associates he had, the places he went, or the things that he did. At that time, it seemed vitally important to separate his two existences even from the woman with whom he was falling in love and would, in a matter of months, marry.

11

THE BUSINESSMAN
GODFATHER

"You're looking at my cock, but it's my leg that's killing me!"

It was on October 15, 1976, that Carlo Gambino died in bed at his Long Island summer home at the age of seventy-four, and though Elliot couldn't fathom it then, this was also the day that the boss of bosses made the greatest mistake of his career. During his twenty-year tenure as *capo di tutti capi*, Gambino had never become an American citizen, never served a single day in jail, and when confronted with deportation in 1969, quietly agreed to pay a local congressman $1,000 a month for life to see to it that the proceedings went away.

An arch traditionalist whose philosophies derived from Maranzano's Sicilian arm of the Honored Society, Don Carlo kept a fanatically low profile, shunning all publicity, eschewing his Massapequa estate to live with his wife in their modest Sheepshead Bay home, but while in his deathbed that day—with John Gotti still in prison—he told his capos that they must choose Paul Castellano, his first cousin and brother-in-law, as their new godfather.

By tradition, a new boss was chosen in a vote of the capos, most of whom would certainly have selected Neil

Dellacroce, the underboss, as Gambino's successor. But in an act that betrayed everything he had stood for, Gambino decided that day to pay back a favor to the Castellano family. Of course, the capos obeyed their godfather's deathbed command and elected Big Paulie boss, but without enthusiasm because Castellano was not admired as a *caporégime*.

Aloof by nature, everyone connected to the Gambino Family understood that it was Castellano's ties to Don Carlo that had made him what he was. Believing that people resented him, Big Paulie rarely forged relationships out of his inner circle, but with the old man's influence became a millionaire selling meat to major supermarket chains and running a substantial wholesale operation called Blue Ribbon Meats. His soldiers, mainly an aging group of loan sharks and bookmakers in Brooklyn, were not nearly so well off, but were still expected to grease Castellano's palms. In the family, Paul was regarded as shrewd, selfish, and very cheap.

Soon after, Castellano would show that he understood the shaky ground that he stood upon by refusing to name his own underboss as tradition allowed and giving Dellacroce near autonomy over crews more involved in blue-collar crimes such as John Gotti's crew of hijackers, loan sharks, and shakedown artists at the Bergin Hunt and Fish Club in Ozone Park. Castellano would focus on the family's white-collar crews, the ones involved in construction bid rigging, labor union racketeering, and stock market fraud like the crew in Bensonhurst that included mob superstar-in-the-making Sammy Gravano.

In effect, Carlo's mistake was compounded by Castellano's, and a riff as old as the American Mafia itself was being played out within the Gambino Family between the Sicilian traditionalists and the Neapolitan iconoclasts. Paul's decision to separate the two chains of command would create two families within the Gambino Family—the Castellano branch and the Dellacroce branch—a move that would cost him his life.

Elliot's first experience with Castellano came in the winter of 1979 when Frank Silvio asked him to pay Big Paulie a visit to check on some swelling the son was complaining about in his leg. Elliot knew that he suffered from NIDDM, noninsulin-dependent Type II diabetes, so it was no surprise that he'd have circulatory difficulties, but his general physician seemed to think a contrast phlebogram of the leg might be in order, which could require some minor surgery.

"No problem," Elliot said, and that evening, he took his Lil' Red Corvette for a drive through the Battery Tunnel and over the Verrazano Narrows Bridge to Staten Island where Castellano lived in his $3.5-million, seventeen-room mansion on Todt Hill.

The mansion was built in 1976 when Castellano took over as boss of the richest and most powerful crime family in the United States, and for him, at the time, it must have seemed like a good idea. Recently released from prison on an IRS charge, Neil Dellacroce was back, temporarily placated, and making money. The family's various rackets were productive, and even Big Paulie's legitimate businesses in New York State, New Jersey, and Pennsylvania were thriving. About the only problem he seemed to have then was the onset of diabetes. The illness, not uncommon, was generally found in people older than forty, particularly those that were overweight like Castellano who despite being a soft-spoken, elegant man, stood six feet, three inches tall, with a large imposing head, big meaty features. He weighed more than 300 pounds.

When Elliot drove up the hill to the mansion, it was dark, but not difficult to see that it was built on the highest land on Staten Island with a view of the Atlantic Ocean and the lights of New York Harbor. The mansion stood surrounded by a park with 120 feet of frontage, secluded from the road by stands of pine trees and an imposing wrought-iron fence built to keep unwelcome visitors out and a pack of vicious Doberman pinschers in. The gates were open when he arrived. He drove up the winding brick road appreciating the splendor of the place. Constructed of large fieldstone and stucco, it was painted white with a curved entrance portico supported by two tall, white columns that resembled the White House.

The estate, truly an awesome sight, told Elliot something about Castellano. This was a Mafia godfather who commanded 3,000 soldiers; was Commission chairman of the five New York families; and a prominent legitimate businessman working with corporate executives on the order of Ira Waldbaum of Waldbaum's supermarkets and Frank Perdue of Perdue Farms chickens. More than a mob boss or stereotype tough guy like Capone or Dellacroce, Paul Castellano saw himself as a modern-day feudal lord, and that was the way he lived, wielding influence enough to shut down the ports of Brooklyn or halt construction of a Manhattan skyscraper with a phone call, while holding life-or-death power over his men, the people he did business with, and others who might not even know his name.

Elliot parked his car, then walked up the white-brick steps, past the columns, to the double-door entrance. He rang the bell, and oddly, it was not a servant as one might expect, but Castellano's wife, the sister-in-law of Carlo Gambino, Nina Manno Castellano, who answered.

An attractive, imposing woman in her early sixties, she seemed amazingly controlled and dignified as she spoke. "Dr. Litner?"

He nodded.

"Please come in," she said in probably the sweetest, most refined voice he'd ever heard.

Elliot entered the thirty-foot-long foyer, decorated with large gilt-framed mirrors that led to a sweeping spiral staircase that rose to the second floor.

"Paul's in the back," she said with a trace of irony as he followed her into an immense kitchen with three huge freezers, a long tiled counter, and a dining-nook table that could seat twelve people.

Passing through the kitchen, they walked through a set of sliding glass doors and stepped into a walled-in area in back of the house that resembled a small park complete with tennis courts, bocce courts, and an Olympic-sized swimming pool. There, dressed in a scarlet satin bathrobe over blue silk pajamas and wearing black velvet slippers, stood the godfather, poolside, smoking a cigar, lovingly watching a dark young woman of thirty as she laughed and frolicked nude in the water in front of the three of them.

"Dr. Litner is here to see you," Nina Castellano said gently.

Big Paulie turned, his expression suddenly sour. "You can leave now, dear," he said dismissively to his wife, looking Elliot up and down as he puffed on his cigar. "You're a Jew, aren't you?"

"Yes, I am."

"Why are all you Jews doctors?" he asked, walking toward one of the reclining chairs that surrounded the pool. "Why not a paisan like Silvio? He comes from Palermo like me and Carlo. Now that it looks like I need an operation, they get rid of the guineas and send in the kikes, is that it? What the fuck." He spread his huge frame over the recliner, undoing his satin robe and pulling off pajamas. "I deal with a lot of Jews in business. When it comes to lawyers and doctors, there's nobody better. Besides, I hear you're a good guy."

"Th-thank you, sir," Elliot answered with a stutter that emerged whenever he got nervous.

Castellano gazed out onto the pool where the girl beamed back at him, striking suggestive poses for their amusement. "She's my maid from Colombia. I call her my 'little clown' because she makes me laugh and can suck the chrome off a Cadillac bumper."

He waved to her as she made her way to the side of the pool where she propped herself up staring at Elliot, breasts pert and gleaming in the sunlight, with a wide-eyed expression like that of a small child. "Is you going to examine him?"

"Yes," Elliot answered, stunned to see that Paul Castellano lay before him, legs spread, penis exposed, watching his young Colombian girlfriend with a glee that seemed almost adolescent. More, though Elliot was no expert, it was apparent to him that along with a swollen left leg and severe varicose veins, Big Paulie had recently undergone surgery to have a penile implant.

"You're looking at my cock, but it's my leg that's goddamned killing me!"

"Yes, let's have a look," Elliot answered getting down to business as he examined the painfully swollen limb. "Has this ever happened before?"

Castellano shook his head in the negative. "Never," he grimaced as Elliot pressed the flat of his hand against his ankle, mapped with varicose veins.

"It's not only your diabetes. You see, veins have valves, every few inches, that open in only one direction—toward the heart—to prevent the backflow of blood. This design reduces the work of the circulatory system, but also makes the valves subject to damage if there is too much back pressure against the valves in the veins. That's what you have here. Pressure that's causing the pain and swelling."

"So you have to amputate my leg?" Big Paulie asked bluntly.

"No, we need to run what's called a contrast phlebogram. It's a simple procedure where a dye is injected into a vein then x-rayed to see how the veins are working. It can be done on an outpatient basis. Chances are this can be treated with medication or something as simple as exercise and periodic leg elevation."

"So he going to be okay?" the godfather's maid asked hopefully.

"No doubt," Elliot answered, without even the hint of a stutter now that they were talking medicine.

"Oh, that wonderful!" she proclaimed, rising out of the water, walking over to him, wet and still naked, as she pressed her lips against his cheek and hugged him.

"Good news, Doc," said Big Paulie, puffing his cigar as Gloria Olarte, his live-in mistress, escorted Elliot back toward the mansion au naturel. "I'll see you at the hospital, tomorrow, first thing."

The next morning, Castellano arrived at the hospital, along with future underboss Tommy Bilotti, driving a factory-new Buick Roadmaster convertible. After some routine tests, it was decided that a change in diet and taking an aspirin daily was all that was needed to prevent future difficulties. But, diabetes and a swollen leg were not the godfather's only problems. By July 1977 with Gotti released from Green Haven prison, after serving time for the McBratney murder, the crown that had been so firmly planted on the head of Carlo Gambino seemed not so snug a fit for Big Paulie. Castellano's strategy to separate the street-crime soldiers under Dellacroce from the corporate soldiers under him worked, but not to his advantage, as he alienated himself further by refusing to fraternize with either Dellacroce's Ravenite Social Club gang in Manhattan or Gotti's Bergin Hunt and Fish Club crew in Ozone Park.

In the eyes of the outside world, Paul Castellano was a successful businessman who'd overcome poverty to become a solid member of society. He dressed well and carried himself with authority. His sons, Joseph, Paul Jr., and daughter Connie attended the finest schools in New York. His wife, Nina, appeared the model wife and mother. But, in truth, there were many sides to Castellano who, not unlike Elliot, had his feet firmly planted in two worlds.

Born in Brooklyn in June 1915, his parents had emigrated from Sicily to New York where his father, Giuseppe, was a butcher and small-time racketeer controlling gambling operations in Bensonhurst. Castellano dropped out of school in the eighth grade to pursue a life in crime, running numbers for local gambling operations. He was arrested on an armed robbery charge in 1934, and proved his mettle by taking the rap alone despite the fact that there were two other accomplices.

During the 1940s, Castellano consolidated his position within the Brooklyn mob by marrying Nina Manno, a childhood sweetheart who also happened to be the sister-in-law of Carlo Gambino, who additionally, was married to Castellano's sister, Katherine. Paul, a reticent man, lacked Carlo's understanding of human nature and the more subtle aspects of crime family leadership. Nevertheless, leaning on Gambino's influence, he gravitated to Mafia stardom, not through the violent tactics used by the Neapolitan genus of the mob run by men like Capone, but through persuasion, influence, and business acumen as members of the Honored Society were taught in Sicily using the more sophisticated methods of Maranzano, Bonanno, and Gambino.

One example of Castellano's brand of corporate crime was the garment business in Manhattan where Tommy Gambino owned most of the trucks and manufacturing firms operating in midtown, where most of the wardrobe of

America's women was designed and produced. Joe N. Gallo, Carlo's *consigliere*, was a major force in the Greater Blouse, Skirt and Undergarment Association, a trade group that negotiated contracts with the district's 800 employees. By controlling the association and the trucking companies, the families controlled the price of clothing and the lives of thousands of workers.

The jewel in Castellano's white-collar empire, however, was the construction business where not a single load of concrete was poured for any contract worth more than $2 million without the consent of the Commission. The point man was a member of the Columbo Family who happened to be Ralph Scopo, president of the Local District Council of the Cement and Concrete Workers' Union. Given Big Paulie's blessing, select concrete-pouring contractors were allowed to be part of what was known as the "Concrete Club." Each of the five New York families controlled one or more of these companies. The only way construction firms could avoid union problems or sudden cutoffs in concrete deliveries was through an understanding with the Commission: union peace in return for a kickback of 2 percent on every contract more than $2 million.

The bid-rigging system for construction projects in New York held genuine appeal for Castellano. When bids were solicited for a project, the Commission decided which of the companies was up for the contract. Once the price was determined, the other companies in the club were instructed accordingly and put in higher bids, netting millions per year for the families while raising the cost of a cubic yard of poured concrete to $85, the highest in the United States.

At about the time Castellano was beginning to feel secure in his new role as *capo di tutti capi*, thirty-seven-year-old John Gotti was named "acting captain" of a crew in Queens, New

York's largest borough. Gotti held a deep disdain for Castellano that everyone in the Gambino Family knew about, not only because he'd superseded his idol, Neil Dellacroce, as godfather, but because Gotti was, like Dellacroce and Capone before him, born of parents from Naples. Gotti was a Neapolitan literally, but also in a figurative sense. He gambled obsessively, often losing $30,000 on a weekend, borrowing from his own loan sharks to make good on his debt. Rumors, too, had been spreading about Bergin crew members like Angelo Ruggiero and Gotti's brother, Pete, dealing drugs, a practice that had been outlawed by the Commission going back to the 1950s.

More to the point, Gotti believed that Castellano questioned his fitness as a family member as much as he questioned Castellano's credentials as head of the family. He understood that Paul, with his typical Sicilian bias, had a low opinion of him. Like his ancestors, Castellano thought Neapolitans were brash, garish, and too emotional to hold positions of power in the modern Mafia. For the most part, it was true. Gotti was a man who saw the fierce, foul-mouthed Capone as an icon. Like Capone and Dellacroce, he cared little for strategies and diplomacy. The underworld was an arena won and dominated by "men's men," not prissy business moguls. Gotti's was a game of intimidation. The Mafia was a world of traditions, but at its core, he had only to look at how a Sicilian like Carlo Gambino had risen to power to see that, in the end, it was a game of manipulation and brute force.

Gotti had a reputation among family members for ruthlessness even then and built upon it by talking to subordinates and enemies in a ferocious style he'd learned from Dellacroce. His crew included three of his six brothers and men he'd known since his teenage, street-gang days. "We're the fucking toughest guys in the fucking world," he once bragged to them after describing how he'd broken a cop's legs, ankles, and jaw with a crowbar. "I told him, 'You want to play more? You want to play more, you cocksucker?' I opened his mouth with my finger and put the gun in. 'You want to play more?' He can't talk, he's crying like a baby."

With Dellacroce in charge because of Castellano's decision to separate family operations, Gotti was in an exceptional position to gravitate up the Mafia ladder, and he knew it. Already held in high esteem for the McBratney revenge killing, it was common knowledge that Bergin crew members identified more with him than with Castellano, cementing that relationship by buying Gotti a new Mark V Lincoln to celebrate his release from Green Haven and hanging a plaque given him during a prison party the night before his release, "To John Gotti—A Great Guy."

To satisfy parole requirements, Gotti became a no-show salesman for the Arc Plumbing and Heating Corporation located several blocks from his Bergin storefront headquarters. There, he and Angelo Ruggiero "scouted locations" for potential projects for Arc mostly via city contracts including a new police station for the 106th Precinct, Shea Stadium, and the National Tennis Center in Flushing Meadows.

Soon after Gotti's release from prison, Castellano reluctantly "opened the books," closed by the ever-cautious Carlo Gambino for fear of inducting a police informer, and initiated Gotti and eight other associates into the family as made men. While Gotti accepted the distinction, it would not temper the disdain he bore for the new godfather. In time, the charismatic John Gotti's power would totally eclipse Paul Castellano's, as the Neapolitan and Sicilian branches of the Gambino Family clashed in a death struggle that would leave only one of the two men standing.

What neither Castellano, nor Gotti, nor Elliot could know

was that an FBI informer had already been introduced into Gotti's Bergin crew. His name was Wilfred "Willie Boy" Johnson.

12

LOVE AND BULLETS

"You know what FBI stands for, don't you? 'Forever Born Ignorant.' They just don't understand people like us, Elliot, and probably never will."

After a six-month courtship, Elliot was ecstatic to find himself marrying, Hanna Shapiro on August 27, 1978. The ceremony, a mixture of modern Jewish and Orthodox customs, was held at the Beth Elohim synagogue in the Park Slope section of Brooklyn, complete with the ritual signing of the *Ketubah*, or marriage contract, and the tradition of the groom veiling the bride, called the *bedikah*, which means inspection.

In keeping with tradition, the family of the bride was on one side of the synagogue and the family of the groom on the other. In attendance on Hanna's side was her father, Mort, standing alongside his sister, Marissa Cohen, and her husband, multimillionaire real estate developer, Herbert Cohen; Mort's physician friends, Dr. Simon Dak, Frank and Dorothy Silvio, and Marc Weiner, doctor-professor of clinical surgery at Columbia University, not to mention politicians like Charles Schumer, former New York Gov. Hugh Carey, and Pulitzer Prize-winning author Norman Mailer.

For better or worse, Elliot's side of the synagogue was

looking a little tattered by comparison. Of course, there was his mother, Etta, decked out in a pink, cotton dress, looking happy, but so tragically alone without his father, Abe, who'd died some years earlier; his brother, Steven, veteran of those unforgettable Cowboys and Indians escapades out in the backies, along with his wife, Deborah, and their seven-year-old son, Andrew; and friends from the old neighborhood, Mr. and Mrs. Micelli, to whom he owed so much; Nick, or course; Joey Fischetti; Sal DiGregorio, now married with three kids; and even Officer Kahler, the cop who patrolled Anthony Avenue and Tremont Street, now retired, standing on crutches suffering from chronic ischemia, an insufficiency of blood flow to the legs.

Despite all of those that were there, Elliot could almost see along with his father, uncles Saul and Lou, those tough and funny Russian Jews who'd trekked to the Bronx from Vinograd to find a safe haven for their families and set up their luncheonettes, laundry, and dry-cleaning shops to support them. He missed their sentimentality. He missed their laughter and stories. But that was life, and though there were no celebrities on their side of the aisle, they had their own history and lives that had been lived to the fullest.

At the end of the ceremony, in keeping with a tradition derived from the Talmud, Elliot stepped on a glass with his shoe and smashed it before the congregation. Then, with the ceremony completed, his new wife, Hanna and he left the synagogue, along with Mort and Etta, for a gala reception attended by 350 guests with entertainment provided by singer Lainie Kazan and comedian Jackie Mason.

Over time, as Elliot came to know Hanna more with each day, he saw in her an aspect that to him would prove both a blessing and a problem. Fiercely loyal, she was also fiercely independent and quite capable of attacking a perceived enemy with the same passion as she would defend a friend. The terrain that lay between those two poles was often not very wide so that he was careful never to show too much of his inner self, especially the part so firmly rooted in the underworld.

During those initial happy days of their marriage, Hanna's response to his private, other life was to leave him alone, often taking trips by herself or with a girlfriend to Switzerland for skiing, Morocco for touring, or Israel for spiritual renewal. Call it genetics, but in that sense, Hanna was exactly like her father, who spoke six languages and had become famous in Brazil during World War II where he led a government-funded team of U.S. physicians in setting up the country's medical system, virtually eliminating a malaria epidemic that threatened to kill thousands. Hanna, like him, was bright, self-contained, and a world traveler. She was pleased to be Mrs. Elliot Litner, but not about to deeply explore any of the peccadilloes that surfaced over the first months of their marriage.

Originally, the plan was to live with Mort near Prospect Park, but Hanna turned out to be fertile. Almost immediately after their honeymoon, she became pregnant with twins. The idea then was to find a place of their own before she gave birth, and so Elliot looked for homes, disappointed to find that during those Carter administration years, inflation was running 20 percent with home-mortgage interest rates not much less than that. Worse, between his gambling, which had consumed more than $250,000 over the previous three years, and nonstop partying with Silvio, Elliot had almost no savings. So that even for a superstar surgeon, getting a $400,000 mortgage wasn't easy. But how do you tell your new wife and father-in-law that?

He'd mentioned his dilemma to Frank Silvio one afternoon washing up after surgery and the next day was contacted by Mount Sinai board member Al Rosengarten. Over lunch, Rosengarten asked him about his financial problems and was very sympathetic. "You know, Elliot, we have some friends in common, and I know they'd like to help," the garment district tycoon offered. "Why don't you let me see what I can do? Would you and Hanna be available for a Realtor friend of mine to show you some homes this weekend?" Elliot agreed, and that Saturday, a representative from Burgdorf took them around focusing very specifically on an estate over the bridge in Englewood, New Jersey.

The house, a Colonial, was situated on a hill with three acres of land. It had five bedrooms, a den, playroom, two balconies, a hot tub, and Olympic-sized swimming pool. "Oh, I really love it, Elliot!" Hanna sighed, nuzzling up to him. What would a place like this cost, he wondered: $1.3 million? $999,000, bid down, maybe? "Oh, not at all, Dr. Litner!" the Realtor answered. "This home goes for $290,000." Well, you could have knocked him over with a straw and a deep breath, and with that, he simply said, "Yes."

The next morning had the same ethereal quality to it as the president of Citibank called him at the hospital to apologize for the problems he'd experienced getting a mortgage approval, personally offering to walk through the $250,000 mortgage he'd be needing for the Englewood house. Then, at day's end, Al Rosengarten came by to see how everything had gone over the weekend.

"I-it's unbelievable," Elliot stuttered to the small, tightly wound, impeccably dressed man before him. "You wouldn't believe the house we're getting, and it's only $290,000. I thought it'd be three times that, but I guess your friends know what they're doing."

"You deserve that kind of treatment, Dr. Litner. You're associate director of cardiac surgery at one of the most prestigious hospitals in the United States, maybe the world. So why shouldn't you get a break now and again. Good fortune is not a disease, is it?"

"No, sir, it isn't."

"You know, Elliot, you're better than you think you are. I spoke with Mr. Castellano, and he thinks highly of you, too. Given your skills as a surgeon and lecturer, there are few positions you'd have trouble rising to. Perhaps, even a directorship if things continue to go as they have."

Elliot shook his head in disbelief. "Why th-thank you, Mr. Rosengarten. That's nice of you to say."

Rosengarten tsked him. "No, no," he said with the wave of a finger, "it's not, Mr. Rosengarten. It's Al. And one more thing, about that house. It was owned by a man named Sonny Montella. He'd worked with Mr. Castellano, and Mr. Gambino before that, for a number of years, but then did a terrible thing, an act of betrayal, really. He became an FBI informer, what we call a "rat." Now he's in their witness protection program. So the place came on the market kind of sudden." Rosengarten shrugged as he turned to leave. "Oh, well, FBI. You know what that stands for, don't you? 'Forever Born Ignorant.' They just don't understand people like us, Elliot, and probably never will."

Al Rosengarten's words that night resonated for Elliot, especially the part about William "Sonny" Montella, a Gambino Family soldier working the Brooklyn waterfront who had, a short time before, disappeared into the Federal Witness Protection Program. Newspaper headlines carried the story for weeks, treating his defection as a major blow to waterfront *caporégime* Tony Scotto, as well as to Castellano. Montella, it seemed, knew all there was to know about mob infiltration of the International Longshoremen's Association, having reported directly to Scotto, who also happened to be vice president of the 16,000-member ILA.

While none of this sounded benign, it wasn't until several months later, with Hanna seven months pregnant, that the Litner family experienced the full impact of the situation. As was his way during these times, Elliot had spent the night at the apartment he kept near the hospital. But the next afternoon when his Corvette finally did pull into the driveway of their Englewood home, he immediately sensed something was wrong.

Standing ominously outside of his front door was a man he'd never seen before, and in the driveway, very near the entrance, was an unmarked industrial van.

"Dr. Litner?" the man called to him before he'd switched off the 'Vette's ignition.

"Yes, I'm Elliot Litner. Is something wrong?"

The man, squat and broad as a professional wrestler, approached him. "Maybe you want come with me, Doc," he muttered, taking hold of Elliot's arm at the elbow.

"What's wrong? Who are you?"

"Just come with me, and everything will be fine. You see, there's been a little misunderstanding that we've come to straighten out."

"What kind of m-misunderstanding?" Elliot asked as he was shepherded through the entrance and into the foyer, suddenly cognizant of a cadenced thudding coming directly from the basement beneath them.

"We've come to get what's ours," the man answered, all business. "My friends are downstairs in your basement. Did you know there was a safe down there, hidden behind the wall in the wine cellar?"

"*Where's my wife? Where's Hanna, she's pregnant and, I swear, if she's been hurt in any way . . .*"

"Don't make this tough on yourself, Dottore. It's the safe we care about, not your wife. She's in there," he said motioning toward the kitchen, "relaxing like you should be."

"Yeah, while your *gumbas* tear my g-goddamned house apart, is that it?" Elliot snapped back, rushing into the adjoining room where Hanna sat at the kitchen table, sipping from her cup, angrier than scared. "Hanna, are you all right? Are the babies . . ."

"I'm fine, Elliot, but I don't know what's happening. I think we're being robbed!"

"No, no, it's not anything of ours they want. It's something in a safe hidden in the cellar . . ."

"Oh, Elliot! They've been here since four o'clock. They said they were friends of yours, so I let them in. Then they made me sit here, threatened to hurt me if I didn't, while the one stayed up here watching me and the others started breaking the basement wall down with sledgehammers!"

He took her into his arms, a deep anger rising up within him. This was *his* house. This was *his* family.

"I hope you know what you've d-done," he sputtered in a voice as threatening as he could make it.

The short, muscular man, dressed in a dark, polyester suit, could hardly keep from laughing. "Oh, don't you worry about us, Dottore. This will all be over soon, and we'll just be on our way."

Elliot cast him a look that left a vibration in the air between them, then turned to Hanna as a sudden explosion erupted beneath them shaking the house to its very foundation.

"We got it! We got the safe!" someone shouted up from below. "Man, this sucker's heavy," one of the two men carrying the safe up the stairs to the side-door exit complained. A third man ran outside to start the van's engine. "Must be $2 million in diamonds and emeralds old Sonny stashed away for himself. That's what Little Pussy promised, and he better be right!"

"Okay, then," the wrestler said addressing them a final time, "but before I go, maybe you want to promise that this little withdrawal of ours stays between us." He took the telephone cord into his right hand and ripped it from the wall. "No need for police. No need to make this more than it is 'cause what was in that safe was ours, not yours, and not Sonny Montella's, *capesci?*"

Elliot swallowed hard, then nodded. *"Capesci."*

Then, the men left, and with the squeal of burning rubber, the van, too vanished from their driveway and into the street so that Elliot and Hanna felt forced to wonder if any of it had happened at all, so surreal had it been.

Like survivors of some natural disaster, the two wandered downstairs into the basement in a daze. The air was thick with dust, the basement, cluttered with debris. Beyond the blown-off door, in what was to have been their wine cellar, there remained a huge hole in the wall where the safe had been.

"My God, Elliot, I'm calling the police!"

"No, no, the phone. It's dead."

"Then I'll go next door to our neighbors. They have to know something's happened, don't they? They've probably called 911 already."

"Then let them! I don't want the police called into this, at least not by us!"

"What?"

"There's n-nothing they can do. And I don't want the publicity."

"What are you saying? Four men just came into our house, held your pregnant wife hostage, then robbed us, Elliot, and you don't want the publicity? What kind of man are you?"

"It's okay, it's okay," he soothed with steely determination. "I'll take care of this. In my own way and in my own time."

Hanna stared at him in disbelief and horror. "You're not telling me you know who these men are?"

"No, but I'm going to find out," he vowed, marching from the kitchen and out the front door toward their neighbor's house as she followed behind him. "We'll spend tonight in a hotel. By the end of the day tomorrow, this will all be cleaned up, I promise."

That night Elliot did something he'd never done before. He called Al Rosengarten and told him all that had happened. "Why that's dreadful, Elliot, *just dreadful*, and, I tell you, I feel responsible. Hanna, is she all right, physically?" "Yes," Elliot assured him, but there were two reasons he'd called. The first was to make certain that Rosengarten was aware that the theft had taken place. The second was to ask him directly that the men responsible be punished.

Less than one month later, while watching the ten o'clock news on television, Gabe Pressman reported, "In Westchester, New York, the bodies of four men associated with mobster William 'Sonny' Montella, who turned state's witness last fall, were found shot through the head 'execution style' this morning...."

Hanna glanced up at the screen. "My... God...."

"What is it?"

"Those men. The photographs of those four men. They're the men who stole the safe from our house."

Elliot barely looked up from the magazine he was reading. "Yes, it looks like them, doesn't it."

"Do you know who they are?"

Elliot shook his head in the negative. "I never met them, but obviously they're 'bad' men. They broke into our house and threatened to harm you. If they are dead, if somebody killed them, I say 'good.' They are the kind of men who deserve to be killed."

Hanna stared at him, her innocent inquisitiveness replaced by a stare that was withering. "I know that you live a complicated life, Elliot. You're a doctor and an intricate man, but once the babies are born, you've got to promise me that all of this will end, or so help me God, I will take those babies and leave you forever."

After that night, the name of Sonny Montella and the incident involving his safe in the basement were never spoken about again. Not by Hanna. Not by Elliot. Not by Al Rosengarten.

13

MOB COURIER

"It's there, stock certificates—IBM, AT&T,
Campbell's motherfucking Soup!"

O f course, Elliot understood who and what Al Rosengarten
was even before the incident with Sonny Montella's
house. Working closely with Tommy Gambino, eldest son
of Carlo, who owned four trucking companies, the two men
virtually monopolized the trucking business in Manhattan's
garment district. In fact, 90 percent of all finished garments
picked up from the cutters and sewing contractors and then
delivered to showrooms and retailers were done in Gambino
trucks. Out of fear of Gambino reprisals, the clothing manu-
facturers went along with exorbitant prices, which were from
40 to 70 percent higher than that charged by independent
truckers. This meant that for every $100 garment shipped in
New York, the mob pocketed from $3.50 to $7, and that after
everyone including Tommy and Al had gotten their cut, they
were still able to send $2 million in tribute up to their godfa-
ther living on Todt Hill.

These days, after a lot of lessons had been learned, Elliot
has adjusted to a more normal existence. But that wasn't the
way he looked at life back then. All that seemed important

was having fun and to him, that meant gambling and women. More, he knew he had to get into a situation that presented real danger to him. It was as if his hand was being forced, not by a need for money, but by a crazy uncontrollable desire to be part of the Gambino Family. Back home, where he rarely spent more than a couple of nights per week, Hanna had given birth to two gorgeous twin girls, whom they named Samantha and Rachel. From his side, however, he'd become an obsessive gambler losing as much as $15,000 on a bad night at the tables in Atlantic City and sometimes more than that.

He partied in Atlantic City with Silvio and his mob pals and even managed to hook up one night after a binge of gambling to catch a show with his old Bronx pals, Nicky Micelli and Joey Fischetti, to see their teenage favorites, Frankie Valli and the Four Seasons, perform some of their hit songs like "Sherry," "Walk Like a Man," "Grease," and so many others. Afterward, Valli invited them backstage where Nick and Joey drank Heinekens while Elliot chugged diet cola reminiscing with the falsetto singer about his growing up in Newark, New Jersey, and they in the Bronx. Not coincidentally, Nicky, through his dad, knew many of the same people as Frankie.

"D'ya ever meet Pete Rodino?" Nicky asked the singer, referring to the New Jersey congressman of Watergate fame.

"Know him? He helped get us started, working tiny clubs down the Jersey shore, standing on floats during the Columbus Day parade through downtown Newark. Yeah, sure, Congressman Rodino, a wonderful guy, just super!"

"How 'bout Tony Boy and his old man Ruggiero—the Boiardos—tell me that estate where they lived in Livingston wasn't a trip, huh?"

Frankie took a swig of Heineken, then just laughed. "I'm going to tell you something, Nick. I did go to that place. Me and the guys played a wedding reception for the family at the

old Terrace Ballroom in Newark back in the midsixties. I went
to the estate, passed through these big iron gates with a goddamned sign that says, NO TRESPASSING! THIS MEANS YOU! Well,
the gates are open, and we think they're expecting us when
just for fun, the old man unleashes a pack of the meanest
Dobermans I've ever seen! Bob Gaudio was with me at the
time, and I tell you, we both almost had heart attacks, these
dogs clawing at our Jaguar while we pass statues along the
one-way road that leads to the main house: statues of his son,
Tony Boy, of his grandson, Richie, his father, and wife, and
then one of him, riding like some kind of Sicilian prince on a
white stallion!"

"Yeah," Joey Fischetti chimed in, "and how 'bout the crematorium? Elliot," he said turning to him, "the old man's got
a fucking crematorium *and a cemetery* built right on his estate!
The old man, he don't want nobody to miss the point, I guess.
These guys were really bad asses. According to my dad, there
were a lot a guys went through those gates and never came
out again."

"How 'bout you, Frankie?" Nick asked. "What are you
and the Seasons up to these days?"

"Touring a little, but to tell you the truth, Bob, who writes
our songs, thinks he's got a couple of winners. This year
we're gonna do a little target practice, try to shoot for a few
top-ten records. It's been a while, you know. Maybe ten years,
but that's the way life is. Good things happen to guys who
don't give up, you know what I'm saying?"

Of course, Elliot understood what he was saying; maybe
not at that moment, but certainly later, when it seemed like
all he could do was give up. But for now, he and the others
took solace in the fact that their teenage singing idol was
back, singing, touring, and recording a new string of tunes
like "Who Loves You" and "Oh, What A Night!" that would
go on to sell something like ten million copies.

They left to hit the casinos one last time once Valli's girl-friend showed up, a knockout, long-legged blonde named Marianne. But meeting Frankie, after all of those years, was no disappointment, *a real player*, they agreed, reminiscing on the drive back home about those simpler days growing up with Abe, Etta, and Uncle Saul in the Bronx.

About two months later, Elliot performed open-heart surgery on the nephew of another Frank, this time Frank Sinatra. The procedure was one that he did routinely, but afterward it was thrilling to hear that Sinatra had come into the hospital with his entourage of half a dozen bodyguards asking to meet him. He'd just gotten out of surgery, with the patient taken to the intensive care unit, when he noticed a commotion and a knot of people nearing reception. Judy Harrow, one of the surgical nurses, ran up to him.

"He wants to meet you," she blurted. "He asked for you specifically, Dr. Litner!"

"Who? What are you talking about?"

"Frank Sinatra. That's him," she said pointing toward the commotion. "He's here to thank you for saving his nephew."

Elliot could only shake his head at the thought of it because thoracic surgery and medicine generally was not like that, but if Sinatra wanted to say "thanks," who was he to deny him his pleasure?

As Elliot approached, the glut of nurses, doctors, and visitors parted, until he was standing in front of him.

"You Dr. Litner?" the singer asked.

"Yes, sir, I am."

"Well, I wanted to shake your hand. My nephew, Jerry, is a very special young man, and his parents are very close to me. So I appreciate what you did for him."

"It's my job, Mr. Sinatra."

Sinatra took a half step back as if to get a better look at a guy like Elliot who he must have thought had just stepped out of a UFO, then he chortled, "Yeah, well, I wanted to thank you anyway."

Then he left, simple as that, leaving Elliot to wonder if this, like so many of the other patients that had been sent his way, had come through a family referral. He never asked and never knew, but about a week later, an entire wardrobe of Oleg Cassini suits showed up at the hospital with a handwritten note:

> *Dottore,*
> *Many thanks for your healing touch!*
> > *Best Always,*
> > *Frank Sinatra.*

Working fifteen hours a day, performing five to seven cardiac surgeries, often on as little as three or four hours of sleep, staying out with Silvio gambling and having sex with women they'd picked up that night until they could barely stand up to take a limousine to Elliot's apartment near the hospital, the pace was withering. No question there was some element of self-destructiveness in all of this, but who cared? He was having fun, or so he thought.

Problematic, however, was Hanna. Given the fact that they were still relatively new to their marriage, one would think that she'd go apoplectic over his behavior, but she didn't. Instead, she chose to ignore it and him, for the most part, shopping nonstop at Sak's, Bergdorf's, and Tiffany's, assuaging the loneliness Elliot thought she'd be feeling with month-long vacations to Paris, Barcelona, and London, often taking the twins and their nanny with her for the duration.

Between his gambling losses, mounting these days into something substantially more than six figures, and Hanna's gift for diverting her potential depression by spending huge quantities of their income, there was not much left in the way of money to sustain their extravagant lifestyle. True, another man might have held a family meeting to discuss finances and ways to better budget the almost one-million-dollar annual income they were spending as if it was Monopoly money, but Elliot was not that man. Instead, yet another "coincidence" happened in his life and career when Dr. Dak called him to his office to discuss the possibility of his doing out-of-the-country lectures, no doubt at the suggestion of board member and major hospital contributor Al Rosengarten.

At around that time, and all through his career, Elliot had been prolific in writing technical papers for some of the world's most prestigious medical journals. Some involved innovations such as "Human Umbilical Cord Vein Fistula: A Novel Approach for Hemodialysis," published in the *American Heart Journal*, or the basic blocking-and-tackling kind of pragmatism found in "Factors Predisposing to Intraoperative Myocardial Infarction during Coronary Artery Bypass Surgery" appearing in the *Journal of Thoracic and Cardiovascular Surgery*.

The idea was for Elliot to make the circuit, attending professional seminars held worldwide under the aegis of the Society of Thoracic Surgeons, the American College of Cardiology, and scores of others, on behalf of Mount Sinai, spreading not only his ideas but adding to the international reputation of the institution.

Of course, he agreed and why not? When a man of Dr. Dak's professional standing asked a young physician to do something so important, he didn't ask questions, he simply did it. So Elliot found himself traveling to various locations, as nearby as Los Angeles, and as far flung as Rio de Janeiro, Brazil, Tel Aviv, Israel, and Geneva, Switzerland.

It was shortly into this new assignment, done in conjunction with his normal workload, that Rosengarten contacted him by phone to suggest they have dinner to explore some ideas that might be mutually beneficial. They met at the board member's favorite restaurant in Manhattan, the Palm, where over a steak and a martini, Rosengarten mentioned that he'd heard Elliot was struggling financially and also that he liked to gamble, a vice to which Al, "Thank God!" had never fallen victim.

"I make no judgments about how a man lives. We leave that to the 'born agains,'" he quipped, "but maybe a friend of ours can help you with your high-interest loan. He has asked if you could occasionally carry a briefcase or parcel for him on some of your trips overseas. He will explain to you how this is done, who to meet, even which customs agent you should look for when reentering the United States. No drugs. Nothing like that. As you know, Mr. Castellano doesn't believe in any of that."

"I don't understand. Why me?"

"You're a doctor with an international reputation. Doctors received only cursory custom's inspections. So we make you a kind of courier carrying family documents of a confidential nature, maybe some uncut gems that some of the fellas like to give as presents to their girlfriends. No sweat, Elliot. Not for you, not for anyone."

Given the fact that Elliot was broke and without a foreseeable way to pay back the $75,000 he owed one of Silvio's loan-shark pals, it seemed more than possible, it was necessary.

"I think that would be okay with me, Al, but how does that help my finances?"

"Simple," he answered. "You carry the goods, we wipe your debt off the books." Then, he clicked his martini glass against Elliot's glass of diet cola. "*Mazel tov!*" he proclaimed in a toast to good fortune.

As promised, Elliot was contacted shortly before his next trip, this time to Brazil, by one of Castellano's twenty-three capos, a large, heavy-set man who Elliot knew only by his first name, Carmine. The deal from his end was easy, he explained. Elliot's itinerary was to be passed on to him via telephone. While out of his room giving a lecture, a parcel would be left for him to carry back in his luggage, then pass along to the capo once he made it through customs. On each trip, Elliot would be given the custom's inspection line number at Kennedy Airport to pass through along with a description of the agent. In advance, it would be arranged with the agent that Elliot was not to be inspected, so there was no chance of a slip-up.

The system seemed foolproof, and on his first two trips, all went well. The parcel was waiting in his hotel room. The custom's line and agent were designated and described in advance. Carmine was outside the baggage claim area, his Lincoln Town Car warmed and ready to receive the package and take Elliot home. But on his next trip, this time on his way back from Geneva, the unexpected happened.

The American 747 landed on time. In his briefcase, Elliot carried notes for his lecture presented to the International Academy of Chest Physicians and Surgeons, a Robert Ludlum spy novel, and a thick accordion folder that he had purposely chosen not to open, hence could not venture a guess as to what it might contain. The customs reentry line that had been designated by Carmine was number twelve. The agent was to be a thin and balding, twenty-seven-year-old man with a mustache.

Elliot studied the terrain. All seemed as it should. Except the agent. He had a mustache, as many of them did. He was, in a manner of speaking, balding, but not really. He was not thin, but slightly overweight. His age? Maybe late twenties, but more like midthirties, and the uncertainty caused the palms of Elliot's hands to suddenly moisten. Anyway, it was close enough to try, he thought, and so Elliot waited in line until the agent waved him forward.

"Where are you coming from?"

"I-I'm Dr. Litner," Elliot answered trying to make eye contact. "I just arrived from a medical conference in Geneva."

Then, the agent asked a question that made Elliot's heart sink. "What's in the briefcase?"

"Papers. Technical papers that I used during my lecture."

"Would you mind opening it up for me to have a look?"

It was at that moment that Elliot heard a click in some atavistic area of his frontal lobe that caused him, wisely, to immediately fall into his best Jerry Lewis impersonation. "Wh-wh-what are you saying? Wh-wh-what are you suggesting?" he blustered, stalling for time enough so that Carmine or someone would see him. "I, sir, am a medical doctor from Mount Sinai Hospital and will not have you or anyone else going through my personal papers!"

The agent was more puzzled than angered or even shocked. "I don't care if you're a doctor or the Wizard of Oz, you will open that bag!"

From that moment on, Elliot was making something a lot closer to sounds than words. But behind the agent, off to his right, he saw another drinking coffee and scarfing down a Dunkin' Donut, obviously on break. He looked to be about twenty-seven. He was thin, and he was balding, no question about that.

"Officer! Officer!" Elliot called out to him in a loud voice. "My name is Dr. Litner, and this man is harassing me!"

The young agent turned with alarm. Recognizing what had happened, he slammed his Styrofoam coffee cup down so hard on the folding table that it smashed and made his way toward the inspection line.

"Hey, Dennis! Maybe you better let me handle this one, huh? I don't think Dr. Litner would mind if I looked through his briefcase, would you, Doctor?"

"No, I suppose not," Elliot huffed. "I just don't like this man's attitude."

Elliot passed through customs five minutes later and hooked up with Carmine, who thought the whole episode was hilarious even before Elliot told him he was so scared, he'd nearly pissed in his pants. Of course, this made Carmine roar all the more. As they left Kennedy for the Long Island Expressway headed toward Manhattan, Carmine lifted up the accordion folder.

"You know what you had in that folder?" Carmine asked.

"No," Elliot answered, physically drained from the experience. "And I don't want to know, either."

"It's these," Carmine said throwing it open and showing a sheaf of parchment covered with engraved letters. "Stock certificates—IBM, AT&T, Campbell's motherfucking Soup! International bonds, letters of credit from a hundred different banks. These, Il Dottore, are better than money. No strings. Nothing to be laundered. Over $2 million worth of this shit, and it's all ours. Yours. Mine. The family's," he laughed.

Later Elliot would learn that Carmine was Carmine Lombardozzi, a Gambino Family capo who specialized in securities theft, stock market swindles, and sophisticated banking frauds, rackets that earned the family millions annually no matter how Wall Street happened to do that quarter or for any other given period.

14

JFK and the Mafia

*"I'm saying Sam fucked me. I spent my life with that guy, and he desert-
ed me. 'It was a slip-up,' he says. But I know Sam, and there ain't no
slip-ups.'"*

So, what was the Mafia, also called La Cosa Nostra, this
"thing of ours"? Where did it start? How much power did
it really wield? These were the questions Elliot asked himself as he became as entrenched in this underworld society
that he'd discovered in the Bronx backies as a boy, as he was
in the world of New York society owing to his position at
Mount Sinai and the family into which he'd married.

Clearly, there were many stories that related to the first
question, but the best he'd heard regarding the formation of
the Mafia came during a conversation with Frank Silvio one
evening over a glass of Chianti at the "21" Club in Manhattan.

"D'you ever see the movie, *Patton?*" Silvio asked. "When
Patton pulls into Palermo standing on that tank with thousands of troops behind him and all the townspeople cheering,
he turns to Omar Bradley. 'Palermo is the most conquered city
in the world,' he says. 'Sicily was the invasion route of conquerors: the Greeks before the time of Christ, the French during the Bourbon monarchy, they were all here, and now it's us,
the Third Armored Division of the United States Army.'

"Well, Patton was right, and every one of those conquerors tramped across Sicily like Nazi storm troopers with no regard for the people, their culture, or customs. So, why are there still Sicilians? How does a population survive for centuries under the boot of foreign conquest? They do it in the way of Machiavelli's *Prince*, by adjusting to those conquerors, pretending to get along with them during the day, while resisting them secretly by subterfuge at night. You see, that peculiar history, and the way the Sicilians dealt with it, was the breeding ground for the Mafioso. But the term means more than just belonging to an organization. It means the qualities someone or something possesses: pride, dignity, guile, and cunning. These are the attributes of a Mafioso."

"But the word, 'Mafia,'" Elliot asked, "where did they get that?"

Silvio leaned forward, talking over the din of conversation around them. "In the thirteenth century, the French occupied Sicily," he explained. "These men were brutal and arrogant, and the population despised them for it. Over the years, the resentment smoldered until one day, a French soldier, who'd lusted over a young girl in Palermo, got drunk. Seeing her on the street with her mother, he tore her away, then dragged her into a dark alley where he raped her with absolutely no fear of consequence. The mother, beside herself with rage, began screaming, 'Ma fia! Ma fia!' 'My daughter! My daughter!' The townspeople were inconsolable. Rioting broke out in the streets, and the mother's cries became a mantra as they chanted 'Ma fia! Ma fia!' But more telling was the reaction of the young woman's suitor, a man named Droetto, who was a true Mafioso. Humiliated and ashamed, he didn't say a word, but methodically sought the soldier out. He learned his identity, talked his way into the military compound, then without challenging him or even identifying himself, Droetto came up behind the man and plunged a stiletto into his heart. That is the way of the Mafioso. It was what Hemingway called 'grace under pressure' with, maybe, a Sicilian flair."

Silvio laughed then, but Elliot never forgot his story or its meaning. These goodfellas, these friends of his, they were different from other men. There was another side to this equation, and it had to do with Droetto and Silvio's story. With these men, these Mafiosi, there was an unspoken pact that being with them sealed forever, and that was that all of the reverse also applied with equal weight. That is, he could never lie. He had to be loyal. He, too, was expected to be generous so that "what was mine was theirs," and anything he could do that was within his power needed to be as good as done if they asked for it.

The final factor in the Mafia equation was probably the most chilling, and that had to do with Droetto and the vast Sicilian appetite for revenge. If one didn't comply with the second side of the calculation, he was reminded of the pact that he'd entered into, knowingly or unknowingly. If, after that reminder, he didn't quite understand what they were saying, he would be reminded again, this time bluntly. If after that, he still had trouble remembering the covenant he'd made, there was no third reminder. Like Droetto, someone very close to him, or maybe someone he had never seen or heard about in his life, would quietly come up behind him, and then he would be dead.

The Mafia, as Elliot was learning, was a club with a life-long membership. When a crew member asked John Gotti about the possibility of being released to another crew, Gotti looked at him in disbelief. "You don't get released from my crew," he answered. "You have lived with John Gotti, and you will die with John Gotti."

That was the way it was, and though it never bothered

Elliot then, a premonition, somewhere on the outer fringes of his consciousness, told him that the cold reality of La Cosa Nostra hung out there for him, and that some day, when everything wasn't so neat and tightly packaged, he would be faced with an irreconcilable dilemma that at that time seemed beyond his comprehension.

One such time, when he felt a genuine sense of discomfort with his role as Mafia doctor, came early Saturday morning in the fall of 1980. The hospital was bedlam, when Elliot was called over the PA system to emergency where he found Dr. Silvio waiting.

"I think you better handle this one. A friend has been asking for you," Frank said quietly, taking him behind a privacy curtain where Lou "Cos" Coscarelli, Carlo Gambino's former strong-arm man, stood holding one of the greasers who'd accompanied Elliot to Sheepshead Bay nearly eight years earlier.

"Jesus Christ! What happened to him?" Elliot asked, motioning Coscarelli to lay the wounded soldier on the examination table.

"He's been shot, Dottore. Three times in the back," Lou answered desperately, placing the limp body before him in a gesture that looked something like a benediction. "Think you can help?"

Elliot removed the wounded man's black leather jacket. The kid, one of Carlo's Zips from Sicily, couldn't have been more than twenty-five-years-old. "I-I don't know. I'll need to have a look, but he's been shot up pretty bad and lost a lot of blood. Frank," Elliot said turning to Silvio, "we need to get him on oxygen and start a transfusion."

After the kid's blood-soaked shirt had been pulled loose from his body, Elliot examined the bullet wounds, one at a time. Best-case scenario, he knew after a cursory exam, was that if they could stop the internal bleeding, the Zip would live. Best-case scenario also meant that with his spine severed as it had been, he would be a paraplegic, and probably on life-support systems, for the rest of his life.

"Doc?" Lou asked.

"It's not good, Cos," Elliot told him as Silvio directed a bevy of nurses and orderlies who moved the kid to intensive care. "I'm putting him on oxygen and giving transfusions to stabilize him while I try to figure out the chances of successful surgery to remove the bullets."

"Yeah?" the huge man prodded.

"In either case, your friend's spine is severed. If I decide to operate, and he survives, he'll be paralyzed from the neck down."

Lou was surprisingly shaken. "Christ," he muttered. "Poor fucking kid. I known him since Carlo had 'im brought here from Castellammere del Golfo. Fucking kid don't have nobody. Just me. I'm the only one, and that's why you gotta help 'im."

"I will, Lou. I'm going to do everything in my power . . ."

Lou stepped forward and put his huge open palm on Elliot's chest. "No, you don't understand, Dottore. I know this kid wouldn't want to live like that, and you need to see that he don't wake up no paraplegic."

"You know I can't do that."

"You can, Dottore," he pressed. "You need to help my friend, and if you do, I'll never forget you for it. Never."

"It's my job to save lives, Lou, not end them!"

"He got no family. The kid got no one 'cept me to look after 'im. Check on him, Dottore. I beg that you let him go with dignity from this world into the next."

Moral ambiguity. It was his Hippocratic oath to "hold yourself far aloof from wrong, from corruption, from the tempting of others to vice," but in truth, as Elliot took the short walk from emergency to the intensive care unit, he wondered what life would mean to an illegal immigrant from a small coastal town in Sicily hopelessly paralyzed or even if he would live through the night.

Once he got to the Zip's bedside, Elliot glanced down at the unconscious young man. He'd already taken several pints of blood to stabilize him. Silvio had put him on life support realizing that he was too weak for surgery. Elliot looked to the telemetry monitor to check vital signs. They were weak and erratic. How difficult would it be? The nurses had cleared out. Silvio was on to his next Saturday morning emergency patient. What was right, and what was wrong?

The question had just passed through his mind when the shrill beep of the cardiac monitor cut through the room. Elliot's eyes shot to the monitor. The white line was erratic, then suddenly flat line. Without thinking, Elliot swiveled down toward the patient's chest and pushed once, twice ... and then not at all, as the thought of saving this young man to live his remaining days in what would probably be his own version of hell crossed Elliot's mind. The flat line held. Elliot straightened up and was standing when two nurses came charging into the chamber. "He's gone," he said succinctly and left.

Later that night, Elliot would arrange for the body to be quietly removed to a Gambino-owned funeral home where it could be embalmed, groomed, and dressed for the wake and Catholic funeral the family would, as a matter of tradition, have for him at Lou "Cos" Coscarelli's request.

Over the weeks to come, Elliot would think back to that moment standing over a man whose name he didn't even know, wondering whether it was best to let him live or let him die. This was as close as it had come so far in terms of making that kind of decision: having to weigh his allegiance to his profession against his allegiance to La Cosa Nostra. Tougher, more consequential decisions were soon to come his way because just as he'd learned about the creation of the Mafia from Frank Silvio, so Elliot was learning about the deadly power that the organization wielded both nationally and internationally, this time from Salvatore "Bill" Bonanno, son of Joseph, who had, himself, run the Bonanno Family as *consigliere* in his father's absence during the mid-1960s.

"The Mafia is a metaphor for the hypocrisy of America," Bonanno explained over a dinner at Patsy's on West Fifty-sixth in Manhattan to a covey of friends including Elliot and a famous former senator. "Like a socially prominent man with a tattooed mistress, he will flirt with her, he will buy her gifts and fuck her, but rarely will he take her out in public. When the government needs the influence of organized crime, they have historically had no difficulty asking for help, usually through the CIA or another of its intelligence agencies. On the other hand, when ambitious prosecutors needed headlines to catapult their careers forward, they had no problem harassing and prosecuting those very same individuals, often using illegal tactics themselves."

An example was Charlie "Lucky" Luciano who, while serving time in Dannemora Prison, was called upon by the Office of Naval Intelligence to help federal agents infiltrate the International Longshoremen's Association. It seemed that in February 1942, more than a year after Pearl Harbor, the luxury ocean liner, S.S. *Normandie*, berthed at a Hudson River pier in Manhattan, had been set ablaze and sunk while it was being converted into an Allied troop ship. Given the rabid fears of a Nazi fifth column already in place in the United States and the fact that German saboteurs had earlier landed by U-boat and were captured on the eastern tip of Long Island, U.S. intelligence was convinced that the fire was deliberately set and prevailed upon Luciano to use his longstanding New York dock influence to help police the harbor.

Later, as part of what was known as "Operation Husky," Luciano was called upon again to use his contacts among the five families to help coordinate sabotage efforts against the Nazis using Mafiosi to blow up bridges, radio towers, and roads prior to the Allied invasion of Sicily. In both instances, Luciano agreed, with the promise that he'd gain a pardon from then-Governor Dewey, and in both instances, he delivered on his end of the bargain. The New York docks suffered no further attacks or labor unrest for the remainder of the war, and the Allies, aided by the Mafia, swept through Sicily virtually unchallenged. Nevertheless, when the paperwork for Luciano's petition for clemency arrived on Dewey's desk, the governor refused to sign and had him deported to Italy.

A second instance of the federal government's betrayal of the mob was carried out by Bobby Kennedy. It wasn't bad enough that the Kennedy brothers used Chicago boss Sam Giancana and his union influence to win Illinois in the presidential election and then have Bobby double-back on him as a key target for prosecution. Even more of a betrayal was the fact that while his brother, President John Kennedy, was recruiting Giancana through the CIA to assassinate Fidel Castro of Cuba, Robert Kennedy, as attorney general, was mercilessly prosecuting not only Giancana, but Miami boss Santos Trafficante and New Orleans godfather Carlos Marcello, both of whom were working in concert with Giancana and the CIA to kill the Cuban leader. Add to this the legendary hatred borne for John and Robert Kennedy by FBI Director J. Edgar Hoover and CIA chief Allen Dulles and an intriguing scenario develops, but not nearly so interesting as a conversation relayed by Salvatore "Bill" Bonanno that night to Elliot at Patsy's that dealt with the Mafia's ultimate payback for personal betrayal: the assassination of President Kennedy in order to stop his brother's prosecutions.

It seemed that while serving a five-year sentence for mail fraud at Terminal Island Federal Correctional Institution in California in 1971, Bonanno ran into Johnny Roselli, Sam Giancana's right-hand man, one day in the prison courtyard. Roselli, nearly seventy years of age at the time, was still handsome in a Hollywood kind of way with meticulously coifed silver hair, a muscular build, and the internal strength and grace of a true Mafioso. It had been years since they'd seen one another, and according to Bonanno, they embraced like long-lost brothers, paisans. Rosselli was only around for a few weeks before being transferred to another facility, but the two got very close during that time.

"What surprised me," Bonanno confided, "was how loose lipped and fatalistic Rosselli was, very out of character, like he just didn't care anymore. Of course, Johnny's name had long been connected to JFK's assassination because of Giancana's role in Cuba. But there was more, like the fact that it seemed to be a general rumor among Cuban inmates, many veterans of the Bay of Pigs, that Rosselli had somehow been involved in killing Kennedy, whom they hated. They fawned over Rosselli, treating him like some kind of hero. Then one afternoon, I finally asked in Italian, 'What the hell is going on with you?'

"'Per cosas,' he answered, meaning 'things.'

"But seeing how strangely he was behaving, I couldn't leave it at that and pressed until finally he let loose with something that must have been eating at him for the past eight years.

"'That fuck!'

"'Who?' I asked.

"'Sam! Sam fucked me. I spent my life with that guy, and

he deserted me. 'It was a slip-up,' he says. But that's bullshit because I know Sam, and there ain't no such thing as 'slip-ups' with him. He wanted me out, Bill, and knew that if I got caught, I'd never, never say a word.'

"I cautioned Rosselli then about talking so openly even to me, but he was inconsolable.

"'It don't matter no more, Bill. All of that's over with now.'

"And he was right. A short time after he got out of prison, Johnny left his Florida home to buy a pack of cigarettes and never returned. A week later, his dismembered body was found in a sixty-gallon oil drum floating in Biscayne Bay."

15

GODFATHERS AND PRESIDENTS

"Can you imagine that? Even the president of the United States is fucking scared of us!"

The first time Elliot met John Gotti was at P. J. Clarke's, a bar-restaurant in midtown Manhattan. Hanna and he had attended a Mount Sinai banquet earlier that evening with Dr. Dak and a table full of the hospital's key supporters when one of them, Tom Shanahan, president of the Bank of New York, suggested they have a nightcap. Dr. Dak was anything but a party animal, but seeing that the institution had just donated $4 million toward the construction of the hospital's new cancer treatment center, he decided to accommodate the banker.

This was no problem for Hanna and Elliot, at least not until they entered the bar where almost immediately Angelo Ruggiero came rushing over, arms spread wide, trailed by mob attorney Barry Slotnick and Gene Gotti, John's younger brother.

"Dottore!" Ruggiero bellowed, wrapping him in a bear hug. "It's good to see you!"

He introduced Elliot to Slotnick and Gene, both of whom treated him like a long-lost brother.

"John's here. D'you ever meet 'im?" Angelo asked. "He's with another friend of ours, Roy Cohn. Come on, lemme introduce you!" he said, taking Elliot by the hand and leading him toward a table as the group he was with, including Hanna, trailed along, dumbfounded.

"How do you know him?" Hanna asked in a harsh whisper.

"Uhmm, ahh, Mr. Ruggiero's nephew was a patient of mine once. I guess he remembers me."

"And the other man at the table. Is that Roy Cohn, the prosecutor from the McCarthy hearings?"

"Yes, I think it is," Elliot replied.

"And the other man, next to him. Don't tell me that's John Gotti, the gangster?"

"It may be. Yes, I'm pretty sure," he stammered unconvincingly. "I mean, it certainly *looks* like John Gotti."

Hanna nodded dubiously, his credibility about as strained as it could get when Cohn, sitting next to John Gotti at the table, looked up and grinned. "I didn't think they let you and Silvio out of your cage before 3:00 A.M. Who said you could leave the hospital anyway?"

Cohn's comment didn't help matters and later fueled one of the few genuine arguments Elliot and Hanna had ever gotten into. After members of Elliot's party, including Hanna, had gone home, an interesting discussion followed with Gotti, who was already making a splash in the New York press. Standing near the bar, sipping grappa and espresso after the kitchen had closed, Johnny Boy, along with Cohn and Ruggiero, were watching CNN as excerpts from a speech made by President Ronald Reagan at the Justice Department earlier that day were being broadcast.

"It comes down, in the end," Reagan stated to the audience of Justice Department employees and the press, "to a simple question we must ask ourselves: What kind of people are we if we continue to tolerate in our midst an invisible, lawless empire? Can we honestly say America is the land of justice for all if we do not now exert every effort to eliminate this confederation of professional criminals, this dark, evil enemy within?"

"Turn that fucking TV off!" Gotti called out to the bartender, and with the television silenced, Ruggiero recalled a recent encounter with the president.

"You know last time that guy, Reagan, was in town, Johnny and me are at the Park Sheraton Hotel about to meet with Neil, and he's there to make a speech. Well, I'm gonna tell you somethin' the Secret Service guys see us, and they don't know whether to shit or go blind. 'Listen,' they say, 'the president is here, and we'd,' what did they say John? 'feel more comfortable' if we'd leave before his car arrived. Can you imagine that? Even the president of the fucking United States is scared of us!"

"That may be, but I wouldn't take what Reagan's saying too lightly. With these new RICO laws a lot can happen," Cohn said.

"Gimme a fucking break, Roy," Gotti shot back. "What are they gonna do," he laughed, "take me down for eatin' pussy? It's still no crime, but if it was, you know I'd get the fucking electric chair!"

"You should listen to me, John. In the next three months, they plan to add 1,000 agents and 200 prosecutors," Cohn warned. "And wiretaps? The cap's been lifted. By year's end, these guys will have the Boy Scouts' latrines wired trying to catch scoutmasters sucking cocks and calling it a RICO conspiracy!"

Gotti didn't seem very impressed with the government's latest maneuvers and probably should have paid more attention, but even Elliot knew that he had a lot on his mind. Though he was still tanned and sporting $1,500 Armani suits with impeccably coiffed silver hair, his face was drawn, and he seemed preoccupied. A short time before, on March 18, 1980, Gotti's twelve-year-old son, Frank, had been killed in a traffic accident two blocks from his home in Howard Beach. Apparently, the boy had borrowed a friend's motorbike and was taking it for a ride when John Favara, a neighbor, was making his way home from work at the nearby Castro Convertible plant. Young Gotti darted out onto 157th Street where Favara accidentally ran him down and killed him.

The NYPD traffic investigators ruled the tragedy an accident, but Gotti's wife Vicki's lust for revenge could not be sated, and soon Favara was receiving death threats. Two weeks after Frank Gotti's funeral, Favara's car was stolen and later found with the word MURDERER spray-painted on it. Not unexpectedly, considering Gotti's reputation for violence, Favara panicked. He and his wife immediately sold their car and put their house on the market. Unfortunately, Favara's intended move came too late as the plans to kill him had already spun into motion when, on July 25, John and Victoria Gotti left Howard Beach for an impromptu Florida vacation.

On July 28, two days before the deal for the sale of his house was closed, as Favara left work, he was confronted by a heavy-set man who clubbed him with a baseball bat. The man then lifted Favara by the belt of his pants and threw him into a blue van. A watchman at the plant where Favara worked witnessed the abduction as did the owner of a nearby diner who ran out to confront the assailant. "Hey, what do you think you're doing?" he called out to him. "Our friend is sick. We're taking him home," the man replied. Both witnesses then watched in amazement as two accomplices got out of the van. One entered a green car parked behind it, the other entered Favara's station wagon before following the speeding van toward the Jericho Turnpike.

John and Victoria Gotti returned from their Florida vacation on August 5. To this day, Favara's body has not been found. Police later received an unconfirmed report that he'd been slaughtered with a chain saw and his body parts placed in a wrecked car that was then compacted into a cube of metal and bone. According to Elliot, even within the Gambino and other families, everyone was very tight lipped on the subject of Favara, though most speculated the killing was carried out by Johnny Boy's closest associates from the Bergin: Angelo Ruggiero, Tony "Roach" Rampino, and Willie Boy Johnson. Another theory, put forward by Frank Silvio, attributed the murder to the barbarous Roy DeMeo, street boss of the Gambino Family car-theft ring and cocaine addicted Studio 54 hanger-on, who specialized in dismembering his victims and making them vanish from the face of the earth. When asked about his missing neighbor by NYPD investigators, John Gotti replied, "I don't know what happened to him, but I'm not sorry if something did happen. He killed my kid."

Adding to Gotti's headaches were many of his own making. Already his reputation as an out-of-control gambler was legendary among family members as well as the FBI, who'd been spying on him for more than a decade. Losses of $40,000 to $50,000 a weekend on card games, horse racing, and other sporting events were not uncommon. He once won $275,000 on the Brooklyn numbers rackets and lost it within forty-eight hours shooting craps. In an FBI wiretapped recording, he was taped talking to Neil Dellacroce while alone one night at the Ravenite Social Club, the underboss' headquarters in Manhattan.

"I'm out $30 [$30,000] so far today with this fuckin' college football ... and there's two more scores to come.... I guess that should put me in enough fuckin' jeopardy for one day." Then, when the two remaining scores came in losers, the bug recorded Gotti smashing a chair against the wall and screaming, "God is a cocksucking faggot!"

At around the time Elliot met Gotti at P. J. Clarke's, larger problems were converging around him that would remain hidden for years like the fact that close personal friend and Bergin crew member Wilfred "Willie Boy" Johnson, known to the FBI by code designation Source BQ 5558-TE, had turned informer as early as 1966, and that despite the best efforts of Gotti and his crew, weeks earlier a bug had been planted within an annex to the Bergin Hunt and Fish Club. The bug would, over the coming months, record many of Gotti's most incriminating conversations, making him choice pickings for the newly activated RICO statutes.

Neither Gotti, nor his boss, Paul Castellano, had the remotest idea what an adversary La Cosa Nostra had in Rudy Giuliani. Giuliani burned with white-hot political ambition and clearly saw the slaying of the Mafia hydra as a platform from which to launch a successful political career. At forty-three, he was associate attorney general under William French Smith. It was in that capacity that he seized a chance to get President Ronald Reagan's ear during a White House cabinet meeting. Giuliani gave an impassioned plea for the administration to mount a "no holds barred" war against organized crime.

The new president must have seen political mileage in the Mafia hobbyhorse because Reagan launched Giuliani's plan on October 14, 1982, announcing a $100-million crackdown on the drug trade and organized crime. His ultimate goal, he told an audience of FBI, INS, and DEA agents with Attorney General Smith, FBI Director William Webster, and Giuliani flanking him, was to "eradicate these dark forces of evil" by launching a "virtual war," led by twelve organized crime task forces armed with RICO and the Justice Department's new ruling that allowed for vastly increased electronic surveillance, centered in the country's twelve largest cities.

The Racketeering-Influenced and Corrupt Organizations statute was the brainchild of Notre Dame Law Professor Robert Blakey. Enacted into law in 1970, it took federal prosecutors years to apply it to actual criminal cases so that even by 1979, only 200 cases had been tried, not one of them having to do with the Mafia. But all of that changed with Giuliani, who did not hesitate to use the sweeping, and many believe unconstitutional, powers of RICO against La Cosa Nostra. Under the RICO statutes, it became a separate crime to belong to an enterprise that engaged in racketeering, and even if the criminal acts were committed by others, a member of the group was guilty of conspiracy for simply being associated with it.

16

TROUBLE IN PARADISE

"You get these gumbas of yours off our property now, or I'm never going to speak to you again."

L ater, when Giuliani became U.S. attorney for the Southern District of New York, he would be on the cutting edge of the Reagan administration's crackdown, becoming the most zealous Mafia prosecutor in the city's history. What was the cause of this obsession, beyond ambition and early childhood warnings from Adelina about his family's past encounters with the "Men of Honor"? Why did Rudy, well along into manhood, carry that blazing personal torch against the mob? Elliot contemplated these questions long and hard during his years as a family associate, maybe to uncover the truth about Giuliani or Gotti, but likely, even he would concede, to try to better understand himself and the motives behind his own double life as respected surgeon and doctor to the Mafia. In Giuliani's case, Elliot was convinced, the answer lay with his father, Harold, and a background that must, in many ways, have haunted the young prosecutor.

Harold Giuliani was twenty-six-years-old when, on April 2, 1934, he and an accomplice hid behind a stairwell in a ten-family residential building in Manhattan, then jumped a Borden's

Farm milkman named Robert Hall. Giuliani, who was carrying a .38-caliber pistol, pressed the gun to Hall's stomach demanding the cash he had collected on his milk run that day. Hall turned over $128 to Giuliani as the second man held him from behind. The robbers were about to make their getaway when a local patrolman, Edward Schmitt, hearing the commotion, burst through the front door of the building, collaring Giuliani as the accomplice escaped out the back door.

Ten days later, Harold was indicted for robbery, assault, grand larceny, and criminally receiving stolen property. Interestingly, it was a Mangano Family associate, Valentine Spielman, who posted Giuliani's $5,000 bail. There must have been more to the story, but aside from Mangano's act of generosity, another strange twist occurred. Hall, a week after the indictment was filed, completely altered his story, swearing this time that it wasn't Giuliani, but his unknown accomplice who carried the gun and pressed it to his stomach.

Why the change in Hall's account? Certainly, this dramatically altered the charges for which Harold would be tried. The answer came from Louis Capozzoli, the assistant district attorney handling the case, who when questioned by the judge explained that Robert Hall had been visited the week before at four o'clock in the morning by three men who threatened his life if he didn't change his testimony. Hall, a simple family man terrified of possible reprisals, changed his story so that Giuliani could switch his plea to guilty for the less-substantial single count of armed robbery in the third degree.

Harold's relationship with La Cosa Nostra didn't end there. Once released from Sing Sing Prison, he went on to become a "collector" for Vincent's, a bar-restaurant front for a gambling and loansharking operation run by Rudy's uncle, Leo D'Avanzo, and his underworld partner, Jimmy Dano. Taking in as much as $15,000 a week with the "vig," or interest, starting at 150 percent, Harold became Leo and Jimmy Dano's "bone breaker," accepting payments slipped to him in envelopes over the bar, using a gun and a baseball bat to break legs, smash faces, and shatter the kneecaps of those who did not pay on time.

The most notorious of Rudy's family connections to organized crime, however, was D'Avanzo's son, Lewis, who, while Rudy was attending law school at NYU, was working the hijacking and car-theft ring with the likes of Gambino Family hit man Roy DeMeo. In June 1969, Rudy's cousin was arrested for the armed hijacking of a truck containing $240,000 worth of mercury and later sentenced to ten years at John Gotti's alma mater, the Lewisburg Penitentiary. While serving that sentence, Lewis was indicted for his real meat-and-potatoes racket, which was running a document-forging operation to cover up the theft of more than $250 million in stolen luxury cars in New York City in 1971 alone.

If the overall scheme appeared white-collar or somehow harmless, one had only to realize that serial murderer Roy DeMeo was lurking in the shadows, which made the operation anything but nonviolent. This became evident to the FBI when five ring members were found murdered gangland style in 1976 and when Lewis D'Avanzo's partner, John Quinn, and his nineteen-year-old mistress, Cherie Golden, were found dead "DeMeo" style one year later. According to FBI informant Willie Boy Johnson, Rudy's cousin Lewis D'Avanzo had put a contract out on Quinn, who'd shared sensitive details about the international car-theft ring's inner workings with Cherie Golden.

In October 1977, while Rudy and his first wife, Regina, were rubbing elbows with former FBI Director L. Patrick Gray and future Attorney General Richard Thornburgh, at their Prospect House luxury high-rise, Lewis D'Avanzo was spotted by two teams of FBI agents on the thirty-first of that month barreling through the streets of Brooklyn in a late-model BMW. Followed by the agents, who held an outstanding warrant and knew him to be "armed and dangerous," D'Avanzo was in the process of switching from the BMW to a Ford Maverick when the first team of agents confronted him. At that point, Lewis jumped back in the car, smashed into the agents' car, then tried to run them down while the others, unknown to Lewis, took aim with a .357 Magnum and a 12-gauge shotgun, firing into his windshield and killing him instantly.

The killing didn't end there on either side. Five months later, another D'Avanzo associate, Michael Manelino, brother of Leo's mistress, Elizabeth, and colleague of Lewis, was assassinated outside of his body shop in broad daylight by the DeMeo crew. Suspecting he, like Cherie Golden, knew too much about the Gambino Family's auto theft enterprise, he was shot in the head, his body stuffed in the trunk of a car, then set on fire.

Interesting to Elliot was the way the web of corruption was spun through almost every aspect of American society. Of course, everyone reacted differently to it. Some, like him, simply accepted the fact that evil existed in every man, understanding that even his best efforts to exorcise those demons of taint could become their own form of corruption like Melville's Ahab with his white whale. But when men like Dewey or Bobby Kennedy or Rudy became fanatical about prosecuting men like John Gotti, who or what are they really prosecuting? What was their motive for doing it? In the case of Giuliani and Kennedy, Elliot theorized that somehow they believed that if they went after members of the Genovese or Bonanno or Gambino families with unmitigated ruthlessness, they were cleansing their fathers' pasts, ripping the taint out like a cancerous tumor so that they could expunge their own family history of crime from the record and from their own consciences.

That may answer the question "why," but when it came to their modus operandi, "how," the logic involved was the most paradoxical of all. Men like Rudy possessed a feral aggression, Elliot surmised, a black hole in their soul that forced them to take the process one step further. They deeply understood the world of power and corruption, and with a sleight of hand worthy of Houdini, "metamorphosed" their own moral disease into a virtue, calling themselves "knights in shining armor" and "societal heroes" chasing down their white whale and killing it, while understanding with a nod and a wink that all of it represented the first leg on a well-paved path to political fortune.

That to Elliot was Rudolph Giuliani in a nutshell: the ultimate political opportunist, armed with the new RICO statutes and no-holds-barred surveillance technologies, wrapped in a cloak of moral certitude, disguised as a Catholic saint. It would be with a combination of these new investigative tools and Rudy's own brand of white-knuckled moral obsession that he would pursue the five families of New York in a landmark prosecution that would bring an entire Mafia empire crashing down into a heaping rubble of traitors, vengeance, murder, and lies.

Elliot's first taste of the imminent disaster that awaited him, Paul Castellano, John Gotti, and even Steve Rubell came in the summer of 1981. Between the incredible hours he was keeping at the hospital, partying with his pals in Vegas and Atlantic City, and doing his part for the Family as an international courier, there wasn't much time left for Hanna and the twins. Beyond the obvious connections that even his wife knew he had with "those people," his friends, new and old, understood he was an easy mark and took full advantage, using his Englewood home like a crash pad where drugs, alcohol, and women were never in short supply.

The drug of choice was cocaine, and though Elliot never used stimulants himself, guys like Nicky Micelli, who he suspected was dealing, and Joey Fischetti and Sal DiGregorio, who'd become wild men when it came to sex and coke, were using a drug called amyl nitrite, which spurred the sex drive in both men and women to the point of nonstop ecstasy. With the Rolling Stones blaring "Miss You" in the background, Elliot remembered having oral sex performed on him while on a poolside lounge chair by one of the "nymphets" Nicky and Sal had brought by along with twenty other "friends," swimming, dancing, or doing the same as he, when Hanna returned from a trip to Boston, trailed by a chauffeur carrying luggage and the twins by her side.

She looked at Elliot. He looked at her. Neither of them said a word. Utterly astounded at finding him there, unabashed, in so compromising a position, with Samantha and Rachel looking on, she left. Simply walked away in disgust, going into the house with the two girls, where she found, to her horror, Nicky screwing the brains out of a long-legged, red-headed casino showgirl in their bed.

Blame it on the amyl nitrite, or just call it terrible luck, but Nicky didn't even look up from his pleasure as Hanna stormed out of the room with twins in tow, out to the pool area where she confronted Elliot. Now, being no fool, he had already put his private part back into his Speedo, gotten rid of Nicky's nymphet, and was sipping a diet cola fifty yards away at the other side of the pool by the time she arrived.

"I want these people out of my house now! Do you understand?" she raged in one of the very few times Elliot had ever seen her livid.

"Now Hanna," he soothed getting up out of the lounge chair, touching his hand to her shoulder, "I realize that you're upset, and you have every right to be . . ."

"Upset? I'm not upset. I'm fucking pissed! Now you get these animals, off our property or I'm never going to speak to you again!"

"O-okay," he stammered, understanding that his marriage was on the line, but stupidly incoherent both in language and logic. "I'll tell them t-to leave, but I'm going with Nicky and the others if you make me do that. We're, all of us," he said getting braver as a group of his whacked-out acquaintances gathered to listen, "g-going to Atlantic City to finish the party."

"I don't care, I don't care what you do anymore," Hanna announced, "just get them out and if you want to go with them, go ahead!"

Hanna left for the main house with the twins as Elliot collected the chauffeur, Nicky, Sal, and Joey for a gambling foray into Atlantic City, making the rounds that night. Finally, they piled back into the limousine, Nicky, Sal, and Joey to kill a bottle of Champagne and polish off a last spoon of coke; Elliot to have his own custom version of a group grope involving simultaneous sex with two hookers he'd picked up playing craps at the tables before making the return trek on the Jersey Turnpike to Bergen County.

Elliot got back to Englewood early the next morning. It was already daylight with the sun bright and shining in a clear, blue sky. He sent the driver home and was feeling every imaginable downside effect of the night before when he entered their house to find it emptier than he'd ever remembered seeing it. Packed, inside and out, and literally crawling with people only hours before, it felt like a mausoleum now, stinking of stale booze, with empty bottles and pizza boxes, furnishings toppled and scattered all over the place.

It was then, walking into the carnage and emptiness of their oversized, newly tiled kitchen that he saw his father-in-law, Mort Shapiro, sitting at the kitchen table sipping a cup of coffee and smoking a Marlboro, looking like the loneliest man on the planet.

"Mort?" he asked.

Shapiro looked up from his cup, a trail of white smoke swirling from his cigarette angled on an ashtray.

"Hanna is leaving you, and she's taking the twins with her," he said sadly and with a sense of finality that made Elliot wonder how much longer he could go on living his life as two people, Dr. Elliot Litner, thoracic surgeon and lecturer, and Il Dottore, the Mafia doctor.

17

THE SPEED OF SOUND

"This girl is Sicilian, Dr. Tick. If her father thought this was anything but appendicitis, her life would be ruined."

One of the nice things about living on two separate planes of existence was that when certain aspects of his Mafia life were worrisome, others concerning his medical career would be soaring. His marriage was falling apart, but under the watchful eye of Al Rosengarten, Elliot's career continued to flourish. His articles continued to be published in the most prestigious journals and highly praised by his peers. When it came to Mount Sinai Hospital, most saw him as eccentric, no one dared question his skills as a surgeon, and since he was avidly nonpolitical, few viewed him as a threat to their progress even though he was seen by most everyone that mattered as the heir apparent to Dr. Dak, director of cardiac surgery.

Occasionally, however, Elliot's two worlds would meld together into something pleasant and important to him in other, more personal, ways than money or good times, ways that Uncle Saul would have talked about if he'd been alive to see it. One moment like that happened around the time of Hanna's leaving him and involved a seventeen-year-old girl whose family had been sent to see him at the suggestion of Tommy Bilotti, Paul Castellano's driver and bodyguard, who he'd met a couple of times while tending to his boss.

It was late afternoon when Elliot was called to his office to find an immigrant Sicilian family crowded into his examining room. The father was a taciturn, hard-working bricklayer who spoke no English; the mother, a strong, loving woman, alarmed by her daughter's rapidly declining health. Then there was the girl lying on the exam table, beautiful with gentle doelike eyes, a flawless complexion, and long black hair, shy and frightened, suffering for more than a week now with severe abdominal pain, nausea, and dizziness.

"Dottore," the mother began, "Mr. Bilotti, he tell me you can help my daughter, Antonia. She been very sick with terrible pain in the stomach."

Elliot nodded, speaking gently to the girl as her father fell into the background, hat in hand, body taut as a piano wire, carrying himself with the square, flat-footed strength of a strict, by-the-rules Sicilian father. "Is this where you have pain," Elliot asked pressing the flat of his hand against her lower abdomen while she nodded tearfully.

"Aside from the stomach pain, what other problems does your daughter have?"

"She dizzy," the mother said stepping toward him. "She fall down two days ago with the fainting. And now she start with the food, no stay in the stomach!"

"Okay, I'm sorry but now I have to ask one personal question to your daughter," he said watching as the mother nodded, almost knowingly, and the father turned away from him. Elliot whispered, "Are you bleeding from down here," gesturing discreetly. Too embarrassed, the girl nodded, and now he understood—everything.

"Sir," he called to the father, who turned back toward him

while his terrified wife hung on his every word. "Your daughter has a damaged appendix," Elliot said drawing a small, imaginary line with his index finger onto the right side of his lower abdominal region. "This is an emergency. We need to operate now, and I need your permission."

Instinctively, the mother swiveled around to her suspicious husband translating Elliot's words to Sicilian with particular emphasis on "*apendicite*" and "*emergenza*," until he understood, reluctantly nodding his consent to whatever procedure would save his only daughter.

For better or for worse, the procedure that Elliot knew was necessary had nothing to do with appendix and everything to do with a life-threatening condition known as ectopic pregnancy. Taken from the Greek word meaning "away from the place," an ectopic pregnancy occurs when the fetus forms outside, rather than inside, the womb. The reason it was so serious was that the growth of the fetus eventually ruptures the fallopian tube causing hemorrhaging that leads to shock and death. Discerning that this young woman's life would be ruined if her devout Catholic father found out she was pregnant out of wedlock, and believing that her mother already knew, led Elliot to be creative with the diagnosis. But there were pressing medical issues, he realized, calling the greenest and most easily intimidated young intern he could think of to assist in the surgery.

The first problem was keeping the real surgery he'd be performing "quiet" while at least trying to make it look like an appendectomy to the intern. The second was that in these cases, the fetus had actually implanted itself in one of the fallopian tubes so that there were a number of surgical challenges, among them internal bleeding and infinitely more subtle, removing the fetus without precluding the patient's ability to later bear children. Given the fact that Antonia was just seventeen with practically her entire life before her, Elliot was hoping to spare her tube and preserve her ability to become pregnant. The bigger problem was explaining why he was involved in a routine appendectomy, but that's when he turned to Silvio's political expertise.

Within hours, Frank Silvio had assembled a surgical team, including Robert Tick, an Irish-Catholic, Georgetown University cum laude, now interning at the hospital, who'd be assisting Elliot in the procedure. Together they observed as the patient's abdomen was washed with soap and antiseptic, her body draped so that only the area of the incision would be exposed.

Elliot began the procedure making a bikini-line incision so the abdomen could be entered. Almost immediately, it became obvious that the fallopian tube had a large hemor-rhagic mass in it—the ectopic pregnancy. The key, he knew, would be to remove it without causing uncontrollable bleeding and then reconstruct the tube. Although he hadn't worked on an ectopic pregnancy in years, he took comfort in the fact that the concept of reconstructing arteries in the heart was no different and even more technically demanding.

During the course of the intensive, forty-five minute pro-cedure, Elliot was able to remove the ectopic pregnancy, pre-serve the ovary, and successfully reconstruct the tube. The internal wound was then cauterized with bleeding controlled and the most dangerous element of young Antonia's surgery completed.

Finally, the remaining phase of their surgery happened when Elliot turned his attention to a small tube of tissue about three inches long, dangling just below the point where the small intestine joins the large one, on the right side of the girl's frail body. It was her appendix. Conjectured to have somehow prevented intestinal infection eons ago, it served no known functional purpose at present, except that day for him, he thought, as he severed the useless appendage from her colon and removed it.

"There it is," he proclaimed, turning to Tick and displaying it. "The source of all this young woman's problems."

The intern looked at him incredulously. "What do you mean?" he asked. "That's the pinkest, healthiest appendix I've ever seen."

"No," Elliot answered, placing the tissue on the surgical table and striking it several times with the blunt end of his laser. "This appendix is obviously infected. Look at the shape and size, swollen and inflamed. Lucky we removed it before it burst."

"Dr. Litner, I don't understand."

"This girl is Sicilian, Dr. Tick. If her father ever thought this was anything but appendicitis, her life would be ruined. That's why, if you want to have a future at this hospital, your report will blame this infected tissue as the cause of her problems."

Tick, who was smart enough to know that he meant what he'd said, looked into Elliot's eyes, then nodded. "May I see that appendix again, Doctor?" he asked.

Afterward, Elliot spoke with the young girl's parents together, taking great pains to show them the damaged appendage, explaining to them what he believed had caused their daughter's ailment. The father listening intently, the mother wisely nodding her understanding of all that he was saying and not saying. His most gratifying moment, however, did not arrive until almost four years later when he received an invitation to Antonia's wedding, delivered in person to the hospital by her appreciative mother. He attended the traditional Catholic wedding ceremony a couple of months later, watching as Antonia's proud father gave her away to her handsome groom. The radiant bride, of course, was wearing a flowing gown of pure white.

This was one of the most gratifying experiences of Elliot's double life, but like the Crosby, Stills, Nash, and Young song says, "traveling twice the speed of sound, it's easy to get burned." And on the whole, the things that mattered most to him were falling apart before his eyes. Though his relationship with his father-in-law stayed cordial, Hanna wouldn't speak to him for months or let him see the twins unless she was in the room with them. Worse, though on a normal basis, he slept only five hours a night, now Elliot was suffering from bouts of insomnia so that even that was getting trimmed to something like three.

Why this sudden mental agitation? Maybe it went all the way back to those early days in the Bronx. The laughing and good-natured kidding that surrounded him there seemed to have evaporated. Instead of thinking about his father or Saul or even Sal, Nicky, and the guys, it was the murder scene that so dramatically changed his life, the one involving the hit and those two men shooting, then smashing the skull of their helpless victim, that seemed to haunt him. In retrospect, this poor man had done, what? Forget to pay a gambling debt? Sleep with the girlfriend of a made man? Elliot would never know, but suddenly, he was asking questions of himself that had never seemed important like what about that man *and what about him?*

18

THE MAFIA AND HOOVER'S FBI

"More recent photos, held by Cohn were even more explicit depicting Hoover having sex with top FBI man Clyde Tolson."

Suddenly and unexpectedly the pressure surrounding Elliot's double life caught up with him, both physically and psychologically. While at the hospital, he was experiencing mind-numbing migraines that could only be sated by strong painkilling drugs like Darvon and Percocet, medications he would never in the past have considered taking. Worse, he was experiencing nightmares, odd and unsettling. In one, he was a child being pursued through his old Bronx neighborhood by implacable gangs of street thugs. In another, more subtle, and haunting, he felt as if he had spent an entire night locked in a room where objects kept shifting their positions, sometimes by no more than an inch or two, but nothing remained exactly in place.

There was no mistaking the meaning of these developments. Into Elliot's life came a general sense that the foundations of the underworld were deteriorating, and that all he'd known before, even within the Gambino Family, was moving irreconcilably toward calamity. He worried about his friends, Nick and Sal and Joey Ficshetti, who seemed to be riding an express train headed straight to hell so far as he could see. For one thing, they were doing cocaine as if it was going out of style. But worse, though Elliot never asked, he knew that Nicky had been secretly buying large quantities of raw cocaine and heroin with family funds then selling it through street contacts in the so-called "Black" or "Cuban Mafia" in Manhattan's West Side and in Harlem.

It was one thing to do hard-core drugs as associates of any of the five families, which was a career-limiting decision, but the sale and distribution of hard-core drugs? That was a life-limiting decision because even though a blind eye was turned to massive deals occasionally made even by traditionalist god-fathers like Carlo Gambino when the risk was small and profits incredible, the ironclad rule for capos, soldiers, and associates was that the dollars from junk weren't worth the risk to the family, and breaches of that rule might well result in execution.

As early as 1947, during a full Commission meeting held on a yacht off the coast of Florida, the subject of narcotics was hotly debated between the traditionalist Sicilian members led by Joseph Bonanno and the Americanized liberal faction led by Lucky Luciano. Bonanno argued that like counterfeiting, drugs risked the possibility of federal intervention. Beyond that, as a traditionalist, he believed along with Vincent Mangano and Joe Profaci that the true Mafioso distanced himself from crimes like narcotics and prostitution while newer players like Luciano, influenced by Meyer Lansky and Bugsy Siegel, saw La Cosa Nostra mostly as a business enterprise where the huge profits in drug trafficking far outweighed the lingering attraction of worn-out Sicilian traditions.

In the end, it was the traditionalist who won out, and at that meeting, three key decisions were made. First, with Lucky in permanent exile, Frank Costello was formally named head of the Luciano Family. Second, Bugsy Siegel would be hit because he'd gone too far in trying to monopolize Las Vegas gambling interests for himself. Third, a specific resolution forever forbidding drug trafficking by the families was enacted. All three of these agenda items were voted upon and decided, but it was the third that resurfaced at Commission meetings held in 1951 and then again in 1956, where against the rising tide of Americanized Mafia voices, the edict to ban narcotics trafficking under the penalty of death was upheld.

Then, in 1956, with the assassination of Albert Anastasia, another hastily scheduled Commission meeting was called by Buffalo boss Stefano Magadinno. Convened at Apalachin in upstate New York, the agenda, which included yet another examination of the Commission narcotics policy, never happened because state trooper Edgar Croswell, sensing a change in the normally quiet atmosphere of the town, investigated the list of guests invited to host Joseph Barbara's estate. They included mob heavyweights Sam Giancana from Chicago; Santos Trafficante, Tampa; Gerry Catena and Frank Majuri from New Jersey; Carlo Gambino, Tommy Lucchese, and Vito Genovese from New York; and even Paul Castellano, a driver for Genovese at this stage of his young career. Soon afterward, Croswell organized a wholesale roundup, arresting dozens of Mafiosi for criminal conspiracy, a charge which—pre-RICO—could not stand up in court. The arrest did cause a furor in the newspapers, proving, once and for all, that the "Mafia" really did exist and that there truly was something called "organized crime."

Up until that time, thanks to the blackmailing of FBI Director J. Edgar Hoover by Frank Costello, even the term Mafia was not used by Hoover or anyone else at the bureau. The go-between in the blackmailing of Hoover was, not surprisingly, the ubiquitous attorney, Roy Cohn. According to Cohn, Lewis Rosenstiel, multimillionaire founder of Schenley's liquor and close ally of Costello, had engaged in bizarre sex orgies with the FBI director for years and had had the presence of mind as early as 1948 to take photographs of Hoover dressed in women's clothing, face daubed with lipstick and makeup, wearing a wig of ringlets while sitting on the laps of unidentified males.

More recent photos, held by Cohn in his office safe at the New York law firm of Saxe, Bacon, were even more explicit depicting Hoover having sex with top FBI man and longtime lover Clyde Tolson. "You know how many FBI agents were assigned to 'organized crime' before Apalachin?" Cohn bragged to a group that included Silvio, Ruggiero, Gene Gotti, and Elliot during one of their lost weekends at Studio 54. "Six. In the whole freakin' country, there were six federal agents investigating the Mafia in the United States, a country of a 170 million. That's the kind of clout a few photographs and a well-placed comment or two will get you. Rosenstiel was the brains, Costello was the muscle. The old Jew and Italian, one-two punch!"

All of that held true, even through the Kefauver Special Committee investigations into organized crime. But it was Apalachin that instigated the McClellan Committee hearings, an entirely new assault, where Chief Counsel Bobby Kennedy relentlessly pursued the entangled relationships between labor leaders like Jimmy Hoffa and the underworld and its leadership. Through all of these changes, betrayals, and power plays, one of the few constants that remained was the ban on drug trafficking. This was the reason that Angelo Ruggiero was so thankful about Elliot's deep-sixing any evidence that might prove his nephew's involvement in the sale of heroin.

Rules or no rules, by the late 1970s, drugs permeated the five New York families, confirming the wisdom of the Sicilian traditionalists, but there was just no stopping it. The drug train was in full gear throttled by incredible profits, ease of entry, and in the end, the delusions of grandeur that only a nonstop high can bring along with it. The collision of the runaway drug train's momentum with stark reality happened for Elliot with the closing of Studio 54. It began when owner Steve Rubell, during an interview with Dan Dorfman of *New York* magazine, let his ego and his addiction get away from him. "Studio 54 is a cash business where profits are astronomical," he was quoted as saying. "Only the Mafia does better!"

Not smart. And if that wasn't enough to whet the appetite of headline-hungry U.S. attorneys, information provided by disgruntled ex-employee Donald Moon was just what the doctor ordered. As part of a witness protection-immunity deal, Moon told federal agents about a secret safe filled with skimmed cash and, worse, about a trove of cocaine and other illegal substances stored in Hefty bags hidden in a gap between the hard and drop ceiling in the club's basement. Inevitably, on December 14, 1979, fifty agents from the IRS and DEA swarmed all over the place. Of course, they headed straight for the basement where, when demands for the accounting books were made by federal agents, the drugged-out ex-model who was running "finance" asked, "Do you want the second set, too?"

Also not smart. So that even when heavyweight attorney Roy Cohn rushed to the scene, comparing the raid to the "wanton acts of the Nazis!" and, ironically, "worse than the McCarthy hearings!" it was too late. According to Rubell, the feds confiscated $900,000 in cash along with a stash of cocaine and amyl nitrite "party favors" he would slip into the palms of celebrity guests, with the street cost of the drugs literally tagged onto them.

But what worried him more, Rubell later confided to Elliot during a late-night sex and drinking binge, was his relationship with Gambino Family loan shark Sam Jacobson, a frequent visitor to Studio 54 offices. IRS agents investigating the club's alternate set of books had discovered a five-column accounting sheet headed "Steve Rubell-Sam Jacobson," Rubell told him, with weekly dates and payoffs ranging up from $2,500 to $25,000 kept by Rubell's co-owner, Ian Schrager. More than the fines and jail time, it was his fear of FBI interrogation about Studio 54's family connection that scared him to death, Rubell confessed. "What if they think I'll rat on them, Elliot? You don't think they'd think that, do you?" he asked, petrified that a contract was about to be put out on him.

On January 18, 1980, Steve Rubell was sentenced to three-and-one-half years and a $20,000 fine for tax fraud. So what did he do? He threw a gala "going-away-to-prison" party that Nicky Micelli, Frank Silvio, and Elliot attended. Of course, it couldn't be the same as the unbelievably wild Halloween or New Year's Eve parties of the past because basically Rubell's "going away" was nothing to celebrate. Steve's old buddies like Andy Warhol, Liza Minnelli, and David Geffen were there while something like 1,000 people partied to the sounds of Gloria Gaynor's "Queen of Disco" and Donna Summer's "Last Dance." Still, somehow, Elliot couldn't help but feel that everything had changed and that guys like Rubell with their arrogance and drug-throttled egos had fucked up everything, the life that they'd been living.

"So, what's with you?" Nicky asked, getting Elliot's attention with a shove that half knocked him over. "We got booze—which I know you don't drink. We got coke—which I know you don't snort. Better, we got broads—which I know you like two at a time—crawlin' out the freakin' woodwork. So what's with you?"

"The place is different, that's all."

"Different? How?"

"Changed—everything," Elliot said, watching Silvio as he danced with a long-legged twenty-five-year-old wearing a white mask, G-string, and pasties with thigh-high platform boots. "I mean look at Frank over there. He looks ridiculous."

"Hey, fuckin' Frank was always ridiculous, you just didn't notice before."

"Yeah, well, for me the whole thing's getting kind of scary. Everybody's screwed up on drugs all the time. Nobody knows what the hell they're doing anymore. I mean, Steve's a friend of mine, but how can anybody be so stupid? Jesus, Nick, if people skim from a cash business, they'll take 10 percent, maybe 15 percent, 25 percent. But these guys skimmed $5 million in one year! Probably 80 percent of their gross."

"Okay, they're assholes. So what?"

"So what? These guys know our people, Nick. They were handing out cocaine and amyl nitrite like candy. They had animals like Roy DeMeo in here bragging about heroin deals, chopping people up like they were veal chops. I mean, what did Rubell and Schrager think was going to happen? What are they doing to people like us?"

"Ya know somethin', Elliot. I know you're a doctor and real fucking smart and all that shit, but sometimes you think too much," Nick said tapping his forefinger to his temple. "Now, I'm goin' to the john to get a taste a some a this Colombian pure I got here in my pocket. And please, when I get back, have yourself a diet soda, and I'll introduce you to a nice piece of Puerto Rican ass, maybe two, if you're nice to me. But don't talk to me no more about this drug shit. I don't like it, understand?"

As Nick left for the men's room, Elliot watched Steve Rubell and Diana Ross make their way up to the D.J. booths where the ex-Supremes lead singer began crooning "My Way" while Rubell gyrated wildly, finally falling backward over the second-floor railing. Fortunately for him, someone caught him by the belt of his pants and pulled him back up, or he might have killed himself. Typical of that night, but untypical of Studio 54, not a soul was laughing and David Geffen shouted at him, "Stop with this 'My Way' shit, and grow up already!"

To Elliot, the collapse of Studio 54 and Steve Rubell was like a metaphor for the way he was feeling about his own out-of-control existence, even Paul Castellano's and John Gotti's. Drugs like some kind of virus had crept into their world, contaminating it so that they all were infected in one way or another, making poor decisions based on greed, violence, and revenge without considering the long-term consequences for rules that had been in place for generations. The world was changing around La Cosa Nostra just as it had changed around Studio 54, and suddenly they were freaks standing naked in the glaring sun of the outside straight world.

In the case of Castellano, it was revenge involving wholesale killer and cokehead Roy DeMeo that would help to bring about his downfall.

According to Silvio, sometime in September 1980 after hearing his son-in-law, Frank Amato, a hijacker and butcher at Dial Poultry, was beating his pregnant daughter, Castellano contacted capo Nino Gaggi, DeMeo's supervisor, and ordered Amato hit. The reason may have been sound, but Castellano's reasoning was not, as DeMeo was more than a car-ring crew leader and murderer. He was a serial killer who had literally butchered at least thirty-seven men and women as much for sport as for business. A drug dealer on the side, he would later be indicted for possession with intent to sell 23 tons of marijuana, 500,000 Quaalude tablets, and 25 pounds of cocaine.

"This is how it goes with this maniac," Silvio, who seemed to enjoy talking about these subjects, confided to Elliot over a drink at Elaine's. "See, there's this apartment in Brooklyn that DeMeo keeps as both an execution chamber and a butchery where he gets to use his skills. When the guy walks in, somebody shoots him in the head with a silencer. He wraps the guy's head with a towel to stop the blood from flowing while another guy stabs him in the heart to stop blood from pumping. After that, they drag him into the bathroom, put him in a shower, bleed him, put him on a pool liner in the living room where they take him apart and package him. The packages wind up, wrapped small and individual, in cardboard boxes that they take to a city dump that Castellano controls so there are never any questions."

"Frank, I like you a lot," Elliot said "but please don't ever tell me anything like that again. It gives me heartburn, really. Promise?"

Silvio agreed, and the conversation ended. But facts are facts, and everything that Silvio had said was probably true because Frank Amato disappeared on September 20, 1980, and was never seen again. The remaining problem for Big Paulie, however, was the fact that he'd allowed himself to be connected to the disappearance of a relative through a capo who was not only a homicidal maniac, but a careless drug addict as well. Realizing the error, Nino Gaggi would once again be contacted by the boss, but this time the hit was on DeMeo.

On January 10, 1983, Roy DeMeo's bloody career ended, his body found riddled with bullets in the trunk of his car. But for Castellano, all of this was too late. The FBI was already investigating DeMeo's multimillion-dollar car-theft ring, along with highly visible New York City labor leader and Columbo Family capo Ralph Scopo, who'd been taped delivering Roy's epitaph. "Paul had to put him away," Scopo was recorded saying. "The guy was crazy and had cast-iron balls."

In the case of John Gotti, it was not revenge but greed that was laying the seeds of his destruction at the hands of nemesis Rudy Giuliani as the *babania* virus wormed its way through to even the most trusted members of his Bergin crew. Through most of his mob career, Angelo Ruggiero remained adamant about steering clear of the huge profits to be made from the heroin trade that his younger brother, Salvatore, had entered into full bore in 1977. Now, in the 1980s, Angelo, too, had become a slave to its allure, participating in international narcotics-trafficking deals with Salvatore and a half-dozen other Bergin associates including John Gotti's brother, Gene.

What Angelo didn't know was that he, along with Scopo and dozens of others, had been named in an electronic surveillance request as a target of a RICO investigation into the Gambino Family. With permission granted, on November 9, 1981, Ruggiero's home was wiretapped and bugged and would remain so for years to come. During that time, the FBI would listen in on conversations about gambling, loansharking, and drugs, but more damning—for him and the world of La Cosa Nostra—a subject even more sacrosanct than the family's longstanding ban on drugs. In a tape-recorded discussion with Bonanno Family associate Frank Lino, Angelo Ruggiero talked about the secret backbone of the United States Mafia, the Commission, a transgression punishable by death.

Angelo "Quack Quack" Ruggiero was not a man without means, however, and through a corrupt FBI agent, he would learn not only about the surveillance, but also about the damning evidence the agency had collected on him. Unfortunately for Angelo, his godfather Paul Castellano would also hear about those tapes and their existence and would set off a civil war between the two families within the family, Dellacroce's and Castellano's that was nothing short of cataclysmic.

When it was all sorted out, Paul Castellano would be shot dead in front of Sparks Steak House on East 46th Street in Manhattan, the FBI would be investigating itself, and John Gotti, an Americanized Neapolitano, would emerge as the most powerful gangster in America.

19

GIULIANI VS. GOTTI

"Stories like that stay with you deep inside like a bright and shiny piece of nuclear waste."

When Elliot thought back on the stories his Uncle Saul told, the Litner family was always running, as if in constant flight, either from something or toward something. He couldn't say for sure what that was, maybe freedom, maybe even from themselves, but in the turmoil after the Russian Revolution with Lenin and Trotsky at the head of the Communist Party and Kerensky leading the Socialists, life became unbearable for the Jews who were blamed for everything bad in Russia.

With their property confiscated and possessions stolen, many traveled from town to town to make a living, but it was quite difficult. The soldiers all had guns. They would hide in the woods, and if a Jew was caught on the road, he was lucky not to be killed. Renegade generals with whatever troops they had would come into a town and round up as many Jews as they could find. Those who couldn't escape were locked up in the synagogue and held for ransom with a deadline to raise money. If their friends and families couldn't raise it, the soldiers would gleefully burn down the synagogue with the Jews inside.

One day, the people of Vinograd heard rumors that a group of these bandits loyal to Kerensky were about to pass through town. They were chasing after Communists, but from which direction, nobody knew. Of course, the townspeople understood what the result would be if they were captured. So they began their exodus taking all they could carry with them. The roads were jammed with people. Saul's family split up with everyone going their own way.

Once on the outskirts of town where the Russian peasants lived, Saul hooked up with two brothers and their sister. Passing open fields and lines of army trenches, they soon discovered that they had taken the wrong road. In front of them, they saw an army of soldiers, some on foot, some on horses, many carrying rifles. They ran back toward the trenches, but the soldiers had already spotted them, and chased after them, cursing, and shooting. The four sat helpless in a trench with bullets flying all around them, thinking that they would never come out alive. One of the brothers suggested they look for shelter somewhere else. Before they had a chance to make a decision, he stood up and was hit in the chest with a bullet. He fell to the ground. This left no choice but for the others to stay in the trench, hoping against hope they could somehow survive.

Inevitably, the soldiers surrounded them, calling them "Jew Communists," until one soldier became so incensed, he picked up his rifle and smashed it into the face of the remaining brother, splitting his eye in half. The boy howled in agony, blood gushing from the wound, as the soldier charged after Saul. But at the moment Saul was about to be bashed, a miracle happened. Another soldier hollered something about "interrogation," saving Saul's life. The first soldier immediately stopped his assault. The second said he would escort the prisoners back to their town for questioning.

As they started back, the soldier asked each of them where they lived. They told him, but he took Saul to the boy's home that was located over a store. He instructed them to wait there until he returned, promising to let them go free once he was sure they weren't Communists.

As soon as they were inside the house, they locked themselves in, waiting to see what would happen when the soldier returned. But ten minutes later, to their amazement, the house was on fire. Saul could hardly believe it. While they were waiting, the soldier had soaked the entire building with gasoline and set it ablaze.

Of course, they ran from the burning structure, simply took off! Saul didn't know what happened to the others, but began walking toward his house. The streets were empty and he didn't see a soul. On the way, he passed his grandfather's house where he discovered his grandmother sitting on the steps, blood all over her face, sobbing. He tried to find out what happened and offered his help, but she begged him to run and hide before they killed him. She wouldn't let him stay with her, so he began running, not knowing where.

It was later that day that he heard the news. Kerensky's men had rounded up dozens of Jews, then held them captive in the town's synagogue for ransom. With no one there to pay, they set it on fire burning all of them alive.

That's another Uncle Saul story, an episode that Elliot and his brother heard maybe 100 times growing up as kids from Saul, the proud owner of 174th Street's finest, and only, laundry, along with dozens of others that spoke of tragedy and outright shock at the hatred their very existence as Jews inspired. Stories like that stay with you deep inside and lie there like a bright and shiny piece of nuclear waste in the pit of your stomach radiating something, maybe hostility or anger or mistrust of the system and the "authority" of which you were supposed to be so respectful or frightened.

Well, Elliot was not so respectful or frightened, and in his own way, if it was hostility he carried around with him, it was hidden even from him at that time and showed itself in ways that were too diffused to see, let alone comprehend. Maybe his incredible appetite for gambling and women was part of that or the fact that he was living a two-track life, one hovering at the top of, or perhaps even above, normal society as a surgeon; the other, equally real and substantive, running below, like some dark underground river that wended its way below society in what was appropriately called the "underworld."

The point for Elliot was that everybody he knew in any kind of power, politicians more than anyone else, carried that same black river within themselves. The difference was that the Mafia guys he knew were honest about it. They rarely pretended to be what they weren't. They knew they were gangsters, modern-day outlaws basically, and they were, in their way, proud of it. They didn't try to tell people they were something other than what they were as Bobby Kennedy and Rudy Giuliani spent their lives doing. They weren't phonies.

Roy Cohn, who genuinely despised Giuliani, told Elliot about a time Rudy met John Gotti on the street when they were both coming up through their respective ranks that said a lot about both men. It seemed Giuliani, U.S. attorney for the Southern District of New York at the time, was driving around Manhattan's Lower East Side with Gail Sheehy, who was writing a story about him for *Vanity Fair* magazine. From Giuliani's standpoint, this was just great. Already graduated from his earlier phase of setting up "New York's finest" for conviction through ex-cop and informer Bob Leuci, he had come to the same realization as Dewey and Kennedy before him: There was a wealth of political capital to be found mining the vein of Mafia takedowns. So what could be better than tooling around Little Italy, bragging to a wide-eyed and best-selling author about your Brooklyn altar boy background and all the macho things you'd done to "bring down" the Mafia?

"'See that place,' Cohn said imitating Giuliani with his monk's face and lisp. 'That's Umberto's, right there on Mulberry Street. It's a piece of mob history because Joey Gallo was hit, there—*right there*—you can still see the bullet holes in the wall outside! And that place. See it,'" Cohn went on with his Rudy routine, "'S.P.Q.R. That's where John Gotti, the famous gangster had dinner *just last night!*' And here is this broad, 'oohing' and 'ahhing,' hanging on every word, writing it down on a notepad, while he's taking her on this 'tour of the underworld' with Rudy no doubt thinking to himself, 'what a freakin' deal I've got here! On the one hand this broad, being Irish Catholic, is going to fall hook, line, and sinker for all my 'I went to Bishop Loughlin prep school' and 'I was thinking about a life as a Christian Brother myself' spiel. So she'll write this sucker up like the second coming of Jesus.' On the other, Giuliani being one of the great cunt-hounds of all time, is probably thinking, 'You know, she isn't half-bad, if I can get her to suck my cock while I'm driving, wouldn't that be great?'

"So now they get to the Ravenite, and the place is crawling with Gotti guys. Maybe twenty or twenty-five of them standing outside, first, because it's a beautiful spring day, and, second, a guy, probably one of Gigante's, took a shot at John two days earlier, but missed. He was tracked down in about twenty minutes, shot in the head four times, then dumped inside the Chin's favorite candy store, to deliver a message. In other words, everybody at the Ravenite is ready for war when this stupid bastard comes passing by like he's driving through Beverly Hills with a 'Home of the Stars' map on his lap, this redhead beside him looking like his Aunt Emily from fucking Des Moines!

"So the guys, who know Giuliani and his gray sedan on sight, stand up and take notice as he slows down. '*Who are those men?'* the broad asks like the awestruck underworld tourist that she is. 'These guys,' Giuliani tells her in his best lispy-wispy prosecutor's voice, 'are what we call made men, professional criminals and part of the Mafia. I know. I can look at them and tell. I can *just feel it.'* *'Aren't you afraid?'* the author squeals. 'No, no, it's just part of the job, you know.'

"Only just as he says that, the pack of guys move to the side, and there, sitting in a chair outside, puffing on a cigar, in a brand new Palm Beach suit, tanning himself, is Johnny Gotti. Well, Rudy's face turns white and bloodless, and he's about to shit in his pants when their eyes meet. Then, Gotti's mouth curls up in that contemptuous grin of his, he raises his hand, cocks his finger like a gun, then pulls the trigger just staring at Giuliani and his lady friend, mouthing the words, 'fuck you!'"

Having observed both men, to Elliot it was obvious that a dangerous chemistry existed between Gotti and Giuliani so that as much as the ambitious prosecutor had Gotti's number so, too, the Mafia chieftain had Giuliani's. In his mind that spring afternoon, Gotti might have been thinking about the *real* Rudy whose father he knew had been more involved with the New York families than his own, who'd spent the better part of his life burnishing stories about Harold's "strait-laced" and "moralistic" father-son talks with him. Sheehy's article later appeared with a boldface, twenty-eight-pica header reading RUDY GUILIANI DOES NOT CHEAT ON HIS OWN INNER CODE. Gotti must have been nauseated! More, just as Rudy had made it his business to analyze and study Gotti and Paul Castellano, John Gotti, who'd read *The Prince* and *The Art of War* at Carlo Gambino's suggestion while in Lewisburg prison, had made it his business to study the mob's implacable adversary, Rudy Giuliani.

Forever playing the high road, Gotti understood that Giuliani was a prosecutorial zealot who would stop at nothing to achieve his childhood goal of being the first Italian-American Catholic president.

So much for Rudy's "inner code." But even the "tough guy" *ginzaloon* image that he swaggered around with in those days had been concocted as men like Gotti, who knew the real Giuliani, could attest. Gotti considered Rudy Giuliani a coward for dodging the draft. In June 1969 Rudy declared himself a conscientious objector. When that failed to keep him out of the military and he was reentered into the draft, he went running to Judge McMahon, the by-the-book, law-and-order judge. McMahon used his clout with the local draft board to help Giuliani connive his way out of his 1A draft-eligible classification.

Giuliani made himself out to be this great moralist, "Could he be a latter-day Savonarola, using temporal power to purge a sin-sodden city?" Gail Sheehy asked in her article. Here was this big patriot and hero, but where was he when it came to the war and draft? "At least I had an excuse," Gotti had once told Cohn when the subject of Giuliani came up. "I was in prison!"

20

TOUGH GUYS
DON'T DANCE

"So go ahead, I'm a tough guy. Do what you need to do. Take my pants off. Give me a blow job if it makes the burning in my stomach go 'way."

John Gotti was no saint when it came to the ladies. While Giuliani was making a splash with his new flame and working nonstop on assembling "enterprise evidence," John, as capo of the Bergin crew, was raking in hundreds of thousands of dollars from JFK hijackings, loansharking, construction-contract rigging, and a subject few talked about, heroin deals arranged through Angelo Ruggiero's younger brother, Salvatore.

The problem was Gotti was spending it just as fast with gambling losses of more than $200,000 in just the final two months of the 1982 football season and a relatively new vice, painting the town red with Shannon Grillo, Neil Dellacroce's beautiful blonde daughter, and a host of other female fans including Lisa Gastineau, ex-wife of the former New York Jets' defensive end.

Gotti's tacit participation in his best friend's international heroin operation weighed heavy on everyone involved including John's brother, Gene, Angelo Ruggiero, and even Dellacroce, underboss to Castellano, all of whom understood that the penalty for active interest in the *babania* trade was

161

death. Hearing rumblings about drug problems within his family, Castellano summoned Gotti and Dellacroce to his White House in April 1982 where he told them that two family members had sworn to him that Pete Tambone, a crew member of the Dellacroce Family, was trading heroin. More to the point, he was going to the Commission to obtain approval to kill the sixty-two-year-old grandfather because getting rid of Tambone would be "a lesson to everyone else in the family." If you deal drugs, you pay for it with your life.

Castellano, both an astute businessman and godfather, was a man who possessed one quality above all others that was respected in mob circles, and that was *fuberia*, a bold slyness that allows people to understand that when you speak, you are saying more than the words that come from your mouth. For Gotti and Dellacroce, who knew that Ruggiero was distributing large quantities of high-grade Sicilian heroin into the midwestern United States and Canada that was netting nearly $1 million per month, this was the most serious kind of warning. While the words talked about "Little Petey" Tambone, the message was that he knew about Ruggiero's operation, perhaps, even their own involvement.

As it turned out, Castellano's petition for the execution of Tambone was stalled when in a Commission vote with only four voting families present, a deadlock ensued. The New York Mafia's governing body agreed then to opt for a less severe punishment, and Pete Tambone was banned from the organization for life, a penalty Ruggiero later told Frank Silvio was "the same as getting whacked." The pass on Tambone's execution did little to relieve the anxiety that permeated Dellacroce and Gotti's Bergin crew, however, and on May 6, 1982, just one month later, Salvatore Ruggiero, and his wife, Stephanie, were the only two passengers aboard a Lear jet flying from New York to Orlando that mysteriously crashed nose first into the Atlantic Ocean. Their unrecovered bodies were believed to have been torn apart on impact.

Soon after, with Angelo "Quack-Quack" Ruggiero singing and being recorded like an opera star for the New York FBI and Source BQ 11766-OC, Willie Boy Johnson, a federal indictment was handed down against Ruggiero, Gene Gotti, and eleven others. The charge was, not surprisingly, narcotics trafficking, but the proof to support the charges was a shocker: FBI tapes derived from bugs placed in the basement, den, kitchen, and dining room of Ruggiero's Cedarhurst, Long Island, home.

The existence of those tapes had a chilling effect on Gotti and his Bergin crew and threw Big Paul Castellano into a rage. Since Ruggiero was a trusted member of Gotti's crew, Dellacroce's faction of the family, and by process of elimination, the godfather himself, there was no telling what damaging evidence had been collected regarding their entire enterprise in addition to Angelo's drug ring. Castellano knew that as a defendant in a federal case, the law required that Ruggiero be given transcripts of his taped conversations, and fearing that he was mentioned in them, demanded that Angelo turn them over to his attorneys, James LaRossa and Roy Cohn, for evaluation. Coming at this from the other side of the street, Ruggiero knew that not only would those tapes incriminate him beyond salvation, but Gotti and Dellacroce along with him, and so he refused.

The dilemma was real for all concerned. Not only had Dellacroce, Gotti, and Ruggiero been pushed by federal agents into a life-threatening conundrum, but Castellano, as boss, was left with a lot to think about. It was Dellacroce's arm of the family that provided the muscle for the Gambino Family. Guys like DeMeo and, more recently, Gotti's new pal, Sammy "the Bull" Gravano, would push a button on most anyone, as much for the fact that they were good soldiers as that they just didn't mind killing people. Dellacroce had always been loyal and as underboss, had coattails that some of his best moneymakers had clung to for years. Add to that the fact that Ruggiero and Gotti had been together since the days of the Fulton-Rockaway Boys and you had the makings of an interfamily war that would see dozens die, millions of dollars lost, and media exposure at the worst possible juncture.

It was at around this time, with the fires of suspicion blazing between the family within the family and Giuliani's RICO case fortified by new information gained from a bug placed in the Jaguar of Lucchese Family boss Anthony "Tony Ducks" Corallo, that Elliot received a call on his emergency pager to come to the Barbizon Plaza Hotel in Manhattan. It was two o'clock in the morning, but he was awake, hanging out with Silvio at Regine's. He hopped a cab, then made his way into the hotel lobby.

The Barbizon Plaza's security men faded into the woodwork, and one of John Gotti's bodyguard/chauffeurs, Joe Corrozzo, walked up to him. Dressed in a suit and a dark gray overcoat, he extended his hand, seeming to know Elliot, though Elliot didn't remember ever having met him. "Dr. Litner?" the bodyguard asked as he accepted the handshake. "Mr. Gotti's upstairs. He'd like to see you."

Elliot didn't bother to respond. What did it matter? If John Gotti wanted to see him, he would go to Gotti's room with no questions asked. Though Gotti, at the time, was not yet the household name that he would become after *Time* featured him on its cover, he was already treated with deference by family members who made it no secret that he was being groomed to become Dellacroce or even Castellano's replacement. More, Gotti's personality had evolved so that unlike the Gambinos, Gigantes, and Castellanos of the world, he had a penchant for the spotlight, hanging out with celebrities like actor Mickey Rourke and baseball star Rusty Staub at Club A, Elaine's, Da Noi, and other midtown spots rather than his old-time haunts in Little Italy.

That much Elliot knew from Silvio. There was a definite aura that one felt when the name "John Gotti" was mentioned. What he didn't know and could never have discerned until he physically examined him, was the Gordian knot Gotti's recent life had become, the complications coming perhaps from Ruggiero's foolishness, Dellacroce's loyalty to him, and Castellano's notions about what a boss could and could not accept.

Corrozzo brought Elliot to the mobster's suite. Another of Gotti's men opened the door. On seeing Corrozzo, he allowed them to enter.

"Mr. Gotti's not feeling too well," Corrozzo explained when they were inside, sounding as if he was the one in pain. "He's in the back. Let me tell him you're here."

Elliot nodded, his eyes scanning the suite's anteroom, plush and modern. There were the makings of martinis on the bar and two bottles of Dom Perignon Champagne already opened. Was this the aftermath of a party, Elliot wondered, or the last gasps of an all-night romp through Manhattan that had led here for a final nightcap?

"Mr. Gotti says you should go into the bedroom."

Elliot followed the bodyguard, walking with him through the anteroom, into a living room, flanked by a long oak dining table with chairs for eight settings. When they came to the door of the master bedroom. Corrozzo motioned him to open it. Elliot was surprised to find an exhausted-looking John Gotti, his normally meticulously coiffed silver hair uncombed, sitting on a sofa watching a boxing match on television, his girlfriend, Shannon "Sandy" Grillo, sitting on his lap.

Gotti, dressed in the remnants of a tailor-made gray suit, with jacket and tie off, and white shirt unbuttoned down to his sternum, barely looked up from the TV screen where two middleweights were going at it. "Do I know you?"

"Y-yes, we've met before, but I don't think you know me."

"What the fuck is that supposed to mean?" Gotti asked, laughing at the inanity of Elliot's remark, then grimacing.

"It means, that I'm an easy guy to forget," Elliot answered, concerned, as he drifted toward the sofa. "Does it hurt you to laugh?"

"It hurts me to breathe!" Gotti moaned, holding his stomach as his gorgeous girlfriend gave Elliot the once-over.

"So who's this, Johnny?" she asked as curious as she was suspicious. "He looks more like a kid who should be dissecting frogs than a doctor. Is it okay for him to be here? With us?"

"My name is Dr. Litner," Elliot answered, already beginning his examination, at least visually. Gotti's stomach, even beneath the shirt, looked distended. "Do you mind if I unbutton your shirt?"

Gotti nodded his assent. "My guy's in Beijing. Fucking doctor thinks he's Richard Nixon! Tommy Bilotti recommended you. You're the guy treated Big Paulie, am I right? The kid Neil calls Il Dottore with the clinics and all that shit.... He told me about you."

Elliot undid the remaining buttons of Gotti's shirt, then hesitated.

"So go ahead. I'm a tough guy. Do what you need to do," Gotti said, talking like a man who hadn't slept in three days. "Take my pants off. Give me a fucking blow job if it makes the burning in my stomach go 'way."

"How long have you been in pain like this?"

"Off and on, maybe a year," he answered eyes still fixed on the TV. "Sandy, get the doctor a martini. Get me one, too

. . ." Then, he leaped from the chair. *"Oh, fuck!"*

"Sorry?"

"Son of a bitch! Did you see that? He just knocked 'im out! This fucking guy Duran gets hit with a fucking two-by-four and smiles. Tonight I bet five dimes on the motherfucker, and he goes down with one fucking right over the top!" Gotti withered back into the sofa. "Can you believe this shit?"

"No."

"What?"

"No, martini, but I'll take a Diet Coke. And, n-no, I can't believe that Hearns just knocked Duran out."

"Sandy! Bring Il Dottore a Diet Coke," Gotti called into the other room. Then he belched. "Fuck! Like I don't have enough fucking problems, I've got what now? An ulcer? Stomach fucking cancer?"

Elliot felt his dilated abdomen. It was hard. "The pain, is it sudden and sharp, or dull and gnawing?"

"Sharp like a fucking knife."

"Have you been vomiting?" Elliot asked without any trace of a stutter. "If you have, is there blood in it? Black blood that looks something like ... coffee grounds?"

"Coffee grounds, huh?" Gotti repeated. Then he grinned in a way that said more than any words could. It was a tired, world-weary grin, so cynical and yet so well grounded that it was chilling. Like if you were torturing him, driving nails through his fingertips with a hammer, he'd still give you that same half-smile, lips slightly curled up, like he knew everything and had lived a thousand lives. "No, there ain't no blood, but every morning it don't feel normal if I don't walk to the bathroom, throw water on my face, go to the commode, then puke my guts out before I brush my teeth."

"What about your stool. Is it bloody? Black?"

"Sometime blood, yeah, but not much. Tell ya somethin',

Doc. Used to be my stomach was made outta fucking cast iron. Now, I eat a slice of pizza, drink a beer, and I got *adjeda* all fucking night. Don't seem right does it? Beautiful broad like Sandy here," he said taking the martini glass from her. "Nice fucking digs. But a goddamned stomach turns itself inside out right when I'm about to make love to her like Rudolph Valentino. So what do we do now, Dottore? What's the fucking verdict?"

"You have what's called a duodenal ulcer, not so uncommon, particularly for a man like you who's very busy and has a lot of stress in his life. What have you been taking for it?"

"Pepto-Bismol."

"Nothing else?"

Gotti shook his head with certainty. "Not a fucking iota more."

"Well, there's nothing wrong with Pepto-Bismol, but I'm going to write you two prescriptions for what's called triple therapy," Elliot explained, scribbling the names of the drugs on a pad. "One is a strong antacid, bismuth subsalicylate. The other is Valium, a mild sedative. Together they'll settle the digestive enzymes that have been attacking your stomach lining. Oh, and Mr. Gotti," Elliot said watching as he sipped his martini, "for the next two weeks, you need to avoid food or drinks that might upset your stomach—alcohol, dairy products, spicy meals."

Gotti held his glass up in a toast. "*Salud!*" he said as if to proclaim "Yes, I'm the toughest fucking guy in the world!" Then, Elliot put the two pieces of paper into Sandy Grillo's waiting hand.

"You should get the prescriptions filled first thing tomorrow. If you run into any more problems or if the pain continues, you need to give me a call. You could have a gastric ulcer, in which case you're going to need an upper G.I. series."

"That all sounds fine, Dottore, except for one thing. Why wait to get these prescriptions? Joe!" Gotti called into the adjoining room. Within seconds, his bodyguard/chauffeur had materialized. "Take these to one of our pharmacies. I want the medicine back here in an hour. Also," he said taking five $100 bills and putting them into the palm of Corrozzo's hand, "take Il Dottore with you. Drop him off anywhere he wants."

Elliot left the suite as quietly as he'd arrived with Gotti sipping his martini on the sofa watching the postfight wrap-up, the adorable Sandy Grillo, wife of Gambino associate, Ernie Grillo, daughter of Castellano underboss Neil Dellacroce, sitting on his lap, giggling as he played with her breasts, now exposed from the black lace negligee that was hanging loose from her body.

It was several nights later that Elliot got a chance to discuss his meeting with New York's most powerful capo with Silvio, who knew a lot more about Gotti and the undercurrents within the Gambino Family than Elliot ever wanted to. The entire episode struck Frank as out of school. "An unspoken La Cosa Nostra rule is that a made man, especially a capo like Gotti, is not supposed to violate another man's wife or children," Silvio explained. "In sleeping with Shannon Grillo, Gotti seems to be violating two sacred oaths with the same woman. Even so, technically, it may not be a violation," he mitigated. "After all, Ernie Grillo is a scumbag who is only an associate, not a made man, and Sandy Dellacroce is not the daughter of Neil's wife, though he's the father of a baby they adopted at birth."

The coming days would be filled with explanations both subtle and profound. But no amount of lawyering, not Cohn's, Giuliani's, or even John Gotti's, could prevent the collision of forces that were building both inside and outside of La Cosa Nostra. For Elliot Litner, even as he saw and felt those forces hurtling about him, there was little he could do but watch and hope that somehow the better men among them would survive. In retrospect, he was uncertain that it came out exactly that way, but in a game of life-and-death poker, he would learn that blood beats technicalities.

21

RICO REDUX

"The Commission's tentacles reached into virtually every aspect of New York City life, but in no instance was their presence more demonstrable than in the construction industry."

Elliot Litner's life had more than the usual share of ups and downs. While the general trend was spiraling downward, there were, to be sure, moments when good fortune came his way. One of those occurred in late 1983 when, after months of living with her father, Hanna and the twins came back to their home in Englewood.

Elliot remembered the rainy November day they returned. That night, after Samantha and Rachel had gone to bed, he and Hanna sat in their living room, a fire blazing in the hearth. From Elliot's standpoint, the subject of reconciliation, temporary though it was, would never have been broached except that Hanna would not let him escape it.

"I love you, Elliot, you know that, don't you?" she asked. "Not in some glamorous, romantic way, but for who you are— especially during moments like this when you're relaxed and able to talk to me like I'm someone important in your life."

"You are important, even if I don't tell you that all the time. You and the girls are all that I live for, really."

"Then why aren't you happier around us? It's like you

think you don't deserve to be happy, or you're afraid to be happy, and so you keep yourself in a constant state of jeopardy with your gambling and friends and other women."

"No, it's just that I have trouble sometimes connecting deeply. I know what I feel, but I can't explain it, and maybe I don't express it very well. I don't know why."

"There's a word for that, you know. It's 'estranged.' You're a man who is estranged. It means you 'arouse enmity or indifference in where there had formerly been love.'" Hanna recited the definition as if reading from the dictionary. "Frankly, Elliot, I think you need to see a psychiatrist."

That was classic Hanna, a woman who had to put everybody in a box, usually on one side of a line or the other marked good and evil. In Elliot's case, however, she'd made a careful exception. He was estranged, not good or evil, *just there*, like an eternal eunuch who for psychological reasons she couldn't engage in either unconditional love or mortal combat.

Understanding that, Elliot resolved to take things as they came, happy to be living with Hanna, ecstatic to be part of his daughters' lives again. Moreover, the reconciliation helped to stabilize him so that for a while, at least, he took a hiatus from Las Vegas junkets and Atlantic City all-nighters to play the role of a caring husband and father. As fortuitous, the combination of high-profile lectures, his work as professor of surgery at Mount Sinai School of Medicine, and the dozens of articles he'd published led the Winthrop-Breon Committee to select him as the recipient for the prestigious American College of Chest Physicians Scholar of the Year Award. That kind of press didn't go unnoticed at the hospital, and around that time, Al Rosengarten suggested they break bread at the "21" Club to "discuss the future."

Entering the restaurant, Elliot was met by Rosengarten in the large anteroom that stood separate from the bar and dining area. Dressed to the teeth in a dark-blue business suit with gold embossed cuff links and a flashy red tie, Rosengarten clasped Elliot's hand and clapped his back as he led him to his table where a snifter of Talisker single malt lay waiting.

"What will you have to drink, Elliot?" Rosengarten asked, angling himself into his chair. "Oh, that's right, you're the 'Diet Coke' man," he said teasingly, "is that what you'll be having?"

Elliot nodded. Rosengarten motioned to the waiter, then took a thoughtful pull from his snifter of Scotch. "You know, we're proud of you, Elliot. Really. Genuinely proud. And impressed. The Winthrop-Breon awards, well, that helps. It helps a great deal."

"Thank you, but I'm not sure I understand, Al."

"I'm telling you that it's official. Dr. Dak will be retiring as director of cardiac surgery at the hospital in June. More to the point, Simon has confided that it's you who he'll be proposing to the board as his successor."

"Me?"

"Yes, Elliot, you. So, what can I say except congratulations! This is a moment of significance," he proclaimed, clinking his snifter of Talisker's against Elliot's glass of Diet Coke, "something worth celebrating, am I wrong? What, with you, Hanna and the twins back together, and now this? These are the times you move, even at an early age, from journeyman to master. From Simon's understudy to one of the cornerstones of the Mount Sinai tradition."

He studied Elliot's expression, one of total consternation, then guffawed. "Look, Elliot, I know what goes on. So does Mr. Castellano and these other friends of ours. The past couple of years have been tough on you and your family. We know that. The pressures of daily surgeries, the travel, the writing. Jesus! No one knows where you get the goddamned energy!" The seventy-six-year-old Rosengarten reached across the table placing his hand, nails manicured and polished, over Elliot's. "What I'm trying to say is this, you've been good to us, and now we want to return the favor. Dr. Dak will put your name forward, and the Mount Sinai board will unanimously approve that nomination. I guarantee it."

Elliot sipped his Diet Coke, "W-why thank you, Al. You've been like a brother to me. And I appreciate what you and Dr. Dak and Mr. Castellano have done for me."

The multimillionaire mogul and Gambino Family stalwart nodded his large head lovingly. His eyes glistened as he withdrew his hand, smiling. "While these two things are in no way connected, Elliot, I did want to bring up one last situation before we start dinner. We need you to carry a package back from Sao Paolo for us. Call it a final gesture on your part. Like before, it will be Carmine that contacts you with the details. Really, it won't be much of anything. A formality, really."

"Sao P-Paolo? Sao Paolo, Brazil?"

Rosengarten took a sip of Talisker. "Exactly."

"But I don't know anyone there. I have no contacts. There are no lecture dates on my calendar. Nothing!"

"What do you mean?" Rosengarten asked incredulously. "Elliot, you're a visiting professor at Prontocor Hospital in Bello Horizonte. This was done by special appointment. Board initiated February 1978."

"Visiting professor? Al, I've never b-been to Prontocor Hospital in Bello Horizonte, Brazil!"

Al Rosengarten sat back in his chair. He held his empty glass out to the waiter, who plucked it from his waving hand. Then, his eyes narrowed, small and shiny. "*Elliot,*" he said as if he was talking to the densest primitive on the planet. "*You're not going to make me go through all of that again, are you?*"

So, that was the way it worked. When the goodfellows

wanted something done, they didn't ask twice. Nor did they think they had to. That's just the way it was in their world. No matter what Elliot did or how he tried to fool himself, at this point, he was entrenched in the Mafia, and there was no way out. More, whether he wanted to admit it or not, like Gotti and like Giuliani, he was hooked on the narcotic of power.

True, he still owed nearly $75,000 from past and recent excursions to Caesar's, the Dunes, Aladdin, and other mobbed-up casinos in Las Vegas and Atlantic City, but the fact of the matter was he coveted that directorship the way a sex addict lusts for a beautiful woman; wanted it badly, and that was all his Gambino Family friends needed to know. It would be several weeks later, in January 1984, before Carmine Lombardozzi contacted him with what eventually became two jobs, one to Tel Aviv, then another, his last, to Sao Paolo.

If the old Bronx and Brooklyn neighborhoods produced anything at all in the hearts and character of its alumni, it was brass balls and an incredible appetite for success. While Elliot was busy trying to become director of cardiac surgery at Mount Sinai, John Gotti was relentless in his pursuit of the title of bosses of bosses within the ranks of the American Mafia.

Still, there was no one among them, incubated in the ghettoes of those virulent New York enclaves, who burned with more white-hot ambition or worked more feverishly than Rudy Giuliani. What Elliot couldn't know at the time, however, was that that feverish work ethic and white-hot ambition were, in effect, turning on him.

Piecing together bits of information gathered from the Ruggiero/Corallo bugs and wiretaps and the testimony of well-placed informers like Willie Boy Johnson, U.S. Attorney Giuliani put together a fifty-one count indictment against Paul Castellano and twenty-one others making it the largest

RICO case ever. Among other charges, the indictment alleged that Big Paulie had ordered Anthony Gaggi to kill Roy DeMeo. While DeMeo was alive, the indictment alleged, Castellano participated in the profits from the multimillion-dollar stolen-car ring that DeMeo ran and that Paul had ordered him, Gaggi, and a third man to kill two Gambino Family con artists who'd staged a phony charity event in 1979 attended by first lady Rosalyn Carter. The scam had embarrassed Castellano, who, a federal witness, later testified considered himself "an upright businessman," to the point where he simply wanted DeMeo dead.

If the godfather's sensibilities were offended by the indictment, considered the worst publicity for the Gambino Family since Albert Anastasia's Murder Incorporated was brought to light, Castellano would find little solace in the proceedings to follow. In sworn testimony, witness Vito Arena, a homosexual member of DeMeo's crew, dubbed "the Gay Hit Man" by the press, recounted the brutal slayings of rival stolen-car dealers Ronald Falcaro and Kaled Darwish by DeMeo killer Henry Borelli. DeMeo then ordered the corpses "cut up," Arena explained, and since it was lunchtime and they were hungry, the team of butchers ate pizza and hot dogs while they dismembered the bodies using small saws and boning knives to parcel arms, legs, and torsos into Hefty bags for later disposal. During the exercise, one of them got so carried away with the dissection of the victim's private parts that a readily identifiable organ slipped through the floor vent and could not be retrieved. "DeMeo went crazy," Arena told the astounded grand jury members, "because he considered it unprofessional."

So how did RICO umbrella this scenario? Dominick Montiglio, Gaggi's nephew, testified that it was he who brought $20,000 in cash payments from the car-theft ring each week to Castellano's warehouse in Brooklyn. Additionally, it was he who accompanied his uncle, Nino Gaggi, to Dial Poultry, a Castellano chicken distribution firm, where sums of cash, at least that large, were turned over to their godfather. Under RICO, this was as clear a case as anyone had ever made. Big Paulie had profited from the car-theft ring and sanctioned all the murders that went along with it including Roy DeMeo's. In other words, racketeering-influenced corruption at its worst and most obvious.

Working with attorneys Roy Cohn and James LaRossa, Castellano was released almost upon arrest on $2-million bail, but still he must have been wondering how the feds, and Giuliani, in particular, had learned so much about his La Cosa Nostra dealings. After all, this was his first brush with either local or federal law enforcement since his arrest on an armed robbery charge in 1934 at the age of nineteen. Now seventy-years-old, he no doubt blamed this latest misfortune on Angelo Ruggiero and his stupidity for talking so openly and allowing his home and telephone lines to be bugged and tapped in the first place. You have to figure that somewhere in the godfather's subconscious, he must have anguished was there more? Additional information that a moron like Quack-Quack was capable of bragging about after two glasses of wine, information about family loansharking, gambling, political payoffs, pornography, union racketeering, construction bid rigging, extortion, drugs, and the dozens of family-related hits to which he could be tied.

But as knowledgeable as Paul Castellano had become during his nine years as godfather and chairman of the Commission, he was not yet aware of two potentially cataclysmic situations. First, in addition to Ruggiero's house being bugged, the FBI had in May 1983 performed a "black bag" job at Castellano's Todt Hill enclave, drugging his Doberman attack dogs with shots from a dart gun, incapacitating the security system and motion-detection devices, then picking the lock to the garage's pedestrian entrance door to gain access to the estate.

Once inside, they knew where family business was carried out thanks to interrogations of Castellano's mistress, Gloria Olarte. The agents planted omni-directional listening devices within the estate so that conversations between Castellano and his capos were transmitted to a command center located in a neighboring house where they were recorded unencumbered. The second problem, that even Castellano couldn't imagine, was that Ruggiero and he were picked up on separate surveillance tape recordings discussing the unthinkable: the Commission and the vast scope of the five families' operations nationally, internationally, and most specifically, in the State of New York.

As Elliot discovered later, it was through these tapes and information obtained from informants that Giuliani put a puzzle together that was custom made for RICO. It was long known that the five families controlled the New York construction industry through their infiltration of the construction workers' unions. For Giuliani, however, a pattern was emerging so that he could now prove there was an organization, the Commission, that acted as a governing body to carry out these crimes. By controlling the unions through bribery, blackmail, and murder, the mob controlled the labor supply at a given construction site as well as the supply of critical building materials such as concrete and steel girders.

The Commission's tentacles reached into nearly every aspect of New York life from trucking to the manufacturing of clothing, entertainment, even garbage collection, but in no instance was its presence more demonstrable than in the construction industry. The Commission had organized the principal building contractors into what they called the "club." If a contractor was not in the club, he couldn't bid on a construction job in New York City. Of all the locks La Cosa Nostra had on unions, there was none more firm, or deadly, than the one it held through Ralph Scopo, a soldier in the Columbo Family and president of the Concrete Workers District Council, LIUNA.

On all concrete-pouring contracts up to $2 million, the Columbo Family extorted 1 percent in kickbacks. Contracts from $2 to $15 million were reserved to a club of contractors selected by the Commission. These contractors were required to kick back 2 percent of the contract price to the families, whose members would split the money.

Thanks to the bugging of Castellano's estate and Ruggiero's loose lips, Giuliani had on tape discussions related not only to the "Concrete Club," but more important to his RICO case, the existence of the Commission. His aim now was twofold. He needed to target Scopo as the definitive link between the unions and the Mafia. As vital to his case, he needed something more than just vague references to the Commission's existence. He needed proof positive of its overseeing role in La Cosa Nostra, proof that would link racketeering with conspiracy. In May 1983, Giuliani saw his golden opportunity with the release of a landmark work on the history of organized crime written by, of all people, Joseph Bonanno, the only living original member of the Commizione del Pace, or the "Commission" as it was called in the United States.

22

STAR WARS

"What can I say about these people? To me, they are strangers."

In his autobiography, *A Man of Honor*, the seventy-eight-year-old Joe Bonanno, then living in Tucson, Arizona, and fifteen years retired, wrote in intricate detail not only about his own extraordinary life, but the formation of the American Mafia. He described his role in establishing the Bonanno Family in Brooklyn, his rise to a position of power among the five families of New York, and the formation and operating procedures of the Commission.

His assault on Mafia overlords, Rudy Giuliani claimed, began one evening when he saw the former godfather being interviewed by Mike Wallace on "60 Minutes." Bonanno was promoting the book, which at the time Giuliani knew nothing about, when the idea occurred to him. "Look at this," he said to his new wife Donna in amazement. "He's describing the Commission. How it started in 1931, how it functioned in the 1960s, how the members were the bosses of the five families from New York, how they coordinated disputes and put out contracts. This is a RICO enterprise!"

Running out to the bookstore the next morning, Giuliani devoured *A Man of Honor*, convinced that he'd discovered the linchpin that could translate FBI recordings, the testimony of informers like Willie Boy Johnson, the targeting of Concrete Workers District Council president Ralph Scopo, and Bonanno's written history, into a racketeering conspiracy indictment.

Soon after, Rudy flew out to Tucson to interview Bonanno, who lay in a bed at St. Mary's Hospital recovering from a heart attack. The goal was to gain a deposition regarding the existence and operation of the Commission, but the meeting turned into something else. Talking to the ailing godfather was one thing, but getting a man as cagey as Bonanno to, in effect, testify against others was an impossible task. Amiable, even talkative, the former boss of bosses had a good time with the forty-year-old prosecutor telling "off-the-record" stories about old pals Frank Costello, Lucky Luciano, Joe Kennedy and his sons John and Bobby, even Al Capone, but nothing about the Commission.

Frustrated by his inability to pin down Bonanno, Giuliani left St. Mary's Hospital angry and with nothing but a copy of *A Man of Honor* in his hand. However that shouldn't have surprised him. Bonanno, a college-educated man and a Mafioso in the Sicilian tradition, was no easy mark and would have died before turning on a fellow member of the Honored Society, even if it was someone he considered a greedy man like Castellano or a raffish one like John Gotti. All Rudy had to have done was read the book for its content, not its value as potential evidence, and he would have understood that, at least in Bonanno's mind, he was up against centuries of tradition, not merely an old, sick man.

Even a man like Elliot who had only a nodding acquaintance with the traditionalist "Mustache Petes," as the younger guys called them, had learned that these old-timers were unshakable. And if he had any doubts about that, they were dispelled in discussions that he had years later on the subject, first with Bill Bonanno, then his aging, but still mentally agile father, Joseph, shortly before his death at his home in Tucson.

"A key component in Mafia relationships is honor," the younger Bonanno told Elliot. "In our world, you defined honor by respect. That has nothing to do with good manners or even deference. It has to do with acknowledging power, yours and someone else's."

"What about Giuliani?" Elliot asked. "When your father agreed to meet with him, was he acknowledging his position, his power?"

"A man of honor is someone willing to acknowledge the power of another, say a legislator, a judge, even a prosecutor, but he isn't willing to accept an insult to his own honor in that relationship. The abuse of the weak by a bully, for example, is an act against honor that a man like Joseph Bonanno would never tolerate or be party to."

Later that same day, Elliot had an opportunity to meet the last living member of the Commission, Joseph Bonanno, a man he'd heard about since his earliest affiliations with La Cosa Nostra. Bonanno spoke in broken English and was dressed in a manner not unlike that of Carlo Gambino, simple and plain. Even his home, a modest, post-World War II split level, was sparsely furnished, and seeing him, sitting on a sofa alone, frail, and ascetic looking, reminded Elliot of the vast differences between these early Mafia kingpins and the newer ones like Paul Castellano, with his estate on Todt Hill, or John Gotti, with his movie-star status and penchant for headlines. Here was a warrior, surely capable of living a life of luxury, who'd shunned the spotlight for all of his Mafia career, choosing instead to live a life as a true Mafioso.

Elliot began by asking Bonanno about a recent movie that had been made about his life. "Did you like it?" he asked.

"Why would you ask me a question like that? The movie is about my life. If I didn't like the movie, what would I be saying about myself?"

"What about your b-book, *A Man of Honor*?" Elliot finally got around to asking. "Why did you write it?"

"It was my declaration that my tradition has died in America. What Americans refer to as the Mafia is a degenerate outgrowth of that lifestyle. Friendships, connections, family ties, trust, and loyalty—this was the glue that held us together. In America, the glue that holds people together is only economic. By that I mean money."

"What do you think of the current leadership, men like Gotti and Gravano from the Gambino Family?"

"What can I say about these people? To me, they are strangers. If they engage in illegal activities, what concern is that of mine? They're all trying to make money. That's all I see. The Mafia is not about money. It is a process, not a thing. Mafia is a form of clan cooperation, and its members pledge lifelong loyalty to it. What makes this process work is that it is based on friendship and honor."

The old man leaned forward then, as if to tell a secret he had kept hidden for a very long time. "Do you know why Americans are so fascinated with the Mafia and movies like *The Godfather*? It's because in it they see people that possess family pride and act with personal honor. The reason Americans are so attracted by this is that they know they are witnessing the erosion of all of those things in their own culture: trust in their government, faith in their religions, belief in a family structure that is falling apart. Americans yearn for *closeness*. They long for family. What they need and want is a father."

If Elliot ever doubted what Rudy Giuliani was up against in trying to get Joseph Bonanno to testify against the rulers of La Cosa Nostra, past or current, he knew after meeting him that day that there was a better chance getting the pope to convert to Orthodox Judaism. Nevertheless, Giuliani would get his revenge.

Months after Giuliani's visit, the ailing godfather was subpoenaed to appear before a grand jury in New York where he would be forced to review passages of his book to have him say yes, there was a Commission. When lawyers argued in court that Bonanno was too sick to travel from Arizona to New York, Giuliani ordered a court-appointed medical staff to Tucson to examine him. When the government's doctors confirmed that Bonanno was, indeed, too weak to travel or undergo the ordeal of testimony, Giuliani was incensed, arguing that if the witness couldn't be delivered to the court, the court would be delivered to the witness. The argument carried, and the conference room at St. Mary's Hospital was converted into a temporary courtroom where Joseph Bonanno was interrogated and videotaped.

As expected, Bonanno, in an oxygen tent suffering from chronic heart problems, held true to his code and refused to discuss anything to do with the Commission, citing Fifth Amendment rights. Giuliani knew that he couldn't indict a man who'd been retired for fifteen years as a conspirator or anything else, so he demanded that the judge cite Bonanno for civil contempt, a charge that would allow the government to jail him for the duration of the trial or until he agreed to testify. So, in an atmosphere that resembled something out of a Kafka novel, the seventy-eight-year-old Bonanno was put on a gurney and taken to an ambulance, rushed to the Tucson airport, flown to Kentucky, and then hustled by medevac to a federal penitentiary in Lexington. There, the mortally ill Joseph Bonanno remained imprisoned for seventeen months until November 1987 when the landmark Commission trial ended and sentences were handed down.

As much as Giuliani's indictments against Big Paulie and

rumblings over Angelo Ruggiero's FBI tapes had exacerbated tensions between the Gotti and Castellano factions of the Gambino Family, Elliot's life within La Cosa Nostra was also being tested. It wasn't until January 1984 that Carmine Lombardozzi contacted him for the second leg of his international travel. This time the destination was Brazil, which Rosengarten had discussed with him. He'd already made the promised "one additional" trip to Tel Aviv.

Contacts had already been made on his behalf either by Al Rosengarten or Dr. Dak, he didn't know which, and all went as planned. He was received by the staff at Prontocor Hospital in Bello Horizonte as a visiting professor and held seminars on two of his favorite subjects, intraoperative cardioplegia and echocardiography, all the while knowing that as he lectured, his room was being entered by a perfect stranger who would place two neatly wrapped parcels deep into the interior of his luggage for him to courier back to family contacts in the United States. Elliot did not know what the parcels contained and did not want to know. The only guarantee he asked for was that they didn't contain illegal drugs such as cocaine or heroin.

Arriving back into the U.S., this time through Newark Airport, Elliot made his way through the preselected customs' line without inspection or hassle of any kind, showing his passport and exiting through the baggage claim area. Outside, waiting for him in his black Lincoln Continental, with engine running, was Carmine. Elliot nodded a curt greeting, then popped open the trunk where he put his luggage, taking from it the two parcels, both tightly bound with string and wrapped in plain brown paper.

Elliot got into the front seat. Carmine extended his hand. "Welcome back, Dottore. How was your trip?"

"Not too bad. I'm here s-safe and sound anyway," he

answered, still petrified with fear from the possibility of getting caught by customs on this, the last of his adventures in smuggling God knew what for these guys.

Elliot shook Carmine's hand then gave him the two parcels, each weighing something like sixteen ounces and about the size of a cigar box. Carmine took them into his right hand, one at a time, gauging their weight, then shaking each one as if to assess their content. Satisfied, he looked into Elliot's eyes, grinned broadly, then placed the two packages between them on the front seat and drove off toward the New Jersey Turnpike.

"You don't look too good, Dottore," Carmine laughed. "Maybe you need a doctor."

"Look, Carmine," he shot back still shaking, "I'm nervous as hell, okay? I'm a damned d-doctor, not a smuggler, can you try to understand that?"

"You worry too much," Carmine said pulling onto the highway.

"I don't even know what's in those boxes. I mean, I swear to God, Carmine, everyone promised it wouldn't be d-drugs, and I just hope to Christ it isn't."

"Well, don't worry, Dottore. It ain't drugs. It's gems. Diamonds and emeralds. About $3 million worth." He turned to Elliot. "Maybe you want a stone for one of your girl-friends?"

"I don't have girlfriends, Carmine!"

Carmine smiled. "I think we both know better, Dottore," he said, eyes twinkling with a secret understanding on the subject of Elliot's sex life that he didn't bother to share. "But that's beside the point because if you have to know, these stones are bought with cash made from drugs, then converted back to cash in Manhattan. I make runs like this twice, maybe three times a month, Colombia, Costa Rica,

Dominican Republic, even Vietnam and Cambodia. What do I pick up? Sometimes it's stones, sometimes it's Treasury bonds, hell, sometimes it's freshly minted American Express certificates. But before you get to feelin' too fucking bad about what we do, maybe you should know that for years, we did most of it with the help of your good old Uncle Sam."

"What are you talking about? The government?"

"You got it," Carmine said with a slow wink. "How do you think the U.S. props up these so-called democracies and tinhorn generals in Central and Latin America? It's no different now than it was in the 1960s with Batista in Cuba, Duvalier in Haiti, or Noriega in Panama. We worked with the CIA side by side, until they realized they didn't need us no more. 'Better to do it in-house,' someone must have figured out. That's why there's all this fucking heat now from Giuliani and these other assholes. Don't you see? We're the goddamned competition!"

Elliot shook his head in amazement. During those days, he was beginning to believe just about anything was possible, even the idea that our own federal government was using money from illegal drugs smuggled into the United States to fund CIA operations and make payoffs to foreign leaders around the world.

"Hey, one other thing," Carmine mentioned, swiveling around to the backseat. "You see that paper there?" he asked pointing toward a copy of that morning's *New York Post*. "Neil told me to give that to you. Said you might be interested."

Elliot retrieved the newspaper. It was turned to page three, with a tiny two-by-two-inch article circled with blue ballpoint ink. MAFIA PUSHER FOUND DEAD IN CAR TRUNK, the headline read.

"Pull over to the side of the road," Elliot blurted.

"What?"

"Pull over to the side of the road *now!*"

Carmine did as he was told, staring as Elliot opened the car door and proceeded to vomit.

The "Mafia pusher" they were writing about was Nicky Micelli. He'd been shot three times through the head execution style in what was suspected to be a "drug deal gone bad." Though he couldn't be certain, parked there on the side of the New Jersey Turnpike that night, Elliot was pretty sure that he knew better.

23

HURRICANES, TORNADOES, AND PESTILENCE

"My friends, the ones you met here at the house and in Manhattan: I'm going to tell you something I probably shouldn't, but even I could get hurt by what's going on with all of this."

There are bad things that run their course or go away in life. Hurricanes, tornadoes, some pestilence are like that, but one of the things that does not go away for members and associates of the Mafia are federal law enforcement agencies, or FLEAS as they are known in the world of La Cosa Nostra. In New York, the Commission investigation had been split into two divisions. One collected interviews from cooperating witnesses, some of whom, like Ralph Scopo, held positions within the families. The second involved evidence gained through electronic surveillance including videotapes and thousands of hours of audio recordings gained through wire-taps and bugs placed in the cars, homes, and offices of mob bosses, most prominently, Paul Castellano.

On both levels, Elliot speculated; federal investigators had pieced together a puzzle, despite the non-cooperation of Joseph Bonanno, that clearly demonstrated the existence of a leadership body called the Commission that ran the New York construction industry. One boss remarked, in context and with remarkable audio integrity, "not a yard of concrete is poured in New York" without the Commission's say-so. Worse for Castellano, not only did the law enforcement agencies have references from multiple sources, such as Ruggiero, about payoffs made through Scopo, but through bugs placed within his Todt Hill estate, agents had learned he'd become partners in S&A Concrete with "Fat Tony" Salerno of the Genovese Family, who saw to it that their company got a greater cut of the jobs!

By September 1984, Giuliani, armed with thirty volumes of evidence, believed he had nearly enough to put forward an indictment, but waited to see what additional secrets the bugs in Castellano's home might yield about the inner workings of the five families. In particular, Rudy was interested in John Gotti, the Bergin crew capo so closely aligned with Gambino Family underboss Aniello "Neil" Dellacroce, who'd recently been diagnosed with cancer of the brain. Through it all, possibly through ignorance, but more likely through arrogance, Gotti remained unconcerned about Giuliani, the fallout from President Reagan's commission on crime, and even RICO. He carried on as if he was still an ordinary soldier hijacking trucks from JFK Airport, despite the fact that within the family, he'd become much more than that.

Even Elliot, from his peripheral vantage point, could see that Gotti's flamboyance could be a huge problem for "Mustache Petes" like Vincent "the Chin" Gigante, who'd already tried to assassinate him after the Bergin's drug connection had been brought to light, and Castellano, who viewed him as unwelcome competition to his throne. Never was the forty-four-year-old capo's poor judgment in better evidence than in September 1984 when Gotti became embroiled in a street fight with Romual Piecyk, a gruff walk-in refrigerator repairman, who soon after must have wondered if he, himself, wouldn't be found hanging dead like one of the animal carcasses his refrigerators were meant to house.

The date was September 11 when Piecyk, a burly six-feet, two-inch strongman, was driving his truck through Maspeth, Queens, and came upon an empty double-parked car belonging to John Gotti and an associate, Frank Colletta, blocking the street. Gotti, there to visit two gambling dens under his control, was shocked to hear the blaring horn of Piecyk's truck.

Who did this guy think he was dealing with? Colletta flew from the Cozy Corner bar, reached through the open drivers' window, and proceeded to bash Piecyk in the face. Piecyk then got out of the truck, and a scuffle began that Gotti joined, smacking Piecyk, kicking him, then taking $325 from his pocket, assumedly a fee for the aggravation he'd caused him. Finally, once Piecyk had had enough, Gotti reached into the waistband of his pants as if ready to draw a gun and growled, "You better get the fuck out of here if you know what's good for you."

No question that after that incident, in their respective graves, Carlo Gambino must have muttered *"Cazu!"* and Al Capone must have sat up and said *"Bravisimo!"* such was the difference in temperament between the Sicilian and the Neapolitan branches of the Mafia. Assuming that Piecyk knew who Gotti was, and understanding that anyone who'd dare to press charges would know they were signing their own death warrant, Gotti and eight other family members including Colletta nonchalantly moved down the street to drink espresso at a local café.

In the meantime, the doltish Piecyk, who understood none of these things, called the police. A car from the 106th Precinct arrived almost immediately, manned by a rookie officer named Ray Doyle. Moments later, when they confronted Gotti and his associates about who had committed the assault, in a show of unity, all ten stood up. Piecyk was insistent, and Doyle handcuffed Gotti and Colletta.

"Do you know who I am?" Gotti asked Piecyk. Then turning to the cop, he said, "Look, why don't you reach into my front pocket. You'll find $3,000 in cash there. Why would I rob a miserable son of a bitch like this guy of $300 when I got $3,000 on me of my own?"

The logic was unconvincing to Doyle, who booked them once Piecyk pressed charges, never imagining that he had just arrested the heir apparent to Carlo Gambino's dynasty. Within weeks, however, Piecyk was hearing and reading about the notorious John Gotti. Now realizing the predicament he'd set himself up for, Piecyk became paranoid, buying a gun and moving his pregnant wife out of their home. He cut off all communication with the Queens district attorney. After having sworn to the crime and identifying Gotti under oath, it just wasn't that simple. The D.A.'s office understood that since Gotti had served two sentences for hijacking and another for the McBratney murder, these two additional felony arrests for assault and robbery could put him behind bars for years.

Enormous pressure was applied by the district attorney's office, but Piecyk refused to testify claiming he'd received telephone threats on his life and that the brakes on his truck had been intentionally severed by Gotti's people. When Sgt. Anthony Falco of the Queens prosecutors' office reminded his star witness that he had no choice but to testify or be imprisoned for contempt, Piecyk made a remarkable turnabout. "I'm not going to testify against Mr. Gotti," he told him. "I'm going as a witness against the government's case on his behalf." This move wouldn't work, either, Falco counseled Piecyk, because in either the first or the second testimony, both given under oath, he would have perjured himself, a crime that would also earn him multiple years in prison.

When Gotti's case did come to trial, a contrast in styles could never have been so evident. Piecyk, who failed to appear at the Queens' courthouse having admitted himself to a local hospital for elective shoulder surgery, was arrested and brought before the jury as a material witness. Having spent the previous night in Falco's office crying his eyes out, Piecyk showed up with arm in a sling, wearing dark sunglasses, and chewing his fingernails. Gotti, on the other hand, with former championship wrestler and one-time Brooklyn District Attorneys' Office superstar Bruce Cutler at his side, sat behind the defense table as nonchalant and voluble as a man watching "Monday Night Football" on TV in his living room.

Tensions were high. Already the subject of media interest, John Gotti was photogenic, even handsome, some would say, but more, tanned and dressed better than most Fortune 500 CEOs, Teflon Don was as charismatic as any movie star. From the first clapping of the gavel, the packed courtroom was abuzz with speculation about what would happen in this the first of many facedowns to come between John "Johnny Boy" Gotti and the federal government of the United States.

"Mr. Piecyk, on September 11, 1984, you were punched and kicked and then robbed in Maspeth, Queens. I ask you to look around the courtroom," said Asst. District Attorney Kirke Bartley, gesturing around him. "Do you see the men who did this to you here today?"

"I don't see them," Piecyk answered looking down at his lap.

"You don't see them here now?"

Piecyk cast a cursory glance around the room, his eyes falling if only for an instant on Gotti, whose lips were curled upward in a small, contemptuous smile that would become his media trademark. "I do not."

Bartley stared at his star witness, stunned. Could Piecyk actually be risking his freedom by perjuring himself in front of judge, jury, and more media than a Queens courtroom had ever seen? Bartley began making very specific inquiries relating to the assault itself in the hopes of untying Piecyk's extremely knotted tongue: questions about the location, the blows that he endured, and what type of clothes his assailants may have been wearing.

"To be perfectly honest, I don't remember anything about the assault at all.... I remember that I was slapped, but I don't know by who.... I have no recollection of who may have slapped me, what they looked like, or even how they were dressed," Piecyk finally blurted back to the exasperated prosecutor.

When the not guilty verdict was announced, Gotti stood up, hugged Bruce Cutler, received hearty handshakes from the dozens of associates, paparazzi, and well-wishers in attendance, then left the courtroom for a massive celebration in Ozone Park. The headline of the *New York Post* probably said it as well as anyone could with the three-inch high, front-page headline, I FORGOTTI!

Over the next three months, John Gotti, stung by Ruggiero's heroin charges as well as Castellano's indictments, would worry about listening devices planted at his Bergin headquarters, the possibility of an FBI rat in the family, and fatal retribution from Castellano over Angelo's stubborn refusal to turn over government surveillance tapes to him. Yet, no matter how low-key Gotti tried to be, at heart he remained the same John Gotti who admired the taciturn Neil Dellacroce, but remained thoroughly enamored of the high-riding, gangster-brute, Al Capone, born in another age and predominant in another time.

On December 9, 1984, when his daughter, Vicki, married Carmine Agnello, twenty-four, proprietor of Gambino-operated Jamaica Auto Salvage, it was not just a wedding. It was a gala bash with more than 1,000 guests in attendance, many of them the nation's most notorious mobsters, with entertainment provided by Jay Black and the Americans, singer Connie Francis, comedians George Kirby, Pat Cooper, and "Professor" Irwin Corey.

Never to be left out when it came to business or social events with so many choice Mafia targets prominent, FBI surveillance teams observed every transaction from vans parked near the entrances and exits of the Marina Del Ray reception hall in the Bronx that night. Elliot's buddy, Frank Silvio, who had a way of being anywhere that seemed like it might be fun, later surmised that within the Gambino's inner circle, this was the moment that high school dropout and former JFK Airport hijacker John Gotti truly arrived as leader of the family. With Castellano under a raft of weighty indictments and just about to get slammed again, there were at least thirty tables occupied only by men, Silvio told Elliot, each of whom took turns paying their personal respects to the father of the bride.

It was almost three months later, on the night of February 26, 1985, that Elliot had the shock of his life while watching local New York reporter John Miller broadcasting the news on NBC. Complete with footage of Paul Castellano being hauled from his Todt Hill estate in handcuffs by a cadre of FBI, while Miller did a voice-over, Elliot saw the first beam in the building that was his life and career come crashing down.

"A Federal racketeering indictment charged nine men yesterday with participating in a commission that governs the five organized crime families in New York City. The fifteen-count indictment said the commission regulated a wide range of illegal activities that included narcotics trafficking, loansharking, gambling, labor racketeering, and extortion against construction companies . . ."

"Hanna! Hanna, come here now! You've got to see this!"

Elliot called out, pressing up the volume on the remote as she rushed in from the kitchen.

"What? What is it?"

"Rudolph Giuliani, the United States attorney in Manhattan, conducted a news conference in the federal office building earlier today," the reporter continued as the picture shifted to background footage of Giuliani standing before a flip chart that diagrammed the Commission's structure. "This case, undertaken by the federal government under newly expanded RICO statutes, charges more Mafia bosses in one indictment than ever before. Paul Castellano, boss of the Gambino Family; Anthony Salerno, boss of the Genovese Family; Gennaro Langella, boss of the Columbo Family; Anthony Corallo, boss of the Lucchese Family; and Philip Rastelli, boss of the Bonanno Family . . ."

Hanna started to say something, but Elliot interrupted.

"Quiet! For a minute! Just listen!"

"Besides racketeering and conspiracy, the indictment specifically cited extortion and bribery charges involving concrete pouring," Miller continued, "charging that the commission established a club of certain construction contractors who poured concrete, controlling the allocation of construction jobs, designating which contractors could make successful bids for contracts, and obtaining payoffs from those concrete contractors . . ."

"Oh, my G-God!" Elliot moaned hitting the channel up button seeing Mary Martin of CBS reporting the story, then ABC's Pablo Guzman, finally stopping at the airing of yet another "live" press conference held by Giuliani outside the federal office building earlier that day.

"Today we exposed the structure of organized crime on a scale never done before," Rudy crowed to a gaggle of journalists including *Daily News* gangland reporter, Gene

Mustain, *New York City Newsday*'s Murray Kempton, and CBS Radio's Eileen Cornell. "This indictment proves beyond a doubt that the Commission was formed in 1931 by Salvatore Maranzano to regulate family relationships and that its current membership used murder as a regulatory tool—the contemporary group had also formed a club of contractors and used extortion to gain control of all concrete jobs in New York City over $2 million."

"Honey, what is it? What's happening, Elliot?" Hanna asked, startled at his horror, as she sat down, putting her arm around his shoulder. "Why are you so upset?"

"Mr. Castellano has been arrested—and Mr. Salerno and Corallo," he lamented, barely able to say their names.

"You know these men? They're friends of yours?"

"Yes, I know them, as patients, but this is unbelievable! Those men are the ones you met here at the house that time and in Manhattan. Silvio, Sal, even Mr. Gotti ... it seems too amazing to believe, but I'm going to tell you something that I probably shouldn't, Hanna, but me, even I could get h-hurt by what's going on with all of this . . ."

"Elliot," she said, the color draining from her face, "I'm frightened. I'm frightened for you and for our family. I want to call my father. I want to tell him everything that's gone on so that he can talk to Dr. Dak and Mr. Rosengarten. Elliot, these friendships, these associations, they could affect your career."

"Don't!" he said, taking hold of her wrist. "Don't talk to anyone now, Hanna. We've got to *think*, to *wait*, until we know for sure what's happening!" His mind raced through these associations like a Rolodex gone wild, each name he scanned involved with the family at least as deeply as himself.

"No," Hanna finally snapped, tearing her arm away from him. "I've listened to you long enough. I don't trust you anymore, Elliot. I don't know who you are anymore, and sometimes wonder if I ever really did. I'm going to call my father. He knows people at the hospital who can make certain no one misunderstands and thinks you're in some way *involved* in any of this."

It was at that moment, as his loving wife of nearly ten years stared at him frightened, with thoughts of his best friend, Nicky Micelli's murder and funeral, visions of himself and the quiet destruction of medical records, all-night sex and gambling sprees, his role as international courier, and his tenement-home upbringing in the Bronx, that Elliot suddenly realized the depth of his vulnerability as a doctor, husband, and human being. The thought of those things, at that particular moment, chilled him to his core. Whether he saw it that way or not, federal prosecutors hearing about Elliot Litner would contend that he was in the Mafia, as complicit as any associate or soldier. The thought of that, and all that went with it, terrified him.

24

THE CONCRETE CLUB

"So, I guess you two Boy Scouts disapprove of me and what I do. That's what it's all about, ain't it? The federal government wakes up one day and decides it don't like the way certain guineas earn their daily bread."

On the night of February 25, 1984, when two FBI agents named Kurins and O'Brien showed up at Big Paulie's estate on Staten Island, the hulking grandfather was speechless and hadn't the slightest idea what the RICO conspiracy charges against him meant. Silently, wearing a bathrobe and slippers, he led them through his home to the kitchen, where his doctor sat with Gloria Olarte as she was preparing a roast beef dinner.

"Do you mind if I change into a suit?" Castellano asked the agents, glancing out of the estate's enormous bay windows where media people were already gathering with video cameras and television crews were setting up for live coverage of the arrest.

"No problem," Kurins responded.

Moments later, as the agents waited in the foyer, Nina Castellano, the godfather's wife of fifty-two years, entered the house along with daughter Connie and her husband, who was holding their one-year-old baby. When Castellano heard the commotion, he reappeared dressed resplendently in a double-breasted blue suit with a striking red tie and Italian black leather, slip-on shoes. He greeted his family, kissed his granddaughter, and watched stoically as his wife, mistress, and daughter cried.

"I think we should go now, Mr. Castellano," suggested O'Brien.

Castellano nodded. The FBI agents handcuffed him as his family looked on, then escorted him out the front door to the flash of cameras and the badgering questions of dozens of newspaper and television reporters who sought to shove microphones in their direction. Though it was already dark, it appeared like daytime at Todt Hill such was the degree of illumination given off by television camera crews trying to capture this moment for the late evening news and posterity.

"Who was it got me?" Castellano asked the two agents as they led him to a team of others waiting to transport him. "Giuliani? Was it Giuliani got me?"

"Yeah, it was Rudy who got the indictment," Kurins answered.

"Well, if you got to get fucked, at least let it be by another paisan, huh?"

The two agents said nothing as Paul Castellano entered the car, one agent on each side of him. "So, I guess you two Boy Scouts disapprove of me and what I do. That's what this is all about, ain't it? The federal government wakes up one day and decides it don't like the way certain guineas earn their daily bread. Okay, fair enough. But don't you two guys ever think that I'm wrong and you're right because it just ain't that fucking simple, and that's the part that burns my ass. Come on. We're not fucking children, are we? Your laws are, how can I say it, a convenience. A convenience when you guys need to fuck a guy like me. A convenience for your bosses when they decide to make some money for themselves and just look the other way."

Castellano, flanked by attorney James LaRossa and "Fat Tony" Salerno's attorney, Roy Cohn, sat through a two-and-one-half-hour hearing after which underbosses arrested that night were released on $1-million bail and bosses on $2 million each. For Castellano, that made a total of $4 million in bail posted to preserve his freedom, a number that caused pause among other family members including John Gotti and rapidly rising Bergin crew member, hit man Sammy Gravano.

Big Paulie's support among the family, especially Dellacroce's faction, never strong, was now further eroding with suspicions that facing lifetime imprisonment and perhaps the death penalty for multiple murders committed by the DeMeo crew, he might make a deal with federal prosecutors and turn state's evidence. As critical, from Gotti's side, was the fact that a mortally wounded godfather might be even more dangerous to him than a stable one in that Ruggiero never had turned over the tapes Castellano had demanded after numerous threats. Further, fully understanding the consequences of narcotics trafficking and the longstanding history of its ban by the Commission, Big Paulie could have Angelo, Gene, the Teflon Don, and even Neil Dellacroce whacked with a simple phone call. "Look at what he did to DeMeo, that cocksucker," one can imagine Gotti arguing to future underboss Sammy Gravano. "He orders Roy to push a button on his slime-bucket son-in-law, then has him iced three fucking months later. Believe me, paisan, it's fucking Machiavelli with this fucking *cazu* every fucking step of the way!"

Soon afterward, motivated on multiple levels, John Gotti began hatching a plot. According to Litner and Gambino Family members who would talk about it years after the event, Castellano had severely underestimated Gotti's savvy and ruthlessness as a blue-collar, street guy and strategist. In a meeting Paul called after his release on bond for his two pending federal cases, Gotti was summoned to Todt Hill where the godfather sought to placate him with an "if I go to prison" scenario that went something like this.

First, Castellano would still run the family from prison. Second, understanding that Neil Dellacroce was dying from cancer, a triumvirate would be formed composed of Carlo Gambino's son, Tommy, Castellano's longtime associate, Tommy Bilotti and, finally himself, John Gotti, who would take over the faction of the family formerly controlled by Dellacroce. When Dellacroce died, Bilotti would be named underboss.

This seemed a remarkable turnaround for Gotti, who played the role of flattered underling. So remarkable, in fact, that he didn't buy it. Gotti knew there existed no example in the world of La Cosa Nostra where three men ever wielded equal shares of power for very long. Always, one was the genuine boss just waiting for the appropriate moment to assassinate his counterparts and take control of the family. Gotti concocted his plan with the knowledge that Castellano loyalists like Frank DeCiccio and Jimmy Failla were having their doubts about Paul, and even members of the Commission had quietly put out feelers among their troops about their growing dissatisfaction.

Out of respect for Dellacroce, Gotti would not kill his godfather until his mentor was finally taken from this world by cancer. Prior to that time, however, Gotti would lure DeCiccio and Failla to his side and put together a hit team made up of his best and most trusted soldiers called the Fist of Five because their secret needed to be held that tightly— Sammy Gravano, John Carneglia, Eddie Lino, Salvatore Scala, Vinnie Artuso—along with backup gunmen Anthony "Tony Roach" Rampino, Iggy Alogna, Joe Watts, and Angelo

Ruggiero all would be recruited for an assassination plot so daring that mob historians would have to reach back to the days of Al Capone and the St. Valentine's Day Massacre to find its equal.

The following year, 1985, was probably the most devastating twelve months in the history of La Cosa Nostra and easily the most gut-wrenching of Elliot Litner's life. In Cleveland, Chicago, Milwaukee, and Kansas City, family bosses were convicted and given lengthy sentences for conspiring to skim vast sums of cash from the Las Vegas casinos that they controlled through the use of teamster pension funds. In Boston, the hierarchy of the Patriarca Family was found guilty of multiple RICO counts ranging from loansharking to murder. In Philadelphia, family boss Nicky Scarfo, target of an all-out federal RICO assault, was sentenced to life in prison.

But it was New York's Mafia leaders who watched in white-knuckled dread because it was there that two federal cases threatened to tear apart the entire structure of organized crime. Both revolved around Ralph Scopo.

It began in October 1984 when after a three-year FBI investigation called "Star Quest," Rudy Giuliani announced a fifty-one-count federal indictment against eleven members of the Columbo Family including its boss, Carmine Persico. In what amounted to a dry run of the Commission case, the Columbos were charged with "a pattern of racketeering that included extortion, theft, loansharking, gambling, bribery and drug trafficking." But the allegation that worried the hierarchy of the families was not any of these single charges. Rather, it was the indictment's primary focus that involved "influencing New York City's construction industry by controlling several unions identified in the indictment."

The reason for this concern was not apparent until after the Commission indictments were released in February 1985 and testimony was underway in the Columbo trial. More than the random acts of greedy union officials looking for kickbacks, Asst. U.S. Attorney Aaron Marcu seemed intent on making Giuliani's larger point in the secretly recorded taped conversations and scores of witnesses and hundreds of surveillance photos he was presenting as evidence. That point being that there existed a Mafia "board of directors" that had ruled the underworld for more than a half century and continued to do so.

If that premise were granted by the jury in the Columbo case, the same information linking payoffs from construction companies through Scopo to the five families that ran the Commission was all Giuliani needed to prove the existence of "racketeering influence" through a "corrupt organization," a RICO win large enough to put away the hierarchy of the New York Mafia for the rest of their lives.

Ralph Scopo couldn't have been enjoying any of the proceedings starting from day one when the indictment was presented to the jury. A grossly overweight chain smoker with a wife and two grown sons, who were also involved with the union, he suffered from angina, hypertension, and as it was later discovered, coronary heart disease. Initially, he may have seen a way out as Marcu read from the indictment charging that from 1981 up to October 1984, he had wrongfully "obstructed, delayed and affected commerce" by extortion while conspiring to obtain the property of the construction companies identified through "actual and threatened use of force, violence and fear."

Up to that point, it might not have seemed too bad to Scopo. The prosecution had a couple of witnesses, who were shaken down, and maybe some tape recordings of telephone conversations that could be incriminating. Scopo's guys had beaten worse in court.

But that was only page 115 of the 230-page indictment. There was more to come, and it was the charges that followed, specifically those made on page 119, that gave Scopo and wizened mob counsel Barry Slotnick something to think about.

During that same period, the U.S. attorney continued, the ruling body of La Cosa Nostra, called the Commission, "organized and controlled" a scheme to extort various New York contractors who poured concrete. The Commission established a club that would designate which contractor would be permitted to make the successful bid on a particular contract. The Commission "controlled the decisions of the Union and agreed to the payment of bribes to coconspirator Ralph Scopo." The Commission enforced the rules of the club by "causing the contractors' supplies of cement to be stopped, as well as other forms of economic punishment, acts of violence, physical harm and murder."

"This is not good," even a tough guy like Scopo must have been concluding at about that time, *"but it's a long fucking way from making accusations about conspiracies and actually proving it. After all, what good were tapes and a pack of pissed-off contractors without a living witness to link it together? And that wasn't gonna happen, so Marcu might as well try to make the jury believe in UFOs 'cause no-fucking-body'd be stupid enough to try to rat out the Commission!"*

The Commission "controlled the allocation of concrete pouring contracts by exercising control over the decisions of the Cement and Concrete Workers' Union and specifically the actions of coconspirator Ralph Scopo," Marcu elaborated. By exploiting its control, coconspirators Anthony Salerno, Antonio Corallo, Christopher Furnari, and Salvatore Santoro and defendants Gennaro Langella and Carmine Persico and "members of the Commission and bosses, and underbosses of La Cosa Nostra families were able to induce concrete-construction companies to join this club and to extort payments from these contractors" in the amount of 2 percent of the contract price of "any concrete-pouring construction job in the New York City area in excess of $2 million" including the $15 million Rivergate Project, Dow Jones & Company headquarters, Manhattan Federal Building, and $30.4 million Jacob Javits Convention Center."

"Holy shit!" Scopo, along with Slotnick, must have realized almost immediately upon hearing the words. *"This isn't just about me or even the Columbo Family. This is about the Commission. This is about the entire, motherfucking organization."* Even Ralph Scopo must have finally understood that *"the link is not some low-level stoolie or empty suit wannabe. The fucking guy who links these two cases together is me!"*

The days following the beginning of testimony in the trial of the Columbos and the announcement of the Commission indictments were no less painful for Scopo. Named as a principal in both cases, his hours in Manhattan's federal courthouse were spent surrounded by attorneys, in the company of his boss, Carmine Perisco, and nine other members of the Columbo hierarchy, listening to witness after witness, tape after tape of contractors describing the manner in which they had been shaken down by the district council president.

In one tape of a meeting between Robert Sisto, a contractor, and Scopo at the Bow Wow restaurant in Howard Beach, Queens, on May 17, 1984, played for the jury, Sisto tells Scopo that he's going to "give him two [now]" and would pay him "four next week." In a second FBI taped conversation of a meeting between Scopo and Carlo D'Arpino, of Cedric Construction, the district council president is heard asking D'Arpino, "How much you got here?" "Fifteen," D'Arpino replies. "Well you still owe me eighty-five," Scopo answers. In yet another discussion between Scopo and Mineo D'Ambrosi, of All-Boro Paving, taped on March 19, 1984, Scopo tells D'Ambrosi "you can't bid on projects over $2 million ... those are awarded to members of the club, who pay two points, not one." When D'Ambrosi complains asking, "Who do I got to go see?" Scopo replies, "You got to see every family. And they're going to tell you 'no.' So don't even bother."

All of this by itself would seem ambiguous and hardly solid evidence in light of the fact that most witnesses were themselves involved in one scam or another and had gotten immunity in return for their testimony. Nevertheless, these were living witnesses who, if they could not testify credibly about the operation of the Commission, could at least support the context and veracity of the tapes in a court of law. More, through their testimony and the subpoenaed financial records of the companies they ran, a detailed accounting of payoffs was created that, representing only a fraction of the Commission's total take, accumulated well into the millions for the years 1981 through 1984: XLO Concrete Corporation, $619,000; S&A Structures, $240,000; G&G Concrete, $117,000; Technical Concrete, $235,000; Century Maxim, $377,000, to name only a few of the dozens the indictment listed.

It was soon after, on November 13, 1985, that an incredible turn of events occurred affecting Elliot irreparably. While listening to prosecution tapes of himself secretly recorded by the FBI in the midst of the Columbo racketeering trial, Ralph Scopo began a response, stared strangely out into the courtroom toward his wife and two sons, then clutched his chest in agony. Struggling for breath, the 300-pound, fifty-six-year-old Mafia capo stood up, grasped the oak railing behind him, then collapsed.

Moments later, Scopo was put on a gurney and rushed to the Beekman Downtown Hospital where he was treated for severe chest pains resulting from angina and hypertension, his condition listed as "serious but not critical."

By year's end, the prognosis for Elliot Litner, M.D., would not be nearly so good.

25

THE HIT ON SCOPO

"Heart disease," he added with a sense of irony that only Elliot could appreciate, "thousands of people die from it every year."

Federal prosecutors held more than one ace up their sleeve for the upcoming Commission trial: two informers within the Gambino Family, Willie Boy Johnson and John Gotti confidant Billy Battista; the tapes recorded in Tony "Ducks" Corallo's Jaguar, along with Angelo Ruggiero's ramblings about drugs and the Commission. Most stunning of all, however, were the secretly recorded dialogues of the boss of bosses himself, Paul Castellano. The prosecution would not waste these legal haymakers on preliminaries like the Columbo trial. They would be held back for the main event, their epic battle to put behind bars the entire leadership of the New York Mafia. Jury selection for Giuliani's Mafia coup de grâce began in September 1985. But even as that was happening, seismic underworld rumblings involving the ongoing Columbo Family racketeering trial and the Gambino car-theft ring trial were setting the stage for the tsunami to follow.

No question Paul Castellano was in ever deepening trouble as chief prosecutor Walter S. Mack's case against ten Gambino Family members and their godfather unwound at federal district court in Manhattan. On December 3, 1985, thirty-seven-year-old Vietnam war veteran and family-associate-turned-government-witness Dominick Montiglio testified to being a "collector" for Castellano's loansharking and extortion activities and a "go-between" in "big narcotics transactions." He went on to tell a hushed jury about rigging hand grenades to automobile ignitions to "blow to pieces" Castellano's enemies and about the murder of nineteen-year-old Cherie Golden, girlfriend of a suspected informer, by DeMeo crew members Joey Testa and Anthony Senter. According to Montiglio, the two hit men flanked the petrified girl in a car, and while Testa drew her attention toward him by talking to her, Senter "blew her brains out" from the opposite side.

If Castellano was concerned about what was going on in his car-theft case, other Commission members like Tony "Ducks" Corallo, Rusty Rastelli, "Gerry Lang" Langella, and "Fat Tony" Salerno must have found the direction of Carmine Persico's Concrete Club trial even more alarming. The reason was simple. More than tapes, which were subject to interpretation; worse than informers, whose own sordid backgrounds could be called into question by clever attorneys like Roy Cohn, government prosecutors had Columbo capo Ralph Scopo, the only direct link between contractors, unions, and the Commission, by the balls.

Day after day, members of the Columbo trial jury were treated to a litany of incontrovertible evidence against Scopo. Too bad if it sealed Persico's fate, but now the Commission indictment had been handed down, and the government's RICO strategy was visible for anyone to see. Scopo's guilt would be used by Giuliani and his prosecutors like a scabbard to gut the Columbo Family hierarchy while establishing the Commission's existence at the same time. Afterward, with the premise of their RICO case in place, the feds would use that

same weapon to convict each one of the defendants for criminal conspiracy, with potential sentences ranging in the hundreds of years. In the minds of these men, starting with
Castellano and Persico, something had to be done about the
"Scopo problem." In other words, he had to be hit.

Of course, all of this was unknown to Elliot at that time,
though a man didn't have to be Albert Einstein to figure out
that somebody, somewhere, would put out a contract on a
witness so important to Giuliani as Scopo. Nearly every
morning and night, Frank Silvio and Elliot would discuss the
latest word on what had evolved into three ongoing government proceedings against "our friends." Some news came
from Silvio's contacts within the family, but most came from
newspapers like the *New York Times*, *Daily News*, and *New York
Post*, all of which relished recounting dramatic details from
the day's court testimony.

On November 21, Barry Slotnick, argued that his client,
who'd been hospitalized on November 13 from hypertension
and angina, couldn't withstand the strain of further questioning during the Persico trial and that his case should be severed. Judge John F. Keenan, who reviewed opinions by doctors for both sides, concluded publicly that there was "no
greater danger to Scopo's life now than at the beginning of
the trial." But according to Silvio, Keenan privately ordered
the government to provide a paramedic along with a wheelchair and oxygen tanks at all future sessions. This, a signal that
while the prosecution maintained Scopo was faking his dizzy
spells, chest pains, and shortness of breath, there was medical
credence to his heart condition that even Judge Keenan was
forced to acknowledge. Elliot didn't press him on the subject,
but Silvio claimed to have seen Scopo's medical records at
Beekman Hospital where he'd been treated earlier and concluded that he suffered from coronary artery disease caused

by atherosclerosis, an accumulation of fatty deposits on the inner lining of the walls of arteries that could indeed be life threatening.

Given the prepping that Silvio had revealed and the fact that constant battering by government prosecutors could only aggravate Scopo's condition, Elliot wasn't totally surprised to receive an invitation to dinner from Al Rosengarten on the afternoon of December 4, just three hours after Judge Keenan decided to sever Scopo's case from the other defendants based on poor health. They met that night at the Plaza Hotel, another of Rosengarten's favorite Manhattan hangouts. He was waiting at the bar sipping a vodka martini when Elliot arrived, and as in the past, they were ushered to his favorite table the minute Elliot got there.

Rosengarten had grown up in Manhattan's Hell's Kitchen, but was now one of the wealthiest men in the city because of his early alliance with Carlo Gambino, and just seeing him would lead a person to assume he was rich—it showed in the way he carried himself, from polished nails to his carefully coiffed, thinning black hair. But while he posed as a businessman-philanthropist, to Elliot, he had the look of a gangster from the old Arnold Rothstein school of crime.

Rosengarten's dress, while meticulous, was overdone, from his custom-made white shirt to the monogrammed cuff links and red handkerchief peeking out from the pocket of his hand-tailored Italian suit. With Al, even polite conversations took on the air of something illicit, his body leaning forward and his right arm hooking around a man's back as he rumbled observations or instructions, staring into his companion's eyes like an ardent lover. Rosengarten's face, tanned from his most recent jaunt to Eleuthera, had a worn look to it, the skin around his eyes noticeably darker than the rest of his face while the eyes, glinting and beguiling, possessed no warmth whatsoever and were capable of transforming midsentence into a withering storm of cold-blooded calculation.

In fact, if there was a single word that came to Elliot's mind, seeing the clever, old businessman-mobster that day, it was "reptile" as Rosengarten finished off his martini with a kind of thirst Elliot never thought him capable of—a sign of the times, he guessed. The small talk was nearly nonexistent as the waiter brought Elliot his Diet Coke and Rosengarten swapped an empty glass of Absolut for a full one.

"Times are not easy," Rosengarten observed. "Our friend in Staten Island has his hands full, and unless things start to straighten up, most people think he won't make it. Maybe you've been following what's going on?"

"Not much. Just the papers like everybody else."

"Well, Elliot, everybody always said you were a stand-up guy. Hell, from the very beginning back in, what was it, the Bronx? It was no different for me. My father was a German Jew and a tailor, can you imagine? When Carlo first laid eyes on me, I was a kid with ambition, smarts, and a set of brass balls. What did I know about life? Nothing. But I knew about suits and dresses, and that was all it took for Mr. Gambino to cut me a break. I'll never forget him for that, God rest his soul. No different for you, I'd venture, and that was the goddamned charm of our world. It was entrepreneurial! No one asked where you came from. If you had the brains and the *cojones*, you were given the opportunity to become an earner. That was the freedom we enjoyed before this bloodsucker Giuliani put his fangs into our lives!"

"Look, Mr. Rosengarten, if you don't mind, maybe we should order something because I've got to get back to the hospital later tonight."

"Right you are, young man!" he said reaching across the table, resting his hand on Elliot's. "These are the virtues that

Simon and I always admired about you. You cut to the chase, Elliot, and that's what I'm going to do tonight. No bullshit!" Rosengarten leaned forward across the table and dropped his voice to a whisper. "So let me tell you now that tomorrow morning a patient is going to be admitted into Mount Sinai for cardiac cauterization. His name is Ralph Scopo. Now, after the testing, he most probably will need to have bypass surgery, which you will also perform." He looked straight into Elliot's eyes. "You know who Ralph Scopo is?"

"I've r-read about him in the *Times*."

"He's the government's key witness in that lynching of Carmine Persico that's passing for justice down at federal district court. And, while he's got nothing to do with Mr. Castellano's current proceedings, he'll also be acting as Giuliani's star witness in this Commission circus they're trying to dredge up. It's a case that's got some important men extremely concerned."

"Yes, I know about that, too."

"Good," Rosengarten concluded, sitting back in his chair, "because if you understand those facts and what it means to these friends of ours, you'll understand why it's got me wondering about the risks involved in a bypass surgery like the one Scopo is about to have. I mean exactly what kind of survival rate is there for a man of Ralph Scopo's age, with his being so overweight and such a heavy smoker?"

Suddenly Elliot could feel the heat of Rosengarten's eyes as they honed in on him. "Well, of course, you're right in saying that age, excessive weight, and the fact that he's a heavy smoker are all negative f-factors, but Mr. Rosengarten, umm, Al, the mortality rate even among patients over sixty-five is low, maybe 1 percent to 3 percent on the outside."

"Exactly! One percent, 3 percent, who's counting? Point is, there's risk entailed in any of these procedures. It's a fact that can't be denied by you, me, even Mr. Castellano. Each of us understands that life doesn't give a pass to every sick man that lies down on the operating table, even when he's in front of a surgeon as skillful as you.

There was a pause and then Rosengarten continued, "After all, you've been a friend since you were a small kid back there in the Bronx when Sal Micelli took you under his wing and helped pay for your education. Favors like that? These are the bridges that lead us from one life and into another, don't you agree?"

"Sure, y-yes," Elliot stammered, understanding more than he wanted to about the intended fate of Ralph Scopo. "I would never want to disappoint you, Mr. Castellano, or Sal Micelli."

"Of course, we know that. Hell, even Dr. Dak brags about your loyalty to him and to the hospital," Al confirmed, patting the back of Elliot's hand again as he motioned for a waiter. "Bobby, why don't you bring Dr. Litner and me two of your best New York strip steaks. One 'rare' like it's still breathing. The other 'well done.' You know about these doctors with red meat. If it don't taste like shoe leather, it's got to be fucking bad for you. Heart disease," Rosengarten added with a sense of irony that only Elliot could appreciate. "Thousands of people die from it every year."

"Yes, th-that's true, Mr. Rosengarten."

"Fine. You just remember that, Elliot. Oh, and one last thing. Your father-in-law, Mort? He's gone to Simon with some wild notions about you and some kind of relationship with organized crime types. Mort's getting up in years and has been depressed since Hanna's mom passed away. We all understand that. Still, that kind of talk is very unwise, Elliot, particularly during these trying times, and so I've spoken with him indirectly about it."

"Spoken with him?"

"A couple of our associates went over to Prospect Park to visit him last night, just as a kind of reminder. I'm sure you can understand our sensitivities about the subject."

26

"New Godfather Heading Gambino Gang"

"Don't feel like the Lone Ranger. The pressure is on everyone. There's a
good chance this city is gonna blow sky high before it's over."

It's odd how things go sometimes.

For months, even years, events can pass by so visible to a
man that he can almost reach out, grab them in space like a
hand of playing cards floating in front of him, then arrange
them with great deliberation for the best possible result. Then
there are the other times when the shit hits the fan and the
episodes that make up a person's life come hurtling at him so
fast and furiously, it's like he's in some kind of perverse *Star
Wars* sequel, having lost anything even vaguely approaching
control, and he knows that God, the Devil, or maybe just Life
in General is about to give him the butt-fucking of his life.

Well, that's how events were shaping up for Elliot. Later
that night, after having been with Al Rosengarten, he stopped
by Elaine's to talk to Frank Silvio. It was not sanctuary he
found, but more chaos, more adrenalin-jolting vulnerability.

"Hey, you look like shit" were Silvio's first words upon
seeing him. It was already after eleven o'clock, it had been a

long day, and it showed, but Elliot's dapper and inexhaustible friend seemed immune to all of that. "Look here," Silvio said pointing to a glass of Diet Coke effervescing on the bar top, "I ordered your favorite while I was waiting."

"Thanks," Elliot muttered. "You have no idea the pressure I'm under."

Frank sipped Glenlivet from a glass. "Maybe I do, but don't feel like the Lone Ranger. The pressure's on everyone, and there's a good chance this city—the 'Volcano' as Joe Bonanno used to call it—is gonna blow sky high before it's over."

"The trials?"

"You don't keep your ear to the ground much, do you, Dottore? Neil Dellacroce died two days ago over at Mary Immaculate Hospital in Queens." Silvio chuckled, amazed himself at the machinations of this world of theirs. "Registered under the name Rev. Timothy O'Neill. That's the alias he used in the old days as a gunman for Albert Anastasia to gain the confidence of the *cafones* he was about to ice. Some sense of humor, huh? No wonder Johnny Gotti loved him so much."

"I read about Dellacroce. It was all over the papers just like these Nazi show trials going on all over Manhattan. Didn't I hear that Gotti was on his way to court along with Dellacroce on RICO charges on the day he died?"

"That's right, but now let me tell you something shocking. Big Paulie didn't show up for Neil's wake. His own goddamned underboss! I was there, Elliot. Gotti, who kept vigil at his bedside through the entire deathwatch, was pissed at the boss like I've never seen. Even capos, guys in Castellano's camp like Frank DeCiccio and Jimmy Brown Failla, didn't like it, and every one of them was fallin' all over John. Now, word is that Big Paulie is going to snub Gotti by naming Tommy Bilotti as his new number two.

"Now there's a mistake even Stevie Wonder could see because whether Paul likes it or not, John controls what Dellacroce has on the street, something like ten out of the twenty-three Gambino crews." He paused for a moment to let his words sink in. "Everyone knows there's been two factions within the family since Carlo passed. Now, with Dellacroce out of the way and Castellano up on three separate indictments, I tell you, Dottore, either John Gotti or Big Paulie is going."

"I'm sorry, Frank," Elliot moaned, covering his ears with the palms of his hands. "I didn't come here to listen to all of this Mafia shit. I've already got a migraine that f-feels like my head is being used for Yankee batting practice. Over dinner tonight, Al Rosengarten tells me Ralph Scopo is coming in for bypass surgery, heavily suggesting a not-so-subtle failure in the surgery. On top of that, Hanna has somehow gotten my father-in-law involved. Now you're telling me the Gambinos are on the verge of civil war! Jesus Christ, do I need this? Do I fucking need any of this aggravation at all?"

"*Scopo*, I should have known," Silvio calculated as much for himself as for Elliot. "It doesn't take much to see what's going on. In fact, it was Simon who asked me to take a look at his charts at Beekman."

"Dr. Dak?"

"Yeah, why?"

"It shouldn't surprise me, I suppose, but Rosengarten brought up his name more than once, and though I know he's on the board and contributes a shitload of Gambino money to the hospital, sometimes I just have to wonder, 'Is there anybody or anything that isn't mobbed up in this city?'"

Silvio lifted his glass in a kind of mock toast. "Until today I might have said you, but I have a feeling that by week's end, all of that will have changed."

Much of what Silvio had told him that night at Elaine's

was on the money, but later when information about the ongoing Gambino disputes came out, as usual, there turned out to be more to the story than Elliot knew at the time. The extent of the rivalry that had developed between Gotti and Big Paulie, for example, was much deeper than even Silvio had imagined. Castellano, who'd been petitioning Angelo Ruggiero for copies of his trial tapes through Dellacroce for months, had obtained transcripts legally in a pretrial motion connected to his own case. In them, he'd read about Angelo's drug involvement in international heroin trafficking as well as the involvement of other Bergin crew members, right under Gotti's nose, and probably with his tacit participation. How else was the Bergin capo going to pay for his enormous gambling debts, averaging as high as $80,000 per month? Certainly not through his formal Gambino interests, the arithmetic of his own cut as godfather simply didn't add up. What's more, in those same transcripts he'd read about Ruggiero's most flagrant transgression against La Cosa Nostra, specific and unambiguous references to the Commission, tied directly to Castellano's name and the names of other family leaders!

Under the rules, Castellano had all the evidence he needed, but beset by his own legal difficulties, did not summon the will to act against the Bergin crew by ordering hits on Gotti, Ruggiero, and the others. Instead, Big Paulie, the spoiled Sicilian businessman, decided to forego violence in the short run for "neutralization," or a series of family demotions for members of the Bergin crew, while Gotti, the razor-edged Neapolitan street thug, plotted the assassination of his own godfather one block at a time.

That night when Elliot returned home, the culmination of his worst fears was waiting for him. Hanna met him at the door in tears.

"Elliot, my father phoned. He sounded very upset and said he needed to speak with you, face to face, no matter what time you came home."

"Jesus, Hanna, it's after midnight!"

"He said he had to see you," she insisted. "He said it was important. I don't know anything more than that, but then again, I rarely do."

By the time Elliot got to Mort Shapiro's place, it was two o'clock in the morning. The old man was waiting for him, nursing a glass of Glenlivet straight up. He motioned Elliot to a chair in the living room of his brownstone, then took a sip of Scotch, his bloodshot eyes peering above the glass. He looked tired and depressed. It was only then that Elliot noticed the red-and-blue blotch around his right cheek and eye.

"Look at me," Shapiro said. "Do I look like I've got my life together? No, I don't. My wife is dead, and I've been drinking myself numb every night for the past five years. But I harm no one, except maybe myself. You? You're different. Walking around like some kind of big-shot genius, pulling the wool over everyone's eyes. Buying fancy cars and fancy gold wrist-watches and fancy thousand-dollar suits, thinking those things are going to make you happy. You think you're leading some kind of double life when all you're really doing is hiding because you're scared of failing, terrified that somehow a low-class Jew like you doesn't really deserve the success you've gotten. Ever thought about that, Dr. Litner, or should I say 'Dottore'? Hell, you've squandered your talents, destroyed our family, and now you're putting the life of your wife and children in harm's way!"

Elliot rose, walking toward him. "You're hurt, Mort . . ."

Shapiro slapped away Elliot's hand as he tried to touch his bruised face. "It was two of your friends, your soldiers or associates, or whatever the hell they're called, did this to me. It seems I overstepped my bounds trying to protect my daughter, daring to confide in my friend of thirty years,

Simon Dak!" He looked at Elliot scornfully. "They've really got you this time, don't they boy? 'In for a dime, in for a dollar,' isn't that what they say? And now they want you to kill Scopo. Kill or be killed. I want you out of my home and out of my daughter's life," snarled the man who'd put his own life at risk both as a civilian in South America and as a front-line surgeon during World War II where he'd won a Silver Star medal for bravery. "I trusted you, Elliot. I trusted you with my only child and grandchildren. I believed in you, in your integrity and goodness, but I was wrong and now it's too late for me to do a damn thing about it."

Elliot left Mort Shapiro's home sick with worry and despair. What the hell did it mean? First, Al Rosengarten a Mount Sinai board member, tries to strong-arm him into murdering a government witness about to come under his care. Next, Mort, an innocent who shared a deep-rooted friendship with both Rosengarten and Simon Dak, is roughed up and threatened for daring to utter a word about his son-in-law's affiliations within the family. Both actions would have been incomprehensible to Elliot at any other time. Could Scopo's assassination be that vital to the New York godfathers' survival?

This was the question caroming through Elliot's mind that morning as he returned by cab to his New York apartment. Within hours, however, he would uncover the motives behind these underworld tremors because nearly simultaneous with those events, Elliot learned that Paul Castellano had summoned his *caporégimes* and announced that he was going to close the Ravenite and assign John Gotti and his crew to other *decimas*, in effect, demoting Gotti to soldier and eliminating the Bergin crew altogether. Next, just as Silvio had predicted, Castellano added another provocation by appointing Tommy Bilotti as his underboss while making it known to anyone that mattered that he was shelving his earlier idea of a triumvirate of acting bosses that had included Gotti.

While Castellano's instincts, blunted by his cushy ride to the top, were failing him, those of the New York tabloids were set in high gear as they observed the roiling broth of politics and violence that was stirring.

As early as March 1985, the New York *Daily News* had run the headline, NEW GODFATHER REPORTED HEADING GAMBINO GANG. As poignant was the acute interest the media was showing Gotti. Now that his mentor Neil Dellacroce was dead, Gotti was the lead defendant in a RICO case based on criminal conspiracy charges for crimes dating back to his hijacking days and three murders including that of Jimmy McBratney for which he'd already served jail time. With his name now at the top of all the court papers, most assumed that Barry Slotnick, a pro when it came to defending against RICO, would be his choice as lead attorney. But based on a deep friendship that was developing between him and one of the family's lesser mouthpieces, Gotti chose another dynamo out of Brooklyn, like himself, Bruce Cutler.

A second significant relationship that had developed over the recent years within the Gotti *decima* was that of rising star Sammy Gravano. Sammy "the Bull," so named because of his awesome strength, wasn't lured into the Mafia, but willingly pursued it. In 1968, he befriended Tommy Spero, whose Uncle Shorty was associated with the Columbo Family. Though he worked construction with his brother-in-law by day, through Spero, his mob career began as a burglar, but soon graduated to murder when Shorty tapped him on the shoulder for a contract to kill a criminal who'd supposedly double-crossed him. Sammy shot and killed the guy, then found out the motive was simply that a friend of Shorty's wanted to fuck the victim's wife, a task that would prove easier for him if she was made a widow. That was no problem for Sammy because as, capos in both the Columbo and Gambino organizations would learn, the Bull was good at two things: muscling percentages out of the New York construction trade and murdering men, known and unknown to him, with absolutely no sense of remorse.

By 1985, with Sammy switched over to the Gambino Family, Gotti and Gravano's destinies were inexorably linked when Neil Dellacroce saved the Bull's life by taking him into the Bergin crew after Sammy committed the cardinal offense of threatening to kill another made man. Despite the fact that both were multiple murderers who relished violence over negotiation, Gotti was from a different world than Gravano, who specialized in construction shakedowns, as opposed to hijackings, gambling, and loansharking. So the diversification and earning power Sammy brought to the Bergin were welcomed.

Gravano held interests in discos, nightclubs, and a popular Bensonhurst bar-restaurant called Tali's. But if Sammy liked the entertainment industry, construction was where he really contributed to the Gambino *borgata*. In addition to hidden interests in plumbing and dry-wall companies, a hardwood flooring firm, and a painting company, with bids fixed through Lucchese Family contacts, Sammy held ownership in Gem Steel and Marathon Concrete. All these companies were deeply involved in construction projects throughout New York. It was only natural that around that time, the Bull would parlay Commission concrete-pouring kickback arrangements brokered through Ralph Scopo into a deal that was consummated by a Commission vote allowing Marathon to enter the club.

Once a member of the Bergin crew, Gravano and Gotti formed something like a mutual admiration society. Gravano, a cold-blooded murderer personally responsible for dozens of hits, admired Gotti's charisma and sense of style. Gotti, the ruthless, Machiavellian leader, had early along seen Gravano as savvy and business minded enough to be competition for him in his climb to the top. Gotti decided to co-opt those talents keeping Sammy out of play while reaping the financial benefits of his work. All of those capabilities Gotti would be calling upon in the days to come as he used Gravano as a messenger gathering support among the Fist of Five and others for his plot to kill Castellano.

First on his agenda was to get Frank DeCiccio and Jimmy Failla on his side. Using Sammy as the go-between, Gotti convinced both that they were never going to make any real money under the boot of the greedy Castellano and his "scumbag" underboss Tommy Bilotti. They agreed. Next, Gotti put feelers out to leaders of the other families. He used Angelo Ruggiero to meet with Gerry Lang of the Columbos who wondered, "What's John waiting for, his own funeral?" Then, he met with Joe Messino, underboss of the Bonannos, who Gotti bragged he had "in his hip pocket." As for Tony "Ducks" Corallo of the Luchesse Family, Sammy was pleased to report back that Castellano was hated by him; more, that Corallo, who'd been secretly recorded talking conspiratorially about Big Paulie, was concerned himself about getting clipped by the Todt Hill godfather, an additional incentive for wanting him out of the way.

The only family boss who would be opposed to a Castellano hit, the plotters of Fist concluded, was Vincent "the Chin" Gigante, aging godfather of the Genovese Family. It was suspected that Gigante, upset at rampant narcotics trafficking within the Bergin crew, had already arranged for a shot to be taken at Gotti outside his Ozone Park headquarters. Beyond that, the Chin was a Sicilian traditionalist who hated the instinctive brashness of the Neapolitans that Gotti represented. He and Big Paulie went back to the founding of the Gambinos and were joined at the hip by loyalty to Carlo Gambino. All agreed that Gigante would never go along with a tradition-shattering plan akin in his eyes to something as unforgivable as patricide. Nevertheless, even someone as powerful at that time as the Chin was not going to stop John Gotti. In characteristic fashion, it was Gotti who puffed out his chest in front of the others and proclaimed, *"Fuck the Chin! We're going after Big Paulie. If it comes down to it, we go to war with the Genovese Family, too!"*

27

A TANGLED WEB

"Busy? I'm never too fucking busy to say hello to my friends."

y early December as the strings of destiny were pulled taut and the lives of Gotti, Giuliani, and Elliot coalesced, the name Ralph Scopo loomed large on the horizon of each. Call it a premonition, but on the morning of December 5 when Scopo's wife and son, a bodybuilder in his midtwenties, met with him for the first time at Mount Sinai, Elliot knew that dice were set rolling that would seriously change his life. If there was a single impression that struck him during their discussion about the surgery to come, it was the family's conviction regarding their husband/father's innocence and genuine concern about his health. When Elliot was with them, they were polite and respectful. But after he left the room, they spoke about him with the kind of reverence reserved for *Reader's Digest*'s "Father of the Year."

According to them, Ralph Scopo was a hard-working family man caught up in a tangled web of FBI and New York City lawmen and prosecutors out to take down anyone who wouldn't cooperate as a state's witness against alleged Mafiosi with little concern for innocence or guilt. In some obvious ways, Elliot's consultation with them was similar to the hundreds of others he'd had over the years. But as he explained the combined right and left cardiac cauterization procedure and got a sense of the kind of people they were, he wondered if Ralph Scopo was, in fact, a corrupt union boss or the victim of an overzealous prosecution machine set into a Mafia feeding frenzy.

Though he'd already determined, after viewing the Beekman charts, that Scopo probably needed aortocoronary bypass surgery to survive, Elliot wanted fresh x-rays of his heart to diagnose exactly where and how the narrowing of his coronary arteries had progressed. This he explained to Scopo's wife and son as the union boss was being prepped for testing.

"This morning we're going to X-ray Ralph's heart using a contrast medium, a kind of dye, that's injected via catheter through an artery in his arm. I know this was done before, but I insist that it's performed before any surgical treatment for coronary heart disease to determine the best possible treatment," Elliot explained, all the while thinking about two men he'd personally known without any mob ties that had been prosecuted and served prison time, their lives shattered, by headline-grabbing prosecutors not so unlike Rudy Giuliani.

"The principal problem that this cauterization procedure helps to diagnose is narrowing of the coronary arteries caused by plaque formation. You see, the arteries feeding blood to the heart are relatively few and small—about the size of the lead in a pencil. The process of plaque formation once it's started, not only narrows the artery, but can enhance the tendency of blood near it to clot," he continued, staring into their faces as he remembered the nightmare Congressman Cornelius "Neil" Gallagher, of New Jersey had lived after forming a subcommittee to investigate FBI/CIA abuses during the late 1960s.

In danger of uncovering "black-bag" break-ins (COIN-TELPRO), brainwashing programs (ARTICHOKE), and assassination squads (PHOENIX), Hoover using the ubiquitous Roy Cohn as a go-between, tried to blackmail Gallagher with phony *Life* magazine exposés based on alleged Mafia connections. That failing, the FBI launched a relentless series of investigations into the congressman, his friends, and family that spanned nearly four decades. By the time the attacks ended, Gallagher, a war hero who'd been awarded three Purple Hearts and Bronze and Silver Star medals during World War II, had served two stints in federal prison, lost his congressional seat, his license to practice law, his good name, and entire life savings. All of this without a single mob-related charge ever having been proven or even substantiated.

"If the clot, or spasm caused by it, is large enough to block the artery, a person can have a heart attack. If the clot isn't that big, but still interferes with the flow of blood, he may experience angina like Ralph did several weeks ago—severe chest pain that results from the heart muscle not receiving enough oxygen. If either heart attacks or angina deprive the heart of oxygen long enough, a portion of the heart muscle called the myocardium dies. The result can range from almost undetectable to immediately fatal," Elliot elaborated, thinking now about Joseph Salvati, a truck driver fingered by a hit man named Joseph Barboza. Salvati served thirty years in prison for a murder he knew nothing about.

In March 1965, during the twilight of Bobby Kennedy's war on the mob, agents overheard Barboza on a wiretap requesting permission from his boss to ice a small-time hood named Edward Deegan, who later turned up dead, shot six times, in an alley. When indictments were handed down, Barboza, the real murderer, was not named because in addition to being a professional killer, he worked as an informant for the bureau. Unbelievably, the four innocent men, including Joseph Salvati, who were named, were subsequently convicted of Deegan's murder on Barboza's testimony with the FBI fully cognizant of their innocence. Salvati, who was targeted because he owed Barboza $400, wound up serving thirty years in federal prison, two others died while serving their sentences, and the fourth man, Peter Limone, was sentenced to die in the electric chair.

"If our testing demonstrates that Ralph's condition warrants, we may go ahead with an aortocoronary bypass procedure," Elliot told them, watching as Marie Scopo's dark and worried eyes met his. "A coronary bypass takes anywhere from two to four hours to perform and is essentially the same regardless of the number of arteries to be bypassed. But just so you understand the procedure, let me briefly take you through what will happen," he said, stopping suddenly as he observed a look of exasperation pass between mother and son. "Mrs. Scopo, have I said something wrong? I don't want to continue if this is upsetting either you or your son." He stared into each of their eyes for some signal about what they were feeling. "I simply wanted to reassure you and your son that bypass surgeries are performed here at Mount Sinai many times each day and that your husband is under the best possible care."

"Dr. Litner, Dottore, we know who you are and have every confidence in your abilities. When we talked about Ralph's condition to people we trust like family, it was you who they recommended. You don't never have to explain what you do to me or to my son. This is all we ask, please don't let my husband and the father of my children die in no hospital. Ralph's no angel, but he's a good man who never did nothing worse than anybody else. He's been a provider to his family and a loving father to his children. He don't deserve to die on no operating table. We love him too much for that."

"I know that you care about your husband very much, Mrs. Scopo. I could see it from the moment you walked into my office. So please don't worry," Elliot vowed. "Everything that can be done will be done."

She nodded, her eyes filling with tears as her son dutifully helped her from her chair, looking more like visiting clergy than the bodybuilding son of a Mafia capo.

"We trust you, Dottore," Joey Scopo stated like the politest, most stand-up guy on the planet. "No matter what happens, we know you'll do everything in your power to fix my father's heart."

It was one in the morning by the time Elliot left Mount Sinai with his initial assumptions about surgery confirmed for Scopo. He was exhausted physically from the work, but more from the nonstop stress. The insulation was gone. For him, it was down to bare wire. With surgery scheduled for 3:00 P.M. that afternoon, he didn't have much time to try to ruminate over just how he would handle the most serious dilemma of his life.

On the one hand, Rosengarten, who carried a lot of weight himself, but not nearly so much as his bosses, had made it about as clear as anyone could that the godfathers who headed the Commission needed and expected Scopo to die on the operating table. On the other, there was the genuine allegiance Elliot held for the Hippocratic oath he was sworn to, along with a sincere liking not only for Ralph Scopo, but for members of his immediate family whom he found to be profound in their story of how this husband and father's life had gone awry. "Misunderstandings of this magnitude were certainly possible," Elliot lamented as he walked from the elevator into the hospital's underground lot. "Just look at me."

Then as he walked toward his 'Vette and switched open

the locks, Elliot noticed a long black Lincoln Continental slowly prowling with lights on bright. It moved like a shark gliding through water, methodical, as it positioned its high beams directly on him, so that he felt like he was an actor on stage caught up in a play no sane man could ever have written. There he stood, just outside the Corvette's driver's door, frozen in the glare of those headlights, waiting for he didn't know what, when suddenly his cell phone rang. Once, twice, three times. Since it was already after 1:00 A.M., he had to believe he was meant to answer it.

"H-Hello?" Elliot asked in a voice so quiet and so frightened that it must have sounded like something between a mouse and a lamb.

"You know who this is, don't you? You do, I know. So don't say nothing. I wanted to call. Let you know that we're counting on you to do the right thing tomorrow. You're a good fucking kid. Everyone says so. Now you get to prove it. Do what we ask, you're the next director of heart surgery at Mount Sinai. Don't, you lose more than your fucking job, *capesci?*"

"Yes, sir," he answered, having recognized immediately the voice of John Gotti, who now that Gravano was a member of the Concrete Club, also had a vested interest in Ralph Scopo's demise. "Thanks for taking the t-time to call. I kn-know how busy you must be," he added stupidly.

"Busy? Never too fucking busy to say hello to my friends."

"Your people, was it them that assaulted my father-in-law, Mort Shapiro the other night?"

"Dottore, on my mother's eyes, I don't know what you're talkin' about, but this much I'll tell you. If your father-in-law was talkin' to any-fucking-body about this trial, about this rat scumbag we both know and these lies he's been tellin' about us, what did you expect? What the fuck did you expect from

234

any of this? You stick your nose up somebody's ass, and you think it's gonna smell like what, roses?"

"No, not roses."

"Good. You remember that 'cause this thing has got to be handled just right, or it's gonna hurt people at very high levels. So you all right with that now? What we were talkin' about?"

"Yes, sir, we're j-just fine."

"Okay, then, let me tell you one last thing. It's about my fucking health. My stomach is good, and my shit still don't look like fucking coffee grounds. That's a good thing," Gotti said laughing. "Now get a good night's sleep, and don't ever forget this conversation."

With those words, the connection went dead. Elliot stood silently watching as the Lincoln's headlights ratcheted down to normal and the black limousine turned around and drove off, its red taillights disappearing into the dark like a mirage that he had to convince himself was real. Then, with hands still shaking, he fumbled with his keys, entered his car, and got the hell out of Mount Sinai's underground parking lot as fast as his Lil' Red Corvette would take him.

28

AN "INTERESTING" LIFE

"Dr. Litner, I was asked by Mr. Giuliani to tell you that if anything happens to Mr. Scopo, the full resources of his office will be devoted to a criminal investigation of you, your business dealings, and medical practice."

Elliot arrived at the hospital at nine that morning, late for him, particularly in light of the full schedule of surgeries that had developed over the past couple of days, not the least of which was Ralph Scopo's. After having been checked in to Mount Sinai, Giuliani's star witness had been deposited via wheelchair on the third floor of the Housman Pavilion along with two armed members of the NYPD Mob-Corruption Unit, who stood guard on a twenty-four-hour-a-day vigil and whose job it was to make certain that Scopo made it alive to the operating room.

Once settled into his office, Elliot mulled over the results of the preoperative tests he'd ordered, recorded by Clark Hinterlieter, the resident surgeon, on a patient's chart. They included an electrocardiogram, blood samples to determine kidney and liver function and cholesterol and mineral balance, blood-cell count, and urinalysis. Also there were the forward and sideways chest X-rays Elliot had described to Scopo's wife and son, along with four units of blood cross matched to Scopo's type that were put aside in the hospital blood bank.

The case, from a medical standpoint, was routine, Elliot was thinking then, but that was where anything simple ended along with any possible pretense of moral ambiguity along with it. No more faking. No more dodging that treacherous crossroad between good and evil. Scopo would either live or die at his hands. But with a poetic twist that even Shakespeare could not have conceived, in murdering a man, he would be saved. In saving a man, he would risk being murdered. It was enough to give a poor Jewish kid raised in the Bronx Excedrin headache #2321!

From his office, Elliot drifted to the eighth floor of the Annenberg Building where, in a large meeting room, about two dozen attending cardiologists and residents met each morning to talk over cases and compare notes. There, he sat sipping from a cardboard cup filled with Diet Coke, so totally preoccupied with this, the dilemma of his life, that he hardly noticed Clark Hinterlieter as he walked up to the front of the room to present Scopo's case.

"This fifty-six-year-old white male has a history of heavy cigarette smoking, is obese, sedentary, and has a family history of coronary disease and elevated lipid levels. The physical exam showed a heart rate of seventy beats a minute, blood pressure 140/75 in both arms, sitting. He was breathing comfortably at fourteen breaths a minute and a febrile . . .," Hinterlieter explained to the group as Elliot wondered what had brought him to this juncture in his life. If there was a way out, he didn't know what it could be at that moment, with little prospect for a breakthrough idea between now and the time of the operation.

Elliot looked around the conference room to his colleagues including Frank Silvio and could tell as soon as Silvio's dark eyes met his own, then darted away as quickly, that

Frank knew everything that was going on. "That's right," Elliot was thinking, "don't get too close, Frankie. Not now because for the moment, I'm still something between a stand-up guy and damaged goods, with the jury still out."

His eyes then fell on Dr. Dak as he observed Hinterlieter's synopsis. "Unusual for him to attend," he was thinking, "but that's no accident." Like nearly every other powerful man he was acquainted with in New York, Simon's name had been thrown around by Al Rosengarten during their dinner at the Plaza. Maybe Dak's being here was a message, yet another intimidation piled atop Gotti's visit and the rest. "Or maybe I've gone over the deep end," Elliot concluded, "become totally paranoid reading meaning into the most innocent coincidence."

Hinterlieter signaled for the angiograms to be shown at the front of the room where the branchlike patterns of Ralph Scopo's coronaries appeared on the ten-by-twenty-foot white screen. "As you can see, there's an 85 percent narrowing of the patient's left main coronary artery just before the vessel divides into its two main branches, the left anterior descending and the left circumflex arteries, which were themselves blocked downstream. The LAD was 80 percent obstructed, and there seemed to be another 99 percent lesion of its first diagonal branch. But because these deposits were spread out along the narrow vessel lining, I wasn't sure whether the artery was bypassable."

As the resident surgeon droned on, Elliot couldn't help but ponder his fate now mere hours away. Exactly what were his options? he anguished, remembering something his Uncle Saul had once told him. "There's a solution to every problem, but most people are either too stupid or too lazy to take the time to figure it out. *Now go know!*" Fair enough. He considered his options. Clearly there are only two outcomes. Either

Scopo lived or he died. If he survived the procedure, there would be only one conclusion killers like Gotti and Castellano could draw, and that is that he betrayed them. And that meant Elliot was dead. If, however, Scopo was to die during surgery or later from complications, this left a mouse hole for escape because the prosecutors' conclusions could never be so clear cut. Anyone interested enough to pick up a medical text could read that there are mortality (death) and morbidity (complication) rates running somewhere between 1 percent and 3 percent attributed to aortocoronary bypass. Why not Scopo? Who could prove otherwise?

"In summary," Clark Hinterlieter lectured, "chest X-rays reflect lung disease, but this does not seem too severe. Angiography shows double-vessel disease in addition to a left-main lesion, with preserved ventricular function. We suspect recent subendocardial infarction involving the anterior wall related to disease in the diagonal branch of the LAD."

Yet, deep within Elliot there was something as strong and visceral as his own survival instincts, and that was his love of healing. True, he'd made many mistakes. He gambled too much. He was unfaithful to his wife and had engaged in questionable activities that jeopardized himself and his family. But not so many that it had totally blunted his need to save, as opposed to snuffing, human life no matter what the motive. He was a healer, not a murderer. Everything he'd learned and been taught by his father, his mother, and uncles sent him hurtling in one direction while all that he had come to know of life since becoming an associate in the Mafia threw him back again where he was trapped, like in one of those 1950s horror films, in the middle of a locked room with stone walls slowly, inexorably, closing in!

"Elliot, do you have anything to add?" Hinterlieter asked.

"Only that I'm bothered by lack of collaterals in this fellow," Elliot shot back, surprising himself with the sharpness of the response. "But, one way or the other, there can be no debate about what to do. Mr. Scopo has the most compelling reason for bypass surgery—a major blockage in his left main artery. Statistically, his chances for survival without the operation are almost nil."

No one disagreed. Afterward as Elliot was leaving the darkened conference room, he found Dr. Dak trailing behind him into the corridor.

"Elliot, may we speak for a moment?" the gnomish seventy-eight-year-old rumbled with his Romanian accent. "There's a man from the Federal Bureau of Investigation who's been asking to see you. His name is Special Agent Hogan. Do you know him?"

Elliot shook his head in the negative, a tingling feeling of dread making its way up from his scrotum to the nape of his neck.

"He says he works with U.S. Attorney Giuliani. I'm sure it has to do with this Scopo fellow, but he wouldn't say just what it was he wanted to talk about. Is there anything I should be aware of, Elliot. Is there anything you would like to tell me before you meet with Hogan?"

"Not that I can think of, Simon. So far as I can see, the diagnosis is very straightforward, almost routine."

"As you know, Dr. Litner, no case is 'routine.' I suspect Scopo's is no exception," Dr. Dak uttered as he ambled down the corridor. "Hogan is waiting in your office. Good luck to you."

Once Elliot returned to his office, Special Agent Peter Hogan, a strapping, red-haired man in his late thirties, was waiting outside along with two other agents, both shorter and dark haired. Hogan stepped forward and introduced himself as his two subordinates faded to the sidelines.

Inside, Elliot offered Hogan a seat, watching from the corner of his eye as the agent studied his diplomas from Syracuse University and Downstate Medical Center, his sharp blue eyes shifting then to family photos of Hanna, the twins, and himself.

"Nice family you have there, Doctor."

"Thank you, Mr. Hogan, but to be honest, I'm busy as hell. Is there something special you wanted to see me about?"

"Yes, there is. I'm here today to observe the operation you're going to perform on Ralph Scopo. I'm pretty sure you know who he is and why his good health is so important to Mr. Giuliani and, really, every American citizen."

"Every American citizen? That's a lot of people. What, maybe two hundred fifty million or so?"

"The men his testimony is going to help convict are the leaders of the five Mafia families that run organized crime in New York. They extort, they steal, and they murder, Dr. Litner. Now, I'm not here to tell you about your work as a doctor, but only to ask one small indulgence on your part and that is that you wear a wire during your preop visit. You know, with Scopo under sedation, he's liable to say things, important things, maybe names, that could be essential to our case."

"Is this Mr. Giuliani's idea?"

"Yes, as a matter of fact, it is. I'm making this request on behalf of the U.S. Attorney's Office."

Elliot stood up behind his desk just then, feeling the heat rise within him, as he considered Giuliani's concept of justice, thinking all the while of his family and its harrowing escape from totalitarian Russia. Here was a sick man, dying for all he knew, lying on an operating table undergoing critical surgery, and these ghouls, brains invaded by ambition as rampant as runaway cancer, wanted him, Scopo's physician, to participate in their mania.

"Mr. Hogan, I won't wear a wire into Mr. Scopo's room or

into anyone else's. I'm a surgeon. I'm not in law enforcement and will not be used by you, the FBI, the U.S. Attorney's Office, or anyone else in any way that might undermine the confidentiality of the doctor-patient relationship. What Scopo says, if anything, while under sedation is no one's business, not even mine. The last time I looked, this was still the United States of America, not the Soviet Union and not Nazi Germany!"

Hogan's pale Irish face reddened noticeably as he sucked a stream of air into his lungs and nodded. "Dr. Litner, I have to make a brief phone call. Would you just wait here for a few seconds while I do that?"

"Not a problem," Elliot said still angry as he glanced to his watch. It was past noon. Ralph Scopo would be prepped and wheeled into Operating Room #2 for surgery in less than three hours.

No more than three minutes had passed when Hogan reentered the room. No question he'd been speaking with the U.S. attorney, who judging by the short time frame, had been standing by for an update.

"Dr. Litner, we're alone so I'll speak frankly. I've just gotten off the phone with Mr. Giuliani. He asked me to tell you that in his opinion you lead an 'interesting' life. We know that you have acquaintances within the Gambino Family. Your name has been mentioned, and you have been referred to, on government surveillance tapes. We need Scopo alive to testify against these thugs in the most important Mafia trial of the century. We'd like you to cooperate by wearing a surveillance wire into surgery. If you refuse, that's your right, but I was asked by Mr. Giuliani to tell you that if anything happens to Ralph Scopo, if, for any reason, he was not to make it through this operation, the full resources of his office will be devoted to a criminal investigation of you, your business dealings, and medical practice. Have I made that point clear to you, Dr. Litner?"

29

THE WORLD ACCORDING
TO FRANKIE VALLI

"It occurred to him that this must be what it's like just before death as a man's life flashes before him."

Operating Room #2 in Mount Sinai Hospital is a twenty-by-twenty-foot chamber with white tile floors and shiny steel cabinets. Like an altar, the operating table was positioned over a pedestal in the middle of the floor with glass-panel windows deep set into the room's walls on either side. The time was 3:35 P.M. Coronary patient Ralph Scopo lay motionless on the operating table, chest bare, electrodes attached to the back of his shoulders, intravenous needles inserted into his right arm and left wrist.

Fifty-six-years-old, grossly overweight, and three-pack-a-day smoker, Giuliani's pride and joy had collapsed three weeks earlier, headlines in the morning papers screaming SCOPO HEART ATTACK DISRUPTS RACKETEERING TRIAL. But there was much more to it than racketeering. This case was an attempt by the FBI and New York City's Organized Crime Task Force to bring down the Commission, the bosses of the five La Cosa Nostra families that governed New York and possibly the nation.

In the background "The Wanderer," a 1961 hit by Dion was playing in place of Verdi or Puccini, Elliot's usual fare.

IL DOTTORE

The anesthesiologist jerked Scopo's head back so the blunt blade of the L-shaped laryngoscope could be put in his throat and a one-half-inch endotracheal tube inserted past his vocal chords. A balloon on the tube's lower end inflated creating an airtight seal as Clark Hinterlieter inserted a Foley catheter through Scopo's penis into his bladder, then nodded to Elliot Litner.

Elliot glanced to his right where outside operating room #2 the Giuliani team of three federal investigators led by Special Agent Peter Hogan awaited the operation's outcome like vultures. Then, to his left where John Gotti's right hand, Sammy "the Bull" Gravano, and two of his underlings loomed nearby the patients' waiting room pacing the floor with equal intensity. "The Brooks Brothers Ivy Leaguers versus the polyester suit *gumbas*," he mused sardonically, the voice in his head sounding like a cross between Woody Allen and a manic Jerry Lewis. "*How the hell did a nerdy, Jewish kid from the Bronx get caught up in a mess like this?*" The feds want Scopo alive to prosecute and "twist" into a government witness. The goodfellas don't want him leaving this operating room alive. Either way, it's understood, Elliot was a dead man.

Dion warbled in the background about Flo on the left, Mary on the right, and Janie being the girl he'll be with tonight. When Janie asks who he loves the best, Dion tears open his shirt to show Rosie on his chest.

> *'Cause I'm the wanderer,*
> *Yeah the wanderer,*
> *I go around, around, around . . .*

The chest was open; the heart-lung machine ready to go. It was impossible to stall any longer. It was time for Elliot Litner, a man who could have been the poster boy for moral ambiguity to choose between life or death: loyalty to La Cosa Nostra or devotion to his Hippocratic oath.

246

"Fifty cc's going in to test the line," the technician announced.

"On bypass," Elliot commanded, "start cooling."

Almost immediately, Scopo's heart slowed.

Judy Harrow, his surgical nurse, held the shiny stainless-steel needle up in the air. She depressed the syringe plunger, and a stream of clear liquid potassium spurted from it.

She handed it to Elliot.

This was it. The moment of truth, for if ever there was a time to see to it that Scopo never awakened from his drug-induced sleep to testify, this was that time.

Elliot took the syringe into his right hand, clamped the aorta, then injected the icy fluid directly into the vessels below the blockages in Scopo's lower aorta.

Ralph Scopo's heart had stopped beating!

The heartbeat indicator read 0. The organ had stopped. Bloodless, motionless, and rubbery, it was the ideal target.

With a Number-15 blade, Elliot cut into the muscle to expose a pale yellow streak on the back of the heart where the major posterolateral branch of the circumflex artery ran. Then, he looked at the front of the heart.

"The distal LAD looks pretty good. We'll put the graft there," he told Hinterlieter. "What's the temperature?"

"Twenty-five," he replied.

"And the flow?"

"Three liters per minute."

Elliot nodded holding a surgical needle at the tip of long-handled forceps, then sewing a series of tiny stitches with near-invisible filament, first in the vein, then in the artery. Still, concentrating with all of his will, Elliot couldn't shake the images that passed through his mind, some related to childhood, most having to do with Hanna, Samantha, and Rachel. Whatever the outcome, he knew his life would never be the same.

"Focus, focus," he repeated to himself like a mantra, his thoughts drifting despite those efforts, back to the events that had led him to this nightmare.

Even as he worked, he could envision the twins frolicking in the water on the lake where they vacationed. He pictured himself and Hanna, early in their marriage, making love, totally consumed with desire for one another. He remembered their family dinners, Hanna singing songs with the kids while Mort cooked burgers on the grill. All of them laughing, savoring the joy and innocence of the children. Then it occurred to Elliot that this must be what it's like just before death as a man's life flashes before him. And, in a way, Elliot was dying because he knew that after today, everything he'd built and worked for would cease to exist. More, he understood that these "friends" of his were no friends at all, but monsters who sucked the marrow from society, threatening and killing everyday people, exploiting their greed and avarice, then subjugating them with mortal terror.

With sutures joining vein to artery, Elliot turned his attention to Scopo's distal LAD, his next and in many ways most important target. "There's a lot of disease in this vessel. But this will turn out to be good for the internal mammary," he observed, picking up the LIMA, which he had left clamped. "See how big it is?"

Judy handed him the finest 7-0 sutures. Once the connection was complete, he unclamped the LIMA, and on the surface of Scopo's heart, branch after branch of tiny vessels immediately turned bright red.

"What time is it?" he asked.

"Four fifty-six," Hinterlieter replied. The heart had been deprived of blood for twenty-one minutes.

"Right on schedule," Elliot calculated, beginning to sew the upper ends of the saphenous vein graphs to Scopo's aorta.

He applied a half-moon-shaped clamp to the massive vessel, isolating a quarter-sized area where the veins would be attached, then punched two circular holes into the vessel through which blood would flow into the new conduits to the heart. Then, eyes focused like lasers, he began attachment, the most critical phase of the procedure, as images of Marie and Joey Scopo flooded his mind.

How could he murder this woman's husband and the young man's father? he anguished. What kind of man would he be to allow Scopo to pay for the bad decisions he'd made during his life? He thought about what Uncle Saul might have advised and the core of the stories he'd told based upon the value and dignity of human life. No, Elliot decided as the final minutes of the bypass surgery approached, he could not be party to another man's murder. Even if it meant one of the family's hit men taking his own life, he would do everything in his power to keep Ralph Scopo alive.

Judy Harrow dabbed a skein of perspiration from Elliot's forehead as he completed his stitching, leaving only the detachment of the heart-lung machine as the final hurdle for the surgical team. He double-checked the grafts. Bulging with blood, there were no kinks or leaks. All had gone smoothly. He could feel the sense of relief in the room as spirits buoyed and "Walk Like a Man," a Four Seasons song began playing over the speaker system.

"Did anyone ever tell you that you had lousy taste in music?" Judy Harrow asked.

Elliot glanced from his patient to the monitor over the table that tracked the state of Scopo's cardiovascular system. The mean arterial pressure was fifty-eight millimeters of mercury; the left arterial pressure was four.

"That's a little low," he told Hinterlieter, who added more fluid to the pump as the blood pressure began to rise. "But to answer your question," Elliot said, attaching pacemaker wires to the right atrium and ventricle, "no. No one has ever told me that I have lousy taste in music. Terrible, yes. Lousy, not until today, but you know what, Judy? Sometimes a man's gotta do what a man's gotta do!"

Then, Elliot sang along with the tape, the surgical team unaware of the incredible sense of freedom he was experiencing at that moment. No one knew what to make of it, but he did because when the chips were down, it was his judgment, his ethics that prevailed, and that was a high the likes of which he'd never experienced before. He reveled, as Frankie Valli crooned the words to his 1963 hit record.

No- thing is worth
Crawling on the earth
So walk like a man
My s-on

Valli was absolutely right.

Finally, Elliot picked up the Bovie and reaching inside the wall of the chest, cauterized any vessels that were still bleeding.

"I think it's pretty dry," he said watching as clear plastic tubes a half-inch in diameter were placed over the front surface of the heart and in the left chest cavity to drain any bloody fluid after the incision was closed.

And that's when an intriguing thing happened. Dr. Hinterlieter reached across to him. "Congratulations, Doctor," he said shaking Elliot's hand. Then Judy Harrow offered her hand. Then Dr. Falk, the anesthesiologist, and Rick Whittaker, the technician, followed by every member of his surgical team.

"Congratulations," "Congratulations," each of them said as they clasped his hand into their own. And, oddly, if this was going to be the last day of his life, Elliot had to admit that, in many ways, it was also his proudest.

THE DEATH OF MYSELF

"Look from now on I don't know you, do you understand that? I want you to take my name out of your Rolodex and out of your address book!"

That night when Elliot returned to his home in Englewood, New Jersey, a 1985 Mustang convertible was parked in the driveway. He understood that this was not his insurance agent, and no doubt someone sent from one of the families, probably the Gambinos, who would be acting a lot more like an undertaker.

Of course, it would have been easy to just keep driving, but Elliot understood the choice that he'd made and its consequences. Now it was time to face the music. He had a family that he loved and a career that had taken him to high places within his profession. He wasn't going to run. He'd done enough of that in his life for reasons that he might never fully be able to explain. Nevertheless, those days, for him, were over.

He parked his 'Vette alongside the Mustang, turned the key to the lock of his front door, and entered to find Angelo Ruggiero waiting for him in a house that looked nearly vacant.

Ruggiero, whom he'd known peripherally for a number of

years dating back to his days in emergency at Brooklyn Jewish Hospital, just stared at him blankly like he couldn't believe Elliot was stupid enough to simply show up as if nothing had happened.

"Your wife and kids have gotten the fuck out, Dottore. There was a group of us came over, which I don't think the missus liked too much. If you ask me, she ain't comin' back. Probably thinks your gonna get whacked, which ain't too fucking far from the truth."

Elliot stood perfectly still in the foyer. Ruggiero walked up to him. Through the archway he could see the kitchen table with a half-empty bottle of Jack Daniel's on it. Ruggiero cocked his arm back then slammed his open hand across the side of Elliot's face, sending him flying back into the closed door.

"Ya know you're a stupid cocksucker, don't ya? Ya know, every-fucking-body that knows your fucking name wants to see you fucking iced, or are you too dumb to know that?"

"I kn-know," Elliot answered, "but I also know that I'm not a murderer. I'm a doctor."

Ruggiero reached over and grabbed him by the front of his shirt, he cocked his hand back again as if to hit him, but then seemed to think better of it. He let go of his shirt and took a step backward, shaking his head at what must have been even to him a pathetic sight.

"Ah, what the fuck! It's all over anyway. I'm a fucking dead man, no matter how all of this shit goes down. Once it's settled, I'm fucked. Like you, I made mistakes. I guess we all make fucking mistakes. Me? I talk too much. Quack, quack," he mimicked, "but I still remember what you did for my nephew. I still remember that."

"What are you going to do to me?"

The brutish, bearlike Ruggiero assessed him. "Everybody wants to kill ya. They say you betrayed us, and that's true. But then Johnny said somethin' that was also true. He said you weren't a made man, hell, you ain't even Italian. Then some guys said that over the years, you done us some favors. So the vote was to let you disappear. Get the fuck out of town. Don't ever show your fucking face in New York or even on the East Coast. You leave your work, which has already been arranged. You get the fuck out of this house, which is now our property, and you live to see another day."

"Thank you," Elliot said.

Ruggiero nodded. "Yeah, right," he said. Then, as Elliot turned to leave, he added, "You're a lucky man, Dottore. Most guys don't get no second chance."

Frontiersman Hotel
Sioux City, Iowa
December 14, 1986

The cramped hotel room in Sioux City was not unlike the one in Cleveland, Ohio, or Rochester, New York, or Madison, Wisconsin, for that matter. Hot and humid, the air was pungent with the odor of sour beer, stale cigarettes, and human smells of every variety. The air conditioner, like the ancient heaters in the winter months, exploded into activity, jarring him from his reverie. He was beginning to feel his inner life was like a kaleidoscope. Sparkles of one mood slipped into another, all of them revolving in his mind. More and more these days, he consulted the mirror. And there he was: Elliot Litner, M.D., face blank and emotionless, a tiny stream of perspiration wending its way down the side of his face as he lifted his Bic pen, jotting the final notes for what would become *Il Dottore*.

In the days that followed the operation, Elliot took the advice given him and went "into the wind," as they say. He bought a Harley-Davidson motorcycle and headed west, at least for a time, but not before contacting two of his most intimate colleagues at the hospital.

When he called Dr. Dak immediately following Scopo's successful surgery, he was informed that there was no longer a place for him at Mount Sinai. It seemed Dak had heard from several board members, notably Al Rosengarten, that Elliot had relationships with "unsavory" characters and perhaps, even ties to organized crime. When Dr. Dak referred this information to Special Agent Hogan, with whom he'd developed a friendship, the U.S. Attorney's Office was quick to corroborate details that would suggest Elliot was in some way associated with the infamous Gambino crime family.

It was much the same with his old friend, Frank Silvio. When Elliot called Silvio's office at Mount Sinai, Silvio couldn't get off the phone fast enough. "Look," he told Elliot, "from now on I don't know you, do you understand that? I want you to take my name out of your Rolodex and out of your address book. I need you to forget that we ever knew one another because this isn't over, Elliot. The shit is about to hit the fan, and I don't want to be involved directly, indirectly, or at all!"

A New Beginning

*"Pity those who learn nothing from the days
that pass each moment before us."*

Of course, Elliot couldn't know what Frank Silvio meant during their final telephone conversation since his old pal was off the phone before he could ask. So, he was left to wonder, but not for long. On December 16, 1986, at 5:30 P.M., Paul "Big Paulie" Castellano and his underboss, Tommy Bilotti, were gunned down by six assassins, all dressed in identical trench coats, as they left their black Lincoln outside of Sparks Steak House on East 46th Street in Manhattan, on their way to a sit-down with Gotti and four other Gambino Family members.

According to detectives piecing together eyewitness accounts, it was Gotti associate Tony "Roach" Rampino who shot Bilotti and John Carneglia who pumped six rounds into Castellano. It was then that a third unidentified killer walked up to Big Paulie's bullet-ridden body and fired a final round at point-blank range into his head.

As planned, it was the assassination of Castellano that established John Gotti as the new boss of bosses and put an Andy Warhol original portrait of him on the cover of *Time* magazine. Unlike Maranzano, Bonanno, Gambino, and other bosses of the Mafia's Sicilian branch, Gotti's reign was high profile, volatile, and ultimately disastrous for La Cosa Nostra. Virtually thumbing his nose at law enforcement after his acquittal in the Piecyk case, Gotti's arrogance fanned the flames of relentless government pursuit. In the years to follow, he would be brought to trial and found not guilty of RICO conspiracy charges in February 1987, as well as four assault and two conspiracy charges stemming from the shooting of union official John C. O'Connor in February 1990.

As the Teflon Don was soon to discover, however, the prosecution did not rest. In December 1990, both Gotti and Sammy "the Bull" Gravano were arrested by FBI agents, charged this time with the murders of Paul Castellano and Tommy Bilotti. So intense was the government's obsession with putting Gotti behind bars that hit-man-turned-government witness John Carneglia would testify that when he offered prosecutors information about an international narcotics-trafficking ring that "made millions selling drugs," they had no interest, stating simply, "Look, what we want is Gotti, and we want him at any cost."

Having been brought to trial four times at that point in the past four years, even the *New York Times* had empathy for the new godfather's plight, sensing something more than the carriage of simple justice in what was happening.

"They arrested John Gotti again the other night the same way they arrested him before," a December 1990 editorial read, "flamboyantly and theatrically ... why all the melodrama, including handcuffs and a platoon of 15 FBI agents? The only obvious purpose is for the prosecution to preen for the cameras."

Denying bail on January 18, 1991, Judge Leo Glasser ordered that Gotti be put in "locked-down" for twenty-three hours a day, then in a move of questionable constitutionality, disqualified his entire legal team of Cutler, Shargel, and Pollock. The prosecution's coup de grâce was, of course, the devastating testimony of Sammy Gravano, who later turned government witness against Gotti.

Involved in no less than nineteen murders, Gravano cut a deal with Asst. U.S. Attorney John Gleeson that let him enter into the government witness-protection program after serving only five years in prison. Hammering away at the credibility of a witness so vested in Gotti's destruction and so jaded by his past as a "sick, serial killer," Gotti's lawyer, Albert Kreiger, suffered a devastating setback when Judge Glasser disqualified five of the six witnesses he had intended to testify on Gotti's behalf.

On April 1, 1991, John Gotti was found guilty of all charges stemming from the Castellano-Bilotti hit and later sentenced to life without parole. Like Al Capone who stood broadly grinning, dressed to the teeth in a "heather-purple pinchback suit" for his sentencing more than sixty years earlier, Gotti wore a $2,000 custom-tailored suit, joking with reporters afterward as more than one thousand of his supporters many holding "Free John Gotti!" placards, turned over cars and set fire to police vans outside the courthouse.

Also like his hero, Gotti died in ignominy confined to a six-by-eight cell at the U.S. penitentiary in Marion, Illinois, without so much as a chair for twenty-three hours a day. Gotti's treatment, clearly punitive in nature, would later be protested by Amnesty International as "cruel and inhuman" since most Marion inmates with life sentences were transferred to regular maximum security within months while Gotti's isolation went on for more than four years.

Finally, after years of battling throat cancer discovered in September 1998, John Gotti, the most powerful criminal in America, died in prison on June 10, 2002.

So far as Rudy Giuliani, the second member of Elliot Litner's Brooklyn-Bronx triumvirate, there remain few unaware of his post-September 11 destiny as *Time* magazine's "Person of the Year" just five months prior to his archadversary's death. What not everyone is aware of, however, is the path that led him there. "Show me a hero, and I will write you a tragedy," F. Scott Fitzgerald once said, and Rudy was no exception.

Much as the targeting of notable crime lords had catapulted Thomas Dewey into the limelight, Giuliani's orchestration of the Commission case transformed him into a modern-day gangbuster and media darling. A *New York Times* headline for Thursday, November 20, 1986, says it all. U.S. JURY CONVICTS EIGHT AS MEMBERS OF MOB COMMISSION, *Giuliani Asserts Decision Will Dismantle Ruling Council*. Sentences ran one hundred years for Anthony "Fat Tony" Salerno (Genovese Family), Anthony "Tony Ducks" Corallo (Lucchese Family), and Carmine "the Snake" Persico (Columbo Family). Anthony "Bruno" Indelicato (Bonanno Family) got forty, Gennaro "Gerry Lang" Langella (Columbo Family) sixty-five; and Ralph Scopo (Columbo Family) who ironically never did turn state's witness, received thirty years.

After his triumph in the Commission case, Giuliani again followed the carefully trodden path of his childhood hero. It was not the conviction of notorious mob figures that deposited Dewey at the gates of the White House, but the toppling of Jimmy Hines, the most powerful man in Tammany Hall. So it was for Rudy, who declared war on Wall Street insider trading, starting with Drexel Burnham investment banker Dennis Levine. Soon after, financial colossus Ivan Boesky, about to be fingered by Levine, not only surrendered voluntarily, agreeing to pay a $100-million penalty, but was persuaded by Giuliani to wear a wire and participate in the successful prosecution of ten additional financial arbitragers charged with inside trading.

Clearly on a roll, Rudy decided to test New York City's political waters by running for mayor in 1989, a move he'd planned since confiding to his Lynbrook High girlfriend, Kathy Livermore, that he wanted to be the "first Italian, Catholic president." Losing to David Dinkins in that round, he tried a second time, launching a successful campaign for mayor against the liberal-minded Dinkins in 1993.

Basing his administration on a "take back the city" agenda, Giuliani became the best-known mayor in America since Richard Daley in Chicago. Crime rate statistics for assault, burglary, auto theft, rape, robbery, and murder plummeted during his term. But the price for these programs was large, particularly for the minority community where police had taken free rein to do what they felt needed to be done with little fear of consequence.

In 1994, Anthony Baez, a twenty-nine-year-old Puerto Rican man, was kicking a football around with his brothers in front of their home when the ball accidentally hit two parked patrol cars. It was then that Officer Frank Livoti put Baez in a choke hold, kneeling on his back while handcuffing him as Baez's father screamed warnings that his son suffered from chronic asthma. Baez died an hour later in a hospital.

In 1997, during Rudy's second term as mayor, Abner Louima, a Haitian immigrant, was sodomized with a stick in a precinct bathroom by arresting officers who mistook him for someone who had tried to punch one of them outside a nightclub. Louima's intestines and bladder were punctured, and he was dumped in a holding cell hemorrhaging.

Then, in 1999, with Rudy's potential Senate bid versus Hillary Clinton heating up, Amadou Diallo, a West African immigrant, was shot at forty-one times, and hit nineteen times in the foyer of his Bronx home by four cops who had followed him home. His fatal mistake, it seemed, was reaching into his pocket for a wallet to show them identification.

No, all was not well for Rudy Giuliani moving into September 11, 2001. Not in his role as mayor, where three months after the Diallo case, Dante Johnson, an unarmed sixteen-year-old, was shot dead by police. Not in his personal life where he was diagnosed with prostate cancer and Donna Hanover was suing for divorce while taking a role in an off-Broadway production of *The Vagina Monologues*. Not in his potential Senate campaign where New York tabloids threatened to expose his love affair with socialite Judith Nathan and he would be forced to answer questions, not about his spouse's conduct like Hillary Clinton, but about his own.

So it was that Rudolph Giuliani became suddenly more human declaring on May 19, 1999, that he was "not a candidate" for the Senate based on health and personal considerations.

Giuliani's fate took an astounding about-face on September 11, 2001, when terrorists attacked and destroyed the World Trade Center towers as part of the most devastating assault on American soil in U.S. history. Acting strongly and bravely, while President Bush was in hiding, he became "America's Mayor" overnight and arguably the most admired man in the nation.

As for Elliot Litner, everything has changed since December 1986 when his world came apart. To some extent, his journey as a person has been like his family's sojourn out of Russia and captivity to the United States and freedom. As a child, he would listen to his Uncle Saul as he told of their chilling flight chased by soldiers as they crossed the frozen Dniester River into Romania on foot, then to Austria and Germany by rail, finally arriving by ship into North America. Like them, he, too, has traveled a great deal in his life over some painful and treacherous geography.

After years of working in various hospitals around the country, in fear for his life much of the time, in 1989, Elliot returned to the East Coast where he established himself as director of cardiac surgery at a well-known hospital in New Jersey. Hanna, who remained separated from him, died of ovarian cancer in 1998. Samantha and Rachel are now fully grown and following careers of their own, outside of medicine.

"So, would you do it again?" the very few Elliot has confided in about his life sometimes ask. "Was it worth all the suffering in the end to live like you did?" Today, he is happy, remarried, and the proud father of a beautiful, three-year-old daughter named Jennifer. So the answer to those questions must be "yes." The reason is that he knows now that each of us must live our own lives and fulfill our own destinies. If, in the end, a man can love himself and others around him, then the things he has done, good and bad, in his life to reach that point must have been correct and an important part of his life's journey.

For those reasons, in part, Elliot Litner decided to share his story. He is not ashamed of the things that he's done because he has learned from them. Pity those who never live, who are neither proud nor ashamed, and learn nothing from the days that pass each moment around them.

EPILOGUE

On May 18, 2002, I flew to Tucson to attend the wake and funeral of Joseph Bonanno, who had died earlier that month. It seemed appropriate in a number of ways, the first being that at this point, two years after we'd met, I considered Bill Bonanno a friend who'd encouraged my writing both with *The Privacy War* and *Il Dottore*. More, during my research, I'd come to better understand him, his father, and the tradition that they wrote about and had lived.

The wake, itself, was a low-key affair held at Bring's Funeral Home in midtown Tucson, attended mostly by family members, a priest with whom Joseph Bonanno had spent many of his last days, and some out-of-town associates, long removed from any business dealings, who out of respect had come to show their faces.

Throughout those days leading to the limousine ride to Saint Peter and Paul Catholic Church, and finally Holy Hope Cemetery where the ninety-seven-year-old godfather was buried, it occurred to me that there could be no conclusion to my book more fitting than this occasion for, truly, with this man an era had ended.

During my time in Tucson, I heard stories that went back generations to Giuseppe Bonanno, patriarch of one of the wealthy families that controlled Sicilian society, who'd been assassinated by a rival faction in 1899. Others about how his son, Salvatore, had promised that if he had a male child, he would offer him to his enemy as a godson to end the bloody feud. It was for this reason that Joseph Bonanno was known as the "Angel of Peace," I learned, a name he lived up to after he came to America in 1924.

Preaching "accommodation" over "violence," he, along with his mentor Salvatore Maranzano, became the architect of the *Commizione del Pace*, an arbitration board created to defuse conflicts between the families. Obviously, in a world as volatile as the "Volcano," his name for the New York underworld, negotiation was not always possible. Despite the fact that he orchestrated "Pax Bonanno," an era of peace that began after Maranzano's assassination in September 1931 and ended with the murder of Albert Anastasia in October 1957, he fought when necessary, driving a bulletproof Cadillac equipped with submachine guns through the Castellammarese War and taking his family "to the mattresses" during the bloody "Banana War" of the late-1960s.

Later, I listened to Bill Bonanno as he recalled one of his father's favorite sayings. "Friendship. Family ties. Trust. Loyalty. Obedience. That is the glue that holds us together." It was at that moment that it became apparent to me why the tradition of what came to be known as La Cosa Nostra could not survive in America. What Maranzano, Bonanno, Profaci, and the others had created was a secret society, a subculture within America, based on Sicilian codes of respect, honor, and dignity. These were not uneducated thugs, but men who had created and lived in an alternate society apart from our own with separate rules, customs, and governing bodies. With the entry of Luciano, the entrepreneur, Capone, the Neapolitan gangster, Meyer Lansky, the corrupt businessman, La Cosa Nostra became the Syndicate, a conflicted enterprise that put American and Sicilian values on a collision course that could only end in self-destruction.

There was another reason why the Mafia, under the steerage of unsophisticated criminals like Joe Columbo, a small-time gambler, John Gotti, a hijacker, Sammy Gravano, a construction worker-murderer, could not survive in America, I concluded. If all you're bringing to the table is an "enterprise," think again, because America is the Ultimate Enterprise. The United States government came to the conclusion sometime during the early 1960s, as the CIA began to flex its muscles, that it didn't need La Cosa Nostra any longer, viewed it as competition, and could use the Mafia to consolidate its power against a created "enemy."

Assassinations, known as "wet jobs," a euphemism for "liquidations within the CIA, could be done in-house. Narcotics trafficking, a multibillion-dollar industry, could be carried out clandestinely, the money used to support secret wars in South America, Southeast Asia, or the Middle East. Gambling, once the stock and trade of the Mafia, could be used as a hidden tax on American citizens, creating huge revenues to help finance state and local governments.

La Cosa Nostra, out in the open since the televised McClellan Subcommittee Hearings, had become a hobbyhorse for law enforcement. Street soldiers, capos, and even godfathers became easy prey for the insurance of government funding in lean times and an opportunity for the institutions of law enforcement to dig their tendrils deeper into citizens' Fourth Amendment rights during good ones, thanks to the star status demanded by Americanized Mafiosi like John Gotti.

I got a taste of this that day when I left Bring's Funeral Home in one of the twelve limousines that made up the caravan headed for Saint Peter and Paul Catholic Church. There were hundreds of people in attendance. Earlier the church had been swept by local police for bombs, and it was clear to me that in addition to the half-dozen television crews present, FBI agents were busy photographing immediate family members and those of us along with them. Since I would probably have to leave early to catch a plane back East, I left my briefcase with the driver, asking that he keep an eye on it until I reclaimed it to head to the airport by taxi.

As it turned out, time became a problem, and I was forced to leave the church about ten minutes before the service concluded. As planned, I walked up to Limousine #3 in the waiting procession of cars, collected my briefcase, handing the driver a $10 bill for his trouble, then walked to the bus stop where a cab had been instructed to meet me.

Paying attention to the main street where cars were passing at a forty-mile-per-hour clip and looking for my cab, I suddenly noticed that two uniformed policemen had walked over to the bus stop. "Good morning, officers," I said, continuing my lookout for the taxi as two more officers approached so that I was now literally boxed in by them. Next, I looked up to see my cab being flagged to the roadside by yet another cop and noticed, to my amazement, that the television crews had converged on top of me and were shooting footage!

"Is there some problem?" I asked the officer nearest me.

"Who are you with?" he asked.

I hesitated. "I'm not with anyone."

"Who do you know here?"

"I know Bill Bonanno. Is that a crime?"

"Is that your briefcase?"

I glanced over to the cab driver, who I'm sure was thinking his next ride if he made it out of town at all would be some kind of latter-day Al Capone. "Yes, it's my briefcase. Why do you ask?"

"Did you just get that briefcase from one of those limousines over there?" the cop asked pointing.

"Yes, I did. It's mine. I gave it to him to hold while I was inside the church for Mass."

"May we look inside that briefcase?" he pressed.

Understanding that I was already late for my plane and would no doubt be held until they could obtain a search warrant, I handed the briefcase over, and they searched it.

"What is this?" one of the cops asked holding up a sheaf of papers, the bag's only contents outside of some pens and a pack of Juicy Fruit.

"It's the manuscript for a book I'm writing. It's about a physician who leads a kind of double life, working at a famous New York hospital, while also working as a doctor with patients in the Mafia. That's how I know Bill. I'm an author. He gave me an introduction to the main character."

The police officer loaded the contents back in my briefcase. "Okay, Mr. Felber, you can leave now. Who knows, maybe someday I'll read your book."

I entered the cab as the television crews, some probably FBI investigators, melted away, repositioning themselves back near the church's exits to cover the mourners as they made their way to Holy Hope Cemetery where fifty doves would be released as Joseph Bonanno, the last founding member of the Commission, was laid to rest.

Afterward, looking at Elliot Litner, his life, and this book, I knew that my initial hunch about doing his story was correct. The experience had allowed me to see through him an intimate history of the Mafia in America that would never have been otherwise accessible. In doing the research for this book, he had taken me along with him on a trip through his experiences with Carlo Gambino, perhaps the last true godfather, to the goring and imminent demise of some imitation of that proud beast, relentlessly pursued by prosecutors like Rudolph Giuliani, served up to them on a silver platter by the last man who would call himself godfather, John Gotti.

Through that period, Elliot had evolved, but in significantly different ways. Unlike the organization that so intrigued and fascinated him, what he saw and felt during those years changed, but did not break him. Early along, I wondered, "Was there a price to be paid for living a double life? What did it cost a man for living too much?" The answer is in a song called "Judy Blue Eyes" by Crosby, Stills, Nash, and Young.

> *Just a word before I go*
> *The les-son to be learned,*
> *Traveling twice the speed of sound,*
> *It's easy to get burned.*

Elliot Litner did both the traveling and the burning. In his case, he was lucky, and the flames that might have consumed him became a baptism of fire that purified the instincts he already had in him and the lessons he'd been taught as a child by relatives like Uncle Saul. If Elliot's first take on life was to yield to the temptations of easy money, friends, and women, the price he paid was the loss of all of those comforts, along with the enduring necessities one genuinely treasures: family, friends, even his identity. Fortunately, he had his heritage and upbringing to save him.

Today the fabric of institutions in the United States are falling apart before our eyes, much as the fabric of La Cosa Nostra fell apart before his: divorce, corporations pushing for productivity at the expense of children, pedophilia in the

Catholic Church, skyrocketing drug dependencies, hypocrisy in politics, bio-weapons and diseases, some of them man made and without cure, all part of the unbridled enterprise mentality.

In that sense, Joseph Bonanno was correct. Americans yearn for *closeness*. They need family. They long for a "father."

INDEX

INDEX

INDEX

INDEX